**WONDER–
FULLY
MADE**

T0339336

What does it mean to be human? The Bible presents a variety of images of our humanity as God bestows it on us; these Scriptural depictions take our bodies more seriously than Christians often do. Kleinig leads readers into the biblical view of that creation of God that is the human body and its proper use and care. He aids Christians in giving witness to our godly regard for and exercise of this complex, magnificent gift of God.

Readers of every age will gain new insights from Kleinig's sensitive and perceptive exploration of the Bible's revelation of what a magnificent gift the human body is. This adventure in searching the Scriptures will enrich the reader's ability to enjoy God's giving us our corporality and to find in it rich grounds for thanksgiving and praise.

**ROBERT KOLB**
Emeritus professor of systematic theology,
Concordia Seminary, Saint Louis

John Kleinig's genius is that he never engages in abstract theologising, but, like the Christian liturgy itself, he enacts God's Word. So rather than a "study of the doctrine of the body" we have here "a theological rhapsody," a song of praise that exalts the human body as a divine creation and exults in the God who gave it. At the same time, this simple and clear book speaks to the earthy realities of human life, with all its pain and messiness, to which Kleinig applies the gospel salve of the God who created our bodies, joined with us in Christ's flesh, and lifts us up to his holy ground through the Spirit. When so much written about the body is polemical, political, or perverse, how good it is to read an author who is on the side of the angels, not the cynics.

**THOMAS M. WINGER**
President, Concordia Lutheran Theological Seminary,
St. Catharines, Ontario, CA

Having taught and written for decades on the theology of human embodiment, I found myself smiling and nodding in agreement as I moved from page to page of this wide-ranging book. John Kleinig has written clearly and convincingly about the wonders of embodiment, grounding his discussion in a rich exposition of Scripture and solid Protestant theology and practically applying his pastoral wisdom for church leaders and members. This book will surely take its place among the growing library of works that treat this fascinating subject. I cannot recommend it too highly!

**GREGG R. ALLISON**
Professor of Christian theology,
The Southern Baptist Theological Seminary

John Kleinig's *Wonderfully Made: A Protestant Theology of the Body* provides a welcome and worthy complement to Catholic and Orthodox theologies of the body by John Paul II and Jean-Claude Larchet. Adopting a six-part structure, identifying the body as created, redeemed, spiritual, sexual, spousal, and living, Kleinig has deftly composed for his readers a biblical and evangelical "rhapsody on the human body" that is at once lucid, poetic, and forthright. *Wonderfully Made* exudes a confidence and directness born from its roots in Holy Scripture, its construction in the classroom, and its shaping in the confessional, with Kleinig the teacher, theologian, pastor, and servant of the gospel in his element. Supported with numerous quotes from Luther to Lewis and abounding in practical examples from life, the liturgy, and the school of hard knocks, this book promises to become a standard go-to text on the agony and ecstasy of physical Christian existence for seminaries, teachers, pastors, parishes, and personal study.

**ADAM G. COOPER**
Associate professor of theology and church history,
Catholic Theological College, Melbourne

Written against the neo-gnostic spirituality of our day, with its focus on the mind at the expense of the body, Kleinig's engaging book is a powerful defence of the embodied spirituality of the Bible. Its deep exegetical and pastoral insights combine to make this a book that speaks to both the head and the heart. Written for a broad spectrum of readers from rank and file Christians to pastors and teachers of theology, the author shows that the body is indeed wonderfully made because it has been created, redeemed, and sanctified by the triune God and is destined for eternal communion with God after the resurrection.

**JEFFREY SILCOCK**
Emeritus, systematic theology,
Australian Lutheran College / University of Divinity

I have one complaint about John Kleinig's immensely valuable contribution to the growing Protestant discussion about the theology of the body: it is too short. Kleinig's theologically saturated reflections about our bodies are delivered in elegant prose, which makes for a reading experience that is as enjoyable as it is edifying. *Wonderfully Made* is a tremendous and accessible guide for Protestants who are beginning to turn (at last!) our attention toward what it means to live in the flesh that God gave us.

**MATTHEW LEE ANDERSON**
Assistant professor, Baylor University,
and founder of Mere Orthodoxy

More than ever we need a book like John Kleinig's *Wonderfully Made*. His rhapsody on the human body addresses today's confusion over our bodies and our sexuality. His positive theological vision of the body offers all Christians a chance to rediscover and rejoice in the beauty of our human bodies, created in the image of God and redeemed through the flesh of Jesus. His biblical theology of marriage as a garden of love embraces the splendor of Christian marriage as a foretaste of our final communion with Christ as our heavenly bridegroom. He extols the blessedness of the single life as those who remain unmarried embody Christ among us through true friendship. *Wonderfully Made* comes from a pastor who preaches the gospel to us through a theology of the body, comforts us with absolution for our failings in the misuse of our bodies, and offers us a place to stand to address our culture with the mystery of the human body fearfully and wonderfully made by God.

**ARTHUR A. JUST JR.**
Professor and chairman of exegetical theology,
Concordia Theological Seminary, Fort Wayne, IN

# WONDER-FULLY MADE

## A Protestant Theology of the Body

John W. Kleinig

**LEXHAM PRESS**

*Wonderfully Made: A Protestant Theology of the Body*

Copyright 2021 John W. Kleinig

Lexham Press, 1313 Commercial St., Bellingham, WA 98225
LexhamPress.com

Print ISBN 9781683594673
Digital ISBN 9781683594680
Library of Congress Control Number 2020950469

Lexham Editorial: Todd Hains, Matthew Boffey, Elliot Ritzema
Cover Design: Joshua Hunt
Book Design and Typesetting: Abigail Stocker

*For my dear wife, Claire,*
*who by God's grace has become one flesh and one spirit with me,*
*and for our dear children,*
*Louise, Timothy, Hilary, and Paul,*
*who are flesh of our flesh!*

# CONTENTS

# ABBREVIATIONS

BoC     *The Book of Concord: The Confessions of the*
        *Evangelical Lutheran Church.* Edited by Robert
        Kolb and Timothy J. Wengert. Translated by
        Charles Arand et al. Minneapolis: Fortress, 2000.

LW      *Luther's Works [American Edition].* 82 vols.
        projected. St. Louis: Concordia; Philadelphia:
        Fortress Press, 1955–1986, 2009–.

WA      *D. Martin Luthers Werke, Kritische Gesamtausgabe:*
        *[Schriften].* 73 vols. Weimar: Hermann Böhlaus
        Nachfolger, 1883–2009.

# PRAYER FOR LIFE IN THE BODY

This order of prayer for our human life in the body invites you to read each chapter in the book as a devotional exercise by yourself. It can also be used by a group in a study of it-with a leader speaking the plain text, and the group the words in bold.

In the name of the Father and of the Son and of the Holy Spirit.
**Amen.**

## PSALMODY

O Lord, open my lips,
**and my mouth will declare your praise.**                    Ps 51:15

You formed my inward parts;
**you knitted me together in my mother's womb.**
I praise you, for I am fearfully and wonderfully made.
**Wonderful are your works.**                    Ps 139:13–14

Your hands have made and fashioned me;
**give me understanding that I may learn your commandments.**
Those who fear you shall see me and rejoice,
**because I have hoped in your word.**                    Ps 119:73–74

The word of the Lord is right and true;
**he is faithful in all he does.**
The Lord loves righteousness and justice;

**WONDERFULLY MADE**

**the earth is full of his unfailing love.**
By the word of the Lord were the heavens made,
**their starry host by the breath of his mouth.**
Let all the earth fear the Lord;
**let all the people of the world revere him.**
For he spoke, and it came to be;
**he commanded, and it stood firm.**
May your unfailing love rest upon us, O Lord,
**even as we put our hope in you.**                    *Ps 33:4–6, 8–9, 22*

### CONFESSION OF FAITH

God has made us his people through our baptism into Christ.
Living together in trust and hope, we confess our faith.

**I believe in God the Father Almighty,**
 **maker of heaven and earth.**
**And in Jesus Christ, his only Son, our Lord,**
 **who was conceived by the Holy Spirit,**
  **born of the Virgin Mary,**
 **suffered under Pontius Pilate,**
  **was crucified, died, and was buried.**
 **He descended into hell.**
 **The third day he rose again from the dead.**
 **He ascended into heaven**
  **and is seated at the right hand of God the Father Almighty,**
 **and he will come again to judge the living and the dead.**
**I believe in the Holy Spirit,**
 **the holy catholic church,**
 **the communion of saints,**
 **the forgiveness of sins,**
 **the resurrection of the body,**
 **and the life everlasting. Amen.**

## PRAYER

Lord, remember us in your kingdom, and teach us to pray:

**Our Father who art in heaven;**
**Hallowed be thy name;**
**Thy kingdom come;**
**Thy will be done on earth, as it is in heaven;**
**Give us this day our daily bread;**
**And forgive us our trespasses, as we forgive those**
**    who trespass against us;**
**And lead us not into temptation;**
**But deliver us from evil;**
**For thine is the kingdom and the power and the glory**
**    for ever and ever.**
**Amen.**                                                    *Matt 6:9–13*

**Almighty God, I thank you that you sustain me and all crea-**
**tures by your life-giving breath, and deliver me from death**
**through Jesus, the Word of life. Protect me from all evil, so**
**that I serve you in all that I do and please you in my daily life.**
**Into your hands I commend myself, my body and soul, and**
**all that I possess, and all those who are dear to me; through**
**Jesus Christ, your Son, our Lord.**
**Amen.**

## ENCOURAGEMENT

Your body is the temple of the Holy Spirit within you:
**whom you have from God.**
You are not your own, for you were bought with a price:
**So glorify God in your body.**                        *1 Cor 6:19*

# BENEDICTION

Our help is in the name of the Lord
**who made heaven and earth.** *Ps 124:8*

Let us bless the Lord. *Ps 103:1*
**Thanks be to God.**
The grace of our Lord Jesus Christ and
the love of God and the communion
of the Holy Spirit be with us all. *2 Cor 13:14*
**Amen.**

1

# BODY MATTERS

In fact, however, the value of an individual does not lie in him. He is capable of receiving value. He receives it by union with Christ. There is no question of finding for him a place in the living temple which will do justice to his inherent value and give scope to his natural idiosyncrasy. The place was there first. The man was created for it. He will not be himself till he is there. We shall be true and everlasting and really divine persons only in Heaven, just as we are, even now, coloured bodies only in the light.

—*C. S. Lewis*

**T**he slogans on two sweatshirts worn by young women recently caught my attention. The first was "My body! My choice!" The second was "Your body may be a temple, but mine's an amusement park." Both sum up how people commonly now regard their bodies. Since it belongs to them and only to them, they may do as they please with it. Therefore they use it for their own amusement in pursuit of physical pleasure for themselves apart from God and any higher purpose in life.

What are we to make of our bodies? That is not a theoretical question for idle speculation, something for philosophers to consider. It is a practical matter that determines the course of our lives. Even if we rarely think about our bodies, our opinion of them and attitude toward them subconsciously govern how we live and act every moment of our lives. Our beliefs about our bodies are always in play because our bodies are part and parcel of what we are. Wherever we are, there our body is with us. Whatever we do, our body does.

But unless something bad happens to me, I mostly take my body for granted, like the air I breathe. Even though it is my constant companion, I seldom consider how I relate to it and what it is meant to be. Yet it is, or should be, obvious how important it is to me and the people around me. It locates me in a particular place at a particular time with particular people in my particular society, family, marriage, and workplace. I am born with my body and die when it can no longer sustain me. The pattern of my life as a whole involves me with my body from childhood to adolescence, marriage to parenthood, employment to retirement, old age to death. My body also marks the daily rhythm of my life with waking and sleeping, dressing and undressing, working and resting from work, eating and drinking, engaging in sexual intercourse and disengaging from it. It governs how I interact with others and how they interact with me. I experience the world around me through it. I live with my body and do everything with it. My human life is, most obviously and simply, life in the body.

Yet I did not make my body; it was given to me and remains given to me as the foundation for my life here on earth. It is never apart from me, nor am I ever apart from it for as long as I live here.

My body is equally important for my life as a Christian. Just as I live my entire earthly life in my human family, my spiritual life in God's family involves my body from its earthly beginning to its final, heavenly destination. My life in Christ is based on a physical event, my baptism. The washing of physical water accompanied by the speaking of certain words joined my body with the body of the risen Lord Jesus, just as the rite of marriage joined my body to my wife's. Jesus now interacts with me physically with his spoken word that I hear with my physical ears, his audible word that animates me with his Holy Spirit and makes me a saint. Jesus also gives himself to me physically in his Holy Supper. There I receive his life-giving body and blood with my mouth and in my whole body. Through his body and blood, he unites me physically and spiritually with himself and all other Christians. He also calls and equips me to serve him bodily—that is, with my actual body and its individual members. So, paradoxically, my spiritual life, the life that is created and sustained by the Holy Spirit, is always lived in the body. It does not take me away from my body or occur apart from it. Rather, it takes me ever further and deeper into bodily life and into fuller embodiment as a human being. It makes me at home in my body as I live here on earth.

All that makes scant sense unless we understand the spiritual life in biblical terms. The biblical understanding of human spirituality differs radically from views commonly and rather vaguely held. Most people see the spiritual as the opposite of the physical and material. Thus, the human spirit is identified either with the conscious mind and its thoughts, emotions, and self-awareness, or with the immaterial soul, the disembodied spirit, of every living person. As such, it can exist and works best apart from the body.

In contrast, the biblical view is that what is spiritual has to do with the Holy Spirit. My spirit is what makes me a person rather than a thing or an animal, a living person animated by the Holy Spirit, the Spirit that gives personal life to every human soul, and eternal life to every believer. The Holy Spirit makes us and our deeds spiritual through faith in Jesus Christ. As Martin Luther says, "The Spirit is whatever is done in us through the Spirit."[1]

Since the spiritual life is produced by the Holy Spirit for people with bodies, Christian spirituality is embodied piety. We human beings are not just spirits, like the angels, nor animated bodies, like the animals, but are embodied spirits, or, if you will, spiritual bodies. We do not just have bodies; we are bodies. They are not just what we are as people but an essential part of who we are. That is why the body is so important. It has been designed to be a temple of the Holy Spirit rather than an amusement park. Like the human mind, it is meant to live in harmony with God and his Holy Spirit. It was created for eternal life with God, not merely temporal life on earth. No matter how damaged it may actually be, every human body is designed for perfection in eternity.

## HIGH REGARD

It is true that some vain people overrate their bodies. Like Narcissus in Greek mythology, they admire themselves. Their bodies serve their own self-glorification. Since their sight is turned away from the world and the people around them, they see nothing but themselves. They confuse the way they look with what they are and identify themselves with their appearance. Despite their self-regard their body is actually underrated, because it is treated as an object, a thing in itself apart from the person and its relationship with others. They idolize their bodies.

---

1. Luther, *Lectures on Galatians* (1535), LW 26:217.

Yet it seems to me that most people do not regard their bodies highly enough. They underrate and despise their bodies. Because they are in thrall to the image of an ideal body, the body beautiful, they do not appreciate how amazing and wonderful they actually are. They belittle their bodies for their apparent idiosyncrasies and supposed imperfections. They fail to see how the value of the body does not merely lie in its total physical arrangement but in its personal use with all its parts. Each body is like a violin made by Stradivarius. In its appearance a Stradivarius is no more attractive than any other musical instrument. It comes into its own when it is used by a master musician to play the piece of music that brings out the best in it. So too with our bodies! We should hold them in high regard for their wonderful construction and their amazing potential, potential that is realized when they are used in the right way to serve others and glorify God.

Sadly, our society as a whole does not know what to make of the body. People disagree on what it is, what it is meant to do, and how it is to be regarded. That is not new. The human body has always been a matter of contention, most of all with regard to its sexual character—perhaps never more so than in Western societies today, in which some of the sharpest social, moral, and religious conflicts have to do with the body! Think of the disagreements in our society over sexuality and gender, marriage and divorce, same-sex intercourse and same-sex marriage, artificial reproduction and genetic engineering, cosmetic surgery and gender reassignment, pornography and voyeurism, sexual abuse and prostitution, abortion and euthanasia, overeating and malnutrition. Think, too, of disagreements in the church over creation and evolution, the incarnation of God's Son and his physical resurrection, the ministry of the church and its use of spoken words and physical objects like water, bread, and wine as the means of the Spirit, the resurrection of the body and bodily participation in eternal life with the Triune God. All these conflicts stem, in large part, from confusion about the body.

Popular culture shows that our society seems to be in two minds about the human body. On the one hand, it is obsessed with the physical body and its health. Our happiness and wellbeing seemingly depend on what we eat and how we feel, how fit we are and how sexually active we are, how we look and what we can do. Since the condition for a good life is a fit, healthy, attractive body, people assess themselves and their bodies by comparison with the images of the socially sanctioned ideal bodies that they see on screen and in print. My ideal self, the person I would like to be, must match that ideal body. Yet that ideal is never fixed. It changes as fashions change. What's more, makeup and photographic trickery ensure that no one ever actually measures up to that artificial ideal. Besides that, even the best body is marred and scarred; it becomes sick and unwell; it ages and dies. No actual body is ever perfect in appearance or in health. No body is ever good enough; it never measures up to what it should be like. Bodily perfection is in fact an illusion, an impossible dream.

On the other hand, an obsession with the body coexists with contempt for the body. Surveys show that most people are so unhappy with their bodies that they would readily trade them in for something better and more attractive. Since they are unhappy with themselves, they project their dissatisfaction onto their bodies and attempt to get rid of its blemishes by the pursuit of bodily self-improvement with diet and exercise, makeup and dress, cosmetic surgery and decoration with jewelry and tattoos. When these efforts fail to deliver the desired outcome, they despise their bodies and treat them harshly as if to punish them for their failure.

In disappointment, more and more of our contemporaries who feel trapped in their bodies try to escape by dissociating themselves from them. Some who have been hurt physically switch off their emotions and live in their minds. Others try to achieve a state of emotional ecstasy through intoxication, music, or spiritual possession. Still others deliberately practice a kind of deep meditation that seeks to transcend the body and reach a state of higher consciousness. It is also true that many Christians who feel uneasy about their bodies reduce the Christian faith to the pursuit of theological knowledge or the cultivation of their own subjective spirituality. Oddly, the focus on the body as the be-all and end-all of human life can result in the unhealthy embrace of a disembodied kind of spirituality.

So neither of these approaches regards the human body highly enough. Both fail to appreciate it properly.

## THE ANIMATED BODY

Up to this point I have quite deliberately refrained from explaining how the human body is connected with the mind and the soul, one's sense of self as a person rather than just a thing. But now an explanation is in order to avoid possible misunderstanding. The connection of the human mind with the body became a central issue in Greek philosophy, and centuries later it remains still pertinent. Like the Greek philosophers, many modern Christians reduce the mind to its cognitive powers and identify it with the human soul. This dualistic view of a person dissociates the mind with its thoughts and judgments from the body with its senses, passions, and desires. Thus, even though modern science shows that the mind cannot be separated from the body, the human mind is still commonly identified with the soul as the spiritual part of a person and as a separate entity from the body. So, for many people, embryos and mentally disabled people are not held to be persons because they are not fully sentient entities with self-consciousness.

But that is not how the human body is regarded in the Scriptures. It could be said that Scripture speaks about embodied minds and mindful bodies. In fact, the Hebrew Old Testament has no terms that correspond exactly to "body" and "mind" in English. The Old Testament speaks more generally about the "flesh" of a person. So does the New Testament. Although sometimes it uses the Greek word for the body in a more technical sense (that is, the human body), the same word is often translated "flesh" to mean not merely the physical body (for example, Gal 2:20) but the sinful self that is opposed to God's Spirit (for example, Rom 8:5–7).

The New Testament occasionally uses *nous*, a Greek word that approximates what we now call the mind (for example, Rom 12:2). The Greeks regarded it as the organ for physical, mental, moral, and spiritual perception. But the Old Testament has no technical term for the mind as we know it. Instead, it regards the heart, the central physical organ of the human body, as the seat of what we now call the mind, much as we now locate the mind in the brain. The heart is regarded as the organ for perception and understanding, thought and emotion, reflection and meditation, memory and enjoyment, imagination and calculation, invention and action, desire and volition. The symbolic use of this physical term presents us with a unitary, synthetic view of the whole person. In this view, the whole body with its respective organs is not only involved in perception and action but also in all mental and emotional activity. So when we think, we speak to ourselves, and when we speak, we think aloud for others to know what we are thinking. We have mindful bodies that interact physically and mentally with the world around them, receptive bodies that need eyes to see and ears to hear and a heart to understand what is presented to them (Deut 29:4; Isa 6:9–10). Thus, for instance, when someone speaks to me, my brain interprets what I hear. So if that part of the brain that deals with hearing is damaged, I can no longer make sense of the sounds that strike my otherwise unimpaired eardrum.

Just as the human mind is associated with the heart of a person in the Scriptures, so human souls are connected with the throat and its breath. Thus, "soul" is the word in Hebrew (*nephesh*) and Greek (*psychē*) for any animate creature, for animals and people who breathe and remain alive as long as they continue to breathe. They die when they no longer breathe as well as when the heart stops beating. Their soul is their life-breath. Thus, the word for soul is also the word for human life (for example, Mark 8:35–36). A human soul is an animate, living person. People do not just have souls; they are souls.

This commonsense way of thinking is carried from the Old Testament over into the New Testament. It has the same holistic anthropology, the same view of the whole person. It employs a range of terms to describe human life from different points of view, different aspects not meant to exclude each other. Thus, when Jesus teaches his disciples about the necessities for physical life on earth in Matthew 6:25, he considers them physically from two complementary points of view, both as persons with living souls and as persons with living bodies. But when he teaches them about death in Matthew 10:28–29, he distinguishes the soul from the body. Similarly, Paul identifies the heart with the mind (Phil 4:7) and the mind with the conscience (Titus 1:15) as complementary aspects of a person. He also distinguishes the body from the mind when he discusses congregational behavior in Romans 12:1–2, and he differentiates among the body, soul, and spirit of God's people when he teaches them about their total sanctification for eternal life with God in 1 Thessalonians 5:23.

This view of the whole person, coupled with the use of the same terms for different entities—like "soul," "flesh," and "body" all referring to the life of a person and to a person's self—can make it hard for us to fathom exactly what we mean when we talk about the body. Take, for instance, Paul's use of the phrase "the body of flesh." In Colossians 1:22 it describes the physical body of Jesus, but in 2:11 it describes the sinful nature of all Adam's descendants. Similarly, in Colossians 2:18 "the mind of the flesh" does not refer to the physical mind but to the sinful mentality that is hostile to God and concerned only with its own spiritual self-advancement.

Human beings do not possess a body or a mind; they are both bodies and minds. They cannot be reduced to either of these. Every person is not just a body or a mind, but both. And yet they are also more than both. As people, they are always much more than self-conscious bodies or embodied minds. Their personal nature and identity, their souls, transcend both their bodies and their minds. So, for example, those who suffer from Alzheimer's disease, or lie unconscious in a coma, are still persons, even though they have lost much of their physical and mental ability. What's more, even though we change physically and mentally in the course of our lives, we still remain the same person. In fact, these changes actually establish and confirm our continuous identity.

Even though we all experience ourselves as the same person for the whole of our conscious lives, our self, our soul, remains a mystery to us. We do not invent our own selves and construct who we are. Our self, our identity, is something given to us together with our bodies to distinguish us from other bodies, and with our minds to make us aware of ourselves as persons, active agents in the story of our lives.

The mystery of our personal identity is understood in three ways in the New Testament. First, the body is distinguished from the soul. Jesus explains it in these terms in Matthew 10:28: "Do not fear those who kill the body but cannot kill the soul. Rather fear him who can destroy both body and soul in hell." He therefore distinguishes the soul from the body and teaches that while the body can be killed physically here on earth, the soul cannot be killed even if the body is killed. It survives the death of the body (Heb 10:39; 1 Pet 1:9; 3:19; Rev 6:9; 20:4). Only God, the Creator and Judge of humanity, can destroy both body and soul in hell. Thus, Jesus asserts that those who have died are still alive to God (Luke 20:38). Thus, my animate human soul animates my body and my mind.

Second, the human soul is associated with the spirit and yet distinguished from it (Heb 4:12). It is the self-conscious, inner self of people in contrast with their physical flesh (2 Cor 7:1; Col 2:5), or their body as their outer self (1 Cor 5:3–5; 7:34). The living spirit of a believer, which has been created and is kept physically alive by God's Spirit, has also been recreated and revived for eternal life with God by his Spirit. It belongs to the spiritual world, together with the spirits of those who have died, angels and demons, the Holy Spirit and Satan, and God the Father of all spirits (Heb 12:9). At death, the spirit of a person returns to its Creator (Eccl 12:7; Luke 23:46; Acts 7:59; cf. Luke 8:55). Thus, in Hebrews

12:23, the saints who have died and are now part of the heavenly congregation are described as "the spirits of the righteous made perfect." Thus, God's Spirit animates my spirit with temporal and eternal life in order to enliven me physically and mentally.

Third, our personal identity is fixed. In Luke 10:20 Jesus teaches that the names of his disciples are written in heaven (see also Phil 4:3; Heb 12:23; Rev 3:5; 21:27). We do not name ourselves. Our parents confer our identity on us by giving us our proper names. They make us who we are. Thus, I am John. If my name is taken away from me, I lose my identity. If I change my name, I change my identity. Ultimately, God gives me my name so that he can call on me by name, introduce himself personally to me, and interact personally with me (Isa 43:1). He did not just give me my personal name, my Christian name, when I was baptized; he also registered it in heaven together with all those who belong to him. He thereby made me a member of his family and a citizen of heaven. As long as my name is written in the book of life, I remain a living person and an heir of eternal life (Phil 4:3; Rev 3:5; 21:27). No matter how much I change, God always considers me the same person in time and in eternity.

## WONDERFULLY MADE!

Our world has many living wonders, many ordinary creatures that are all quite extraordinary. This array of wonders ranges from a simple cell to the supremely complex human body. From every point of view, each embodied person is the most amazing visible being on earth. Our human bodies, linked as they are to the whole web of life on earth and the life of the living God, are indeed "fearfully and wonderfully made" (Ps 139:14).

Yet the more we examine our bodies and learn about them, the more we discover how little we actually understand them and their complexity. Our vision of ourselves is always partial, incomplete, and one-dimensional, often a reflection of how others see us and of what they tell us about ourselves. We never see ourselves directly, or fully, either by looking at ourselves in a mirror or by thinking about what has happened to us. We only ever see bits and pieces, moments and episodes, in the story of our physical lives on earth—mere snapshots at various stages of our lives, rather than a complete video of our entire embodied life from all points of view.

There is only one who sees us fully at each moment and entirely in our whole existence. He sees us physically and mentally, personally and spiritually. The only one who has an accurate vision of us is the living God, the author and director of our bodily lives. That's the message of Psalm 139. He is the only one who knows my heart (1 Kgs 8:39; Ps 44:21, Acts 1:24; 15:8). He knows how I think and what I feel; he knows what I am and why I act as I do. He is "acquainted with all my ways" (Ps 139:3). Even though I cannot see him physically, he sees me completely (Ps 139:1–12). Thus, the royal singer of this psalm not only praises God for his wonderful creation but also praises God for God's even more wonderful vision of him (Ps 139:13–18). He pictures his whole life from the moment of conception as a process of waking up from a deep sleep to discover God's presence with him:

> For you formed my inward parts;
>> you knitted me together in my mother's womb.
> I praise you, for I am fearfully and wonderfully made.
> Wonderful are your works;
>> my soul knows it very well.
> My frame was not hidden from you,
> when I was being made in secret,
>> intricately woven in the depths of the earth.
> Your eyes saw my unformed substance;
> in your book were written, every one of them,
>> the days that were formed for me,
>> when as yet there was none of them.
> How precious to me are your thoughts, O God!
>> How vast is the sum of them!
> If I would count them, they are more than sand.
>> I awake and I am still with you.

The eyes of God see what is hidden from human eyes. They see the whole life of each human body from the womb to the tomb. God's thoughts and purposes, his intentions and plans, are precious to the psalmist, because they encompass his entire physical and mental life. God does not program and script its entire course with little or no room for improvisation; he follows his outline and purpose for it as he works with each person in staging it. Like a producer who devises a play together with his actors, he supervises its enactment.

But unlike most dramatists, God is also the main actor and allows for improvisation in the play. He therefore interacts in a hidden way with the characters that he has scripted. As the creative author and active producer in the drama of our bodily lives, he sees and understands us fully in all the dimensions of our existence. Most amazingly, by speaking with us he shares his vision of us with us, as well as his plan to disclose himself to each of us. His thoughts are precious to us, because he wants to bring us to himself on the everlasting way that leads from earth to heaven (Ps 139:18, 24). Thus, our vision of our bodies comes from his vision of us. He wants us to revise our self-vision according to his vision. That process of revision can only come from him and through him.

The body matters much more than we usually imagine it does. It matters because it locates us in time and space here on earth. It matters because we live in it and with it. It matters because through it we interact with the world around us, the people who coexist with us, and the living God who keeps us physically alive in it. It matters even though it is so fragile and so easily damaged. It matters even though we rebel against our Creator and abuse our fellow creatures on earth. It matters even though it is finite and doomed to die. Most of all, it matters to us because it matters so much to God. He is the supreme philanthropist, the lover of humanity (Titus 3:4).

The sacred Scriptures show us how much the human body matters to God, and why. From Genesis to Revelation, Scripture paints two pictures of bodily life on earth. On the one hand, it shows us how God regards the human body, the body that he creates in his image, redeems by the incarnation of his Son, and sanctifies for life with him through the Holy Spirit. On the other hand, it also shows us how completely it has been corrupted by rebellion against God, how badly it has been misused to damage other people and the world around it, and how tragically it is doomed to die. Yet it would be wrong to give equal weight to both these portrayals, for the bright vision of its glory far outweighs the gray vision of its misery. Thus, in 2 Corinthians 4:17, Paul exclaims that each momentary affliction of the body is preparing us for "an eternal weight of glory beyond all comparison" with anything that we have yet experienced.

## THE THEOPHANIC BODY

Like a composer who values all musical instruments in an orchestra as well as their skillful players, God prizes our bodies and us as embodied people for what he plans to accomplish through us individually and corporately. Since he has made each of us and the whole of humanity in his image, the value of the body does not depend on its worth to the person who owns it; it does not come from its social status or usefulness, nor is it derived only from its place and function in the natural world. The worth of the body is conferred by its divine Creator. The triune God designed it for himself and for participation in his own eternal life. He made it as it is so that he could give himself and his gifts bodily to people on earth and work with them in caring bodily for others and the world, which is their natural habitat. He designed it so that he could show himself bodily to other embodied people and give them bodily access to himself by his theophany, his physical appearance to them in Jesus.

The human body was made to bridge two realms: the invisible, eternal realm of God and the visible, temporal realm of his creation. Created as they were in God's image, all human bodies were meant to be holy even as God is holy. Thus, human bodies do not just belong to this world, but also to the eternal world of

God. They are meant to reflect the triune God bodily in their life and behavior, all in keeping with their own unique characteristics and according to their unique calling. Each person has been made to represent him partially in their bodily life on earth. None of them represents God fully except Jesus; he is not just a man made in God's image, but he is God's image, the visible likeness of the invisible God (2 Cor 4:4; Col 1:14).

As a result of human rebellion against God, people serve God poorly and badly. They are far from the glory of God (Rom 3:23). Like rooms with cracked and dirty windows, they do not let the light of God shine in them and out through them. Like a damaged and mistuned musical instrument, they eke out an off-pitch tune. They are not as they should be, nor do they any longer function properly. They have lost their access to God and live corruptly apart from him.

But through God's Son, who took on a human body to reclaim us bodily for fellowship with God the Father, our bodies once again become what they were meant to be. By our faith in Jesus and union with him, our bodies share in his holiness by being filled with the Holy Spirit. They become temples of the Holy Spirit (1 Cor 6:19). As shrines where God resides, they share in his hidden glory and display it by word and deed to the world. So, through our bodily union with Jesus, we are filled with all the fullness of God (Eph 3:19). We glorify God and honor him with our bodies (1 Cor 6:20). Through him our bodies once again become what they were meant to be: agents of God and instruments by which he shows himself and gives of himself to other people on earth. By their union with Jesus they become theophanic; they manifest God to people on earth. As disciples of Jesus and recipients of his Spirit, we exhibit the grace of God the Father bodily in the course of our earthly lives. As blameless, innocent, and unblemished children of God, we are enabled to "shine as lights" in a dark and crooked world (Phil 2:15). What greater honor could be conferred on us and our bodies than that?

So then, the value of each body is not inherent to it, that is, does not come from itself. It has its worth from God and receives its full worth, its glory, from its union with Christ. Each human body was made to be part of his body. Or, to change the picture, each body was crafted to be a living stone, set—together with and upon Jesus—in its proper place in God's holy temple (1 Pet 2:5). Each human body has its proper place there with God. It will not come into full view and be itself until it is there. Only there will it be as it was meant to be, just as our bodies are, even now, visible and colored only in the light.

## IN PRAISE OF THE BODY

Some years ago, a prominent Christian journalist addressed a conference for pastors here in Australia. His topic was how best to communicate the Christian faith and a Christian worldview to the cultural movers and shakers who had nothing but disdain for Christianity, to opinionated critics who were, all too often, biblically ignorant and theologically illiterate. He observed that Christians often reinforced their contempt for Christianity by attacking public immorality and lobbying politicians to impose Christian morality on the whole of society by the prohibition of abortion, euthanasia, same-sex intercourse, and same-sex marriage. That project has, in fact, proved to be rather counterproductive, as it has led to counter-legislation to sanction these measures, as well as the use of popular media to cast them in a positive light and depict Christians as angry, self-righteous killjoys.

In contrast with that rather self-righteous, censorious stance, he advocated a positive approach that was neither naively optimistic nor cynically pessimistic. He noted that the Christian faith and Christian moral teaching are best communicated positively, by providing an attractive vision of what is right and good and true, a theological vision of the beauty of physical human life and of the world as God's creation, an appealing vision of the beauty of marriage and sexual intercourse between husband and wife, a persuasive vision of the beauty of sexual chastity and marital faithfulness—and all of that personally by example, rather than by argument! Such a vision is best communicated physically in word and deed, image and reality, art and life.

I must say that I agree with him. It is better to light a candle than to curse the darkness, as it's been said. The negative, somewhat distorted vision of the body needs to be countered by a positive, rightly ordered vision of it in its beauty, no matter how flawed our bodies may be. As Paul says in Philippians 4:8, "Whatever is true, whatever is honorable, whatever is just, whatever is chaste, whatever is commendable, if there is any excellence, there is anything worthy of praise, think of these things." That is what I want to do in this study; that is what I want its readers to do as they read what I have written.

I am sure that this is the right approach to our Christian consideration of the human body. Presently, we are confronted with so much physical, social, moral, and spiritual ugliness that it is easy for us to be enraged and deranged by it. As we consider how badly the body is used and abused, we can all too easily side with the cynics rather than the angels. But if we listen to what God has to say about it, we can see it as he sees it, both in its potential, eternal glory and in its actual, present misery. Thus, the view of the human body that will be sketched out in the following chapters comes from God's word. It is not based on my own observations but on the sacred Scriptures, as they throw light on what we could not otherwise see with our human eyes unless they were enlightened by God's Spirit. I will not use God's word to critique the abuse of the body but to provide a positive theological vision of its creation by God, its redemption from corruption by Jesus, and its renovation by the Holy Spirit.

## MY POINT OF VIEW

This book is a pastoral-theological meditation written from a Lutheran perspective. Its purpose is to consider the body theologically and anthropologically in light of what God says about it in his word, and to contribute some all-too-little-known insights from the classical Lutheran tradition for the ongoing ecumenical discussion of this topic.

Two convictions motivate me in this reflection on the human body. On the one hand, I am convinced that we Christians will not be heard and heeded by our critics in our teaching of various aspects of bodily life unless we paint an attractive picture of it in its potential and actual beauty. To be sure, that beauty is not always obvious and is seldom self-evident, even when we get some glimpses of its splendor. It is, in fact, mostly hidden from human sight. Its hidden beauty is seen most clearly and accurately in the light of God's word. On the other hand, I am also convinced that abstract arguments and reasoned explanations, no matter how good they are, cannot inculcate a bright vision of its true beauty. God's Spirit-filled word alone can do that by enlightening our imagination; it alone has the power to heal our broken bodies and make us truly at home with ourselves, God, and others in our bodies. This is a lifelong process, for we shall see our bodies in their true light only when we have become like him in every way and see him as he is; then when we see him as he is, we shall see ourselves fully reflected in him (1 John 3:2).

This book considers the human body theologically as God's creation, so that we may regard it as he does and treat it as he desires. It is, if you like, a theological rhapsody on the body—a written reflection in praise of the human body, meant to appeal to the imagination and evoke a vision of its divinely given splendor. More correctly, it is written in praise of the triune God who has created the human body to reflect his glory, rescues it from death and destruction, and makes it holy. Thus, the next three chapters will consider the body from those three points of view. Then, after that, the last two chapters will consider the sexual character of the body in the light of its creation, redemption, and sanctification at the expense of other possible applications, since sexuality is such a current, controversial topic in our society. Each of the first three main chapters will conclude with a pastoral section on how best to practice the chapter's teaching.

Every human body, no matter how plain it may appear or even how disabled it may be, is destined for eternal glory. This glory is mostly hidden from human sight and only ever partially seen by those who have eyes to see it; it is a far greater glory than anything any human eye has seen or mind has yet imagined (1 Cor 2:9–10). Already now, God sees each body as it will be in eternity. He looks beyond outward appearances and sees the hidden person of the heart that is beautiful and precious in his sight (1 Pet 3:4). We are therefore challenged to see them as God sees them and regard them as he regards them. More than that, since every human body is destined for eternal glory, we would do well to take good care of our bodies. We need to treat them wisely and use them well because God values them so highly. Since our bodies matter so very much, what we do with them matters equally so. Every human body is, indeed, somebody.

2

# THE CREATED BODY

As a human being a person is a whole, not a body
without a spirit or a spirit without a body. ... Thus,
the whole unitary person is the object of all God's
acts from the bestowal of dominion over the earth
to the resurrection of the dead and the end of the
world ... nobody acts with just one part of the
self. When somebody thinks, that person actually
thinks with the body, and every bodily function
is also at the same time a function of the soul
and the spirit.

—*A. F. C. Vilmar*

**W**e cannot appreciate the complexity, beauty, and mystery of the human body unless we realize that it is given to us. We do not make bodies; they are made for us. They are provided for us with all their main characteristics. We receive them as a gift. But from whom, or what?

Our bodies are obviously made from the physical and biological material that is provided for them in the natural world. In that respect our bodies do not differ in kind from the animals that live on earth with us. Yet we do not actually get our bodies from the natural world; we inherit them from our parents, our mother and father, together with the unique genetic codes that determine so much of what we are and what we can be. We receive our bodies from our ancestors.

But the mystery remains! Who, or what, gives me my body through my parents? While our bodies could perhaps have just been developed, long ago, by an impersonal natural process in an amazing series of unlikely accidents, the most likely and satisfactory answer is that they, like the whole world, were created by some supernatural being. By rational reflection we may then infer that our bodies were created, but we cannot infer who made them. That can only be disclosed by our bodies' supernatural creator or by other supernatural beings who witnessed their creation.

Jesus teaches that this is so! Paraphrasing Genesis 1:27 and 2:24, he asserts this momentous truth about a husband and his wife in Mark 10:6–8: "From the beginning of creation, 'God made them male and female.' 'Therefore a man shall leave his father and mother and hold fast to his wife, and the two shall become one flesh.' So they are no longer two but one flesh." When Jesus speaks of the beginning, he alludes to Genesis 1:1 and its declaration that God created the whole cosmos. We therefore receive our male or female bodies from God through our parents and ancestors, going all the way back to the creation of the first man and woman. Their creation is both an initial act in primordial time and a foundational act that lasts for all time. Their creation is also our creation. Here is how Luther explains it:

> God divided mankind into two classes, namely, male and female, or a he and a she. ... Therefore each of us must have the kind of body God has created for us. I cannot make myself a woman, nor can you make yourself a man; we do not have that power. But we are exactly as he created us; I am a man and you a woman. Moreover, he wills to have his excellent handiwork honored as his divine creation, and not despised. The man is not to despise or scoff at the woman or her body, nor the woman the man. But each should honor the other's image and body as a divine and good creation that is well pleasing unto God himself.[1]

Our vision of the human body cannot be separated from what God himself tells us about its creation. And that is what I would now like to explore by looking at how God's creation of the body is depicted from two different perspectives in Genesis: a universal, cosmic perspective in 1:1–2:3 and an earthly, social perspective in 2:4–3:24.

### THE COSMIC HABITAT FOR THE HUMAN BODY

Before God created Adam and Eve with their bodies, he built a home for them to live, an ordered cosmic habitat for the body that provided what was needed for its survival and prosperity. In broad outline, Genesis 1:1–2:3 sketches out the cosmic order for it in two main ways.

First, in a series of ten decrees, God the Creator of heaven and earth establishes the order of dependence in it; he provides what

---

1. Luther, *The Estate of Marriage* (1522), LW 45:17–18.

is needed for the body to live physically on earth. The human body occupies its own niche in the much larger physical order that encompasses and sustains it. That niche is the dry land on earth, which human beings share with the other land animals akin to them. The habitat for animal and human life on earth stands at the apex of a set of orders within a larger cosmic order in which each consecutive order depends on what was before it for its existence. There is the order of light that keeps the darkness in its place, the order of sky as a separate domain from the earth, the order of earth with its oceans and continents, the order of vegetation that is produced by the land, the order of the sun, moon, and stars that move in the sky above the earth, the orders of fish in the sea and of birds in the sky, and, last, the order of animals and human beings on earth. Each higher order depends on what is under it for its existence, like vegetation that needs dry land for its growth, while the complete order has been designed to support all life on earth, whether it be the life of plants, fish, birds, animals, or humanity.

Second, the same divine utterances also establish the order of government in this cosmic order. While the sun, moon, and stars rule over the sky and the earth, humankind was created as God's regent to rule over the fish, the birds, and the animals on earth. By means of these agents, God governs the whole of his created order. Thus, the human body has its own allotted place and receives its proper function in that cosmic order, its God-given ecosystem. The human body depends on it for its survival and exercises dominion on earth.

With the human body properly placed within it, the cosmic order receives God's full approval, his unabashed appreciation and delight. Six times in Genesis 1 we hear that when God sees what he has created, he recognizes that it is "good"—the light (1:3), the dry land (1:10), the vegetation on earth (1:12), the constellations in the sky (1:18), the birds in the sky and the fish in the sea (1:21), and all the animals on dry land (1:25); each of these is indeed lovely to behold.[2] But when he has made Adam and Eve and housed them in their proper habitat, he is even more pleased. He recognizes that they, together with the whole physical life-support system for them, are "very good" (1:31). Excellent, perfect, and utterly splendid! In 1 Timothy 4:4, Paul sums up God's approval of his physical creation with the assertion that "everything created by God is good." So, too, the human body. All that follows in the rest of the Bible and its account of God's dealings with humanity presupposes God's approval of the human body. Thus, any disparagement of it as something bad, or contempt for it as unfit for God, is ruled out of order by the first chapter of the Bible.

## THE MYSTERY OF THE BODY

Besides the depiction of the visible cosmic support system for human beings with their bodies, Genesis 1:1–2:3 alludes, rather briefly and enigmatically, to the invisible mystery of the human body by mentioning its eternal orientation and its likeness to God, two themes that are merely introduced without any elaboration. That comes later in the Bible.

We get a hint about the human body's eternal destination when God rests on the seventh day, the culmination of his creative acts. At first the seventh day seems out of place; it does not fit in with what precedes, for on this day God says nothing and creates nothing. He merely "rests" from his completed work of creation. After blessing the fish and the birds and man, he "blesses" this day and "sanctifies" it by resting on it. Yet despite its apparent misfit, it is the climax of the whole account, and it touches on three mysteries. First, the culmination of God's creative work for six days in his rest on the seventh sets the weekly rhythm and pattern for the human body: work and rest. For six days, man and woman were to work with God on earth; on the seventh day they were to rest with God in order to receive his blessing. Second, God sanctifies

---

2. The Hebrew word that is used here, like its Greek translation, means both "good" and "beautiful."

the seventh day so that by resting bodily with God on that day, which was later called the Sabbath, they could share in his holiness (Exod 20:8–11; 31:12–17). Third, unlike every other day, there is no mention of the beginning and end of the seventh day. Since it is God's day, it is eternal. While it is set in the time for human life on earth, it transcends all time; it belongs to eternity. It shows that the human body had been created for eternal life by resting with God in heaven rather than just for temporal life on earth with care for its plants and animals.

Genesis 1 discloses another aspect of the mystery of the human body by saying that it was created in God's image. That's what makes humans theologically different from the animals, which, like them, also received physical bodies and the power to procreate. In simple terms, human beings are the only physical creatures made to resemble God. Thus, God announces what he proposes for human bodies with the very words by which he creates humankind: "Let us make man (Hebrew *'adam*) in our image, after our likeness" (Gen 1:26). Then follows this poetic description of man's creation:

So God <u>created</u> man (Hebrew *ha'adam*) in his own image,
in the image of God he <u>created</u> him;
male and female he <u>created</u> them. (Gen 1:27)[3]

These three step-like lines, with their repetition and variations, play on the four senses of *'adam* in Hebrew: "man" as the term for any human person, humankind as a whole (which includes people of both sexes), a male person, and the primordial male figure Adam. Later on, after the account of the fall, we have this third summary in Gen 5:1b–2:

When God <u>created</u> man,
he made him in the likeness of God.
Male and female he <u>created</u> them,
and he blessed them and named them Man (*adam*)
when they were <u>created</u>.

---

3. All parenthetical notes in Scripture quotations in this volume are the author's addition.

As in 1:27, we have the puzzling transition from a singular noun and a singular pronoun to the plural pronouns for male and female persons. This emphasizes that both men and women were created in God's image.

The two key terms in these three passages are "image" and "likeness." The more concrete term, "image," is used elsewhere in the Old Testament for a painted picture of Babylonian soldiers (Ezek 23:14) and the statues that served as idols of Baal (2 Kgs 11:18). The more abstract term, "likeness," derived as it is from the verb "resemble," is used for the resemblance of Seth to his father Adam (Gen 5:3), the resemblance in a painting of the Babylonian soldiers to high-ranking officers (Ezek 23:15), and the assumed resemblance of an idol to its deity (Isa 40:18). Thus, they are virtual synonyms, even though they are used to make a fine distinction in Genesis 1:26 between "in our image" and "after our likeness." Even though a human being is made to be like God, no human is divine by nature; no human is *the* image of God, as an idol was supposed to be the image of its deity by physically embodying it.

God's spoken word for human creation in Genesis 1:26 and its interpretation in 1:27 and 5:1b–2 tell us five things about humankind. First, all people were created by a divine, creative utterance for bodily life on earth with each other and all other living creatures (Gen 1:26). That divine decree, that performative word, makes them what they are; it determines their status and purpose as human beings. Therefore, they derive their human nature and identity from God. They do not name themselves as they name all the other creatures (Gen 2:19); God himself names them so that he can address them personally and converse with them (Gen 5:2).

Second, unlike the idols of pagan gods in the ancient world and the kings of Egypt, they were not made *as* images of God but were only created "*in* his image." In their humanity, they were to resemble the living God by reflecting him in what they were and what they did. They were to be holy as God himself was holy (Lev 11:45; 19:2; 20:26; 1 Pet 1:16). But we are not told who or what that image is. It is only in the New Testament that we discover that God's Son, Jesus, is *the* image of God the Father, the one in whose image human beings were created (2 Cor 4:4; 1 Cor 15:49; Col 1:15; cf. Rom 8:29; Col 3:9–11; Heb 1:3). So, to be in God's image is to be like Jesus by union with him and participation in his communion with his heavenly Father. In his human body, Jesus shows us God the Father, so that when we see his Son, Jesus, we see God the Father (John 12:45; 14:9); by his human body we are remade in God's image (Rom 8:29; 1 Cor 15:49). So even though God is spirit, a spiritual being without a body (John 4:24), he has designed our human bodies to manifest himself visibly and personally, just as idols were supposed to display pagan deities, and to foreshadow his incarnate Son and our bodily union with him.

Third, human beings were created in God's image as male and female. In Hebrew, the terms "male" and "female" describe both their biological sex (Lev 12:2, 5, 7; 15:33), which they share with all the animals (Gen 6:19; 7:3, 9, 16), and their corresponding gender, their sexual identity (Lev 27:3, 4, 5, 7; Num 5:3). Both are given by God in their creation. So, both their sexual status and their gender are aspects of their creation in God's image. Men and women were designed to reflect God's character, his qualities, and his activity, each separately in their devotion to Jesus and together in their conjugal sexual union with each other.

Yet this account of their creation does not show us how they were to do this. It could be that they were to cooperate with him as the Creator in sexual procreation. However, that is not necessarily the result of their creation in God's image, because the birds and fish and animals also procreate by their engagement in sexual intercourse. The answer to that is given much later, by Paul in Ephesians 5:22–33. They were created as male and female in God's image to reflect Christ's self-giving, self-sacrificing love for the church as his bride. His one-flesh union with the church is correlated, imperfectly and yet really, with the one-flesh union of husband and wife in marriage.

Fourth, God did not just create some part of them with some of their faculties, such as their mind with its rational self-consciousness, or their soul with its capacity for personal relationships; he made the whole of them in his image in order to represent him. The mention of their sexuality shows that this includes their bodies. Likewise, in Genesis 9:6, the reason for capital punishment for murder is that the victim is made in God's image. The violation of a living, human body is an attack on God. The whole human being as a soul, a living person, with a human body and a human mind, was designed by the living God to reveal himself—however partially and imperfectly—in the person's life on earth. The body of each person was made for theophany, for God's human manifestation on earth, the visible disclosure of his glory in human terms. That is what human bodies were designed to do and what they have failed to do ever since the rebellion of our primordial parents (Rom 3:23). And that is what Jesus regained for all humanity to compensate for that failure (John 1:14, 16–18).

Fifth, even though the passages that speak about the creation of humankind in God's image do not explain how they were meant to resemble him, they do describe what they were meant to do as creatures made in his likeness. As God's vice-regents, they were to "have dominion" over all the fish and the birds and the land animals (Gen 1:26, 28). Just as God maintained the whole cosmic order and supervised its proper operation, all human beings, rather than just a few powerful kings, were to maintain proper order in the animal kingdom on earth, so that all animals, each in their own niche and in their own way, would thrive on earth together with all humankind. As managers of God's earthly estate, they were to "subdue" the earth (Gen 1:28). They subdued it by farming it properly and protecting it from exploitation and abuse, so that its vegetation would provide food to maintain and sustain human and animal life on earth (Gen 1:29–30). Humankind was to be like God by serving as good stewards of the earth and its animals.

## THE SMALL WORLD OF THE BODY

After painting the big picture of the created world that puts the human body in its life-sustaining cosmic context, in chapter 2 Genesis depicts the creation of man and woman for local life in their domestic context. It focuses our attention on the small world of actual bodily life, the much more limited life of a farmer and his wife. The accent here is on the *ground* (Hebrew *adamah*)—the ground that was to be farmed by the man (Hebrew *adam*, 2:5; cf. 3:23; 4:12), the ground that was irrigated by steams of water (2:6), the ground from which the man was formed (2:7), the ground from which ornamental trees and fruit trees grew (2:9), the ground from which the land animals and the birds were formed (2:19).[4] The panoramic view of the human body in its cosmic context is replaced by the close-up picture of the human body as it lives with plants and animals on earth.

Genesis 2:4–25 shows us two basic aspects of human life in the body: its location and its marital vocation. Here God is depicted in down-to-earth, hands-on terms as a potter or sculptor who "forms" the man and the animals from the soil (2:7, 19) and as a builder who "constructs" the woman from the rib of the man (2:22). The account begins with the formation of the man (Hebrew *adam*) from the ground (Hebrew *adamah*) and ends with the construction of the woman/wife (Hebrew *ishshah*) from her man/husband (Hebrew *ish*). Surprisingly, its goal is the one-flesh union of husband and wife (2:24).

Like the bodies of the animals, the body of the man was "formed" from the ground and made from its "dust" (2:7; 3:19). It was made of the same elements, the same physical material, as them for physical life together with them on the ground. Like the animals, human bodies come from the dust of the ground and return to the dust when they die (3:19). Yet unlike the animals, whose bodies are indirectly animated by God, they are directly

---

4. See also the subsequent mention of the curse of the ground by God (3:17; 8:21), the return of the human body to the ground at death (3:19), Cain's offering of fruit from it to the Lord (4:3), and Cain's banishment from it for his murder of Abel (4:10–12).

animated by God, who "breathes the breath of life" into Adam's mouths and lungs (2:7b). That supernatural intervention makes Adam and his descendants spiritual beings who have been created in God's image. So, like the angels, they are spirits. Yet unlike the angels, they are spirits with bodies; they are embodied spirits.

Like the animals, they do not have the breath of life as a permanent possession; they have it as an ongoing endowment from God contingent on their connection with him. They are life-receiving creatures. He does not just animate them initially, like a lifeguard who resuscitates someone who has stopped breathing. Rather, they are like deep-sea divers with oxygen tanks; God keeps on breathing the breath of life, his life-giving Spirit, into their nostrils. He enlivens the human body with the life-breath that comes from him (Job 33:4; Is 42:5). In bestowing his breath he also quickens the mind with all its powers (Job 32:8; see also Prov 20:27). So human beings keep on receiving the breath of life from God for the duration of their life on earth (Job 27:3). Should God withdraw it and no longer animate them, they would all die (Job 34:14–15; cf. 1 Kgs 17:17). God's breath, the breath of life that he breathes into them, makes them what they are, with all their physical and mental powers. They depend on him and his Spirit for their survival.

God did not create only the spirit of Adam, but of all of Adam's descendants, by their creation in the womb (Job 33:4; Is 42:5).[5] He creates the bodies and souls of all people, even after Adam and Eve fell into sin.[6] That rules out the common teaching of the soul's preexistence, either with God in the spiritual realm, as taught in Plato's philosophy and in Mormonism, or its incarnation in a previous being, as taught in Hinduism and in Buddhism. It also rules out any notion of reincarnation in the body of another person, for at death the spirit returns to God its giver (Eccl 12:7).

---

5. See the Formula of Concord: Solid Declaration, 1. 7, BoC (533).

6. See the summary in the Formula of Concord: Epitome, 1.4, BoC (488): "For God created not only the body and soul of Adam and Eve before the fall but also our body and soul after the fall, even though they are corrupted. God also still recognizes them as his own work, as it is written, Job 10[:8], 'Your hands fashioned and made me, together all around.'"

Besides forming the human body from the ground, the Lord God sets the man in the garden that he had planted for him (2:8), a good garden with trees that God produced from the ground to nourish the man physically with food and provide for him a lovely physical environment (2:9a, 16a), a productive garden for the man to tend and keep in good order (2:15). God grounds Adam's body there and keeps it grounded there. He establishes an earthly home for it in its life with him; he provides food from the trees in the garden by which he nourishes the body; he gives Adam a well-watered garden full of ornamental trees to delight him; he gives Adam work to do with his body, work in which he cooperates with God in caring for the garden that God had provided for him and his wife.

## TWO BODIES, ONE FLESH

The creation of Adam's body from the ground sets the backdrop for God's creation of the woman. The Lord God does not, as we might expect, form her from the ground like he did Adam. Like a master plastic surgeon, he constructs her from his rib, so that she would be of the same basic nature as him, or, perhaps even from his side, so that she would be next to him.

The context for her unique creation is vital for making sense of that miraculous intervention. The Lord God had decided that it was not good for the man to be and live alone with his body on earth (2:18). That judgment did not imply that his solitude was, in itself, a bad thing. It would always remain with him, because his self-conscious embodied soul separated him from all other things and all other animate bodies. But it was even better for him to have some human company as well. It would be good for Adam if he had a physical "helper" and a "partner" (2:18, 20), but it would also be good for God, because by relying on each other they would learn to rely on him. On the one hand, it was good for Adam to have someone to help him in his work, a coworker and collaborator, so that there would be a division of labor between them in a common enterprise. On the other hand, and much more enigmatically, it would also be good if that helper would also be his "partner," a "fit companion" for him. In Old Testament Hebrew, this rather unusual term is not used elsewhere as a noun, but only as a preposition for what is "in front of" or "opposite" a person or thing. Here it describes a partner who corresponds with him as his opposite, his proper match; she is meant to be his counterpart who will complement him, his other half who will be both like him in some respects and yet unlike him in others. Together they will round themselves off and sharpen each other physically and mentally, so that they will fit together well and work well together as they keep on adjusting to each other.

God's creation of a helper and partner for Adam proceeds in two stages. First, he forms the birds and animals from the ground for him so that he could have many companions to keep him company. Since they are formed from the ground like Adam, they are in that respect like him, and so, in some ways, fit for him. Yet when the Lord God presents them to him to appraise their suitability for companionship, he finds them wanting. While some of them, like pet cats, could keep him company, he could use others, like donkeys, to do some physical work for him. But none of them could be a personal helper and suitable partner for him.

Only after Adam does not find a personal partner for himself (2:20), then and only then does the Lord God create the woman for him and present her to him. God is the supernatural matchmaker and celebrant of their union; he gives the woman to the delighted man as his lovely wife (2:22b). Thus, Luther says: "No other beautiful sight in the world appeared lovelier and more attractive to Adam than his own Eve."[7] At the sight of her, Adam exclaims that she was bone of his bones and flesh of his flesh (2:23). That biblical idiom is normally used as a stock formula for close physical kinship in a human family or clan or tribe (Gen 29:14; Judg 9:1–3; 2 Sam 5:1; 19:12–13), people who not only share the same ephemeral flesh but also have the same much more substantial bones, the same basic nature. She is his body mate, as close to him as his

---

7.  Martin Luther, *Lectures on Genesis*, LW 1:67.

closest relatives, yet even closer than that, because she is physically part of him.

Their personal partnership, with the physical union that it establishes, is described in three ways. First, and most mysteriously, in an initial act that is never repeated, the Lord God creates the woman from the ribcage of the man. By doing that, God does not clone Adam in order to replicate him, nor does he, as some suppose, create a male and a female from a hermaphrodite, a single asexual or bisexual primordial human being. Rather, by creating Eve from Adam's ribcage, the Lord God creates a strong physical affinity between them with the urge to reconnect physically once again. He does not make her from Adam's head, so that she would dominate him, nor from his feet, so that he would oppress her, but from his side, so that she would be next to his heart.

Second, at the sight of her naked body, Adam describes the physical connection between them by making two puns on the two senses of the Hebrew word *ish* ("man," or "male person," and "husband") as well as on its Hebrew opposite *ishshah* ("woman," or "female person," and "wife"). Since she has been taken "from" a man (Hebrew *meish*), her physical orientation is toward man (Hebrew *ishsha*h)—but not just any man: *her* man, the man who is her counterpart (1 Cor 11:8–9). That correlation of the woman with her man establishes the dynamic polarity that creates a kind of sexual magnetic field in marriage. Without the union of opposites, marriage does not work as it should.

Third, her unique creation from the man results in their bodily union with each other, their conjugal sexual union in marriage (2:24). With their bodies they have a common physical life on earth, rather than just occasional physical interactions with each other. In their convivial union the two of them become "one flesh." Oddly, that unusual term remains unexplained. It is a riddle that plays on the paradox that, in this case, one plus one is one. While the focus of this saying is on the body, it includes the whole person. It alludes to their physical union in marital cohabitation, their sexual union as husband and wife, and to their procreative union that results in the birth of a child as the foundation of a new family. Their two bodies become one flesh, even though they still remain separate from each other. Yet their union is even closer and more permanent than two fraternal twins. They complement each other bodily in a common life where they are meant to work together as interdependent partners. Nothing could be more physical than that! Little could be more wonderful than that! Their marital, sexual union is the culmination of God's creation of them as a man and a woman.

## THE NAKED BODY

The bodily creation of our first parents for bodily union with each other culminates in the mention of their unashamed nakedness: "the man and his wife were both naked and were not ashamed" (Gen 2:25). That is an apt indication of their dignity and beauty, the dignity of their bodies and the beauty of their sexual union. They are not ashamed of themselves and their nakedness; they delight in their nakedness, because they have nothing to hide from each other and God. Unlike children who are not ashamed of their naked bodies because they are not self-consciously aware of them, they are well aware of their nakedness. They are quite at ease with their appearance, because they both are what they appear; they both show how they think and feel by their physical appearance. They have, as it were, transparent bodies, bodies that disclose their minds and their souls perfectly without distortion and misrepresentation. Because they have nothing to hide, nothing unsightly, no dark self, no dark thoughts and no dark feelings, no dark actions and dark reactions, they are not afraid of being seen by each other. Unashamed of their bodies, they are happily at home in them and physically at ease with each other.

Oddly and sadly, a sense of shame is now an ingrained mark of our embodied humanity. It is both intensely physical and intensely personal. As far as we can tell, animals are not ashamed of themselves and their bodies. Yet a shameless person is less than fully human. Such a person is not fit for life in community, life in the body together with other people. That applies most of all in sexual interactions. Sexual shamelessness breeds sexual abuse, and vice versa. The sexual modesty that clothes provide is an essential requirement for life in the public domain. People hide the naked body from public view and reserve it for willing, physical self-giving to another chosen person in private sexual intercourse. Unlike the animals, we now clothe our naked bodies. We dress in order to present ourselves publicly to others; we undress in order to present ourselves privately to a chosen spouse in the safety of our homes. Through dress we manage our bodies.

Even though we all experience shame, we find it hard to say why we do and even harder to explain how it works. It has to do with our honor as a person in our community, our social standing with others in that community, and our sense of personal worth in the eyes of our associates. We gain honor and retain it based on how those around us regard us. By their approval they give us our "face," our sense of worth. By their disapproval and rejection they shame us. So, when we know that there is something wrong with us, something shameful that makes us unacceptable and unpresentable, we cover up. We hide ourselves from public view and try to present an acceptable face instead. We avoid exposure.

This sense of shame is most evident in our sexuality, for there our whole self is at stake personally, emotionally, and physically. It has the power to make or break us as men and women. In that fraught arena we experience shame as nowhere else. Sexual rejection undermines our sense of self. It dishonors us more than anything else. So we need to protect ourselves from the shame of sexual dishonor and abuse. Since we identify that sense of shame with our genitalia, we cover them up from visual violation. We dress our naked bodies, and thus we can safely undress them for our spouse, a chosen person who has pledged to love us, honor us, and never reject us.

Sexual modesty is a much underrated, indispensable condition for sexual safety and enjoyment. Both shameful sexual prudery and shameless sexual exposure dishonor our bodies and their divine

Creator. Sexual exhibitionism damages sexual intimacy because it offers the naked body on display to others rather than as an exclusive, personal gift to a spouse in a committed relationship. But the practice of sexual modesty, with its use of appropriate dress, protects the body from intrusive public, visual abuse and reserves sexual intercourse for private use. In fact, modesty facilitates safe sexual self-giving with its call for physical intimacy and visual self-disclosure. So, as Paul reminds us, we (paradoxically) honor our sexual organs by treating them with greater modesty than the other more publicly presentable parts of our body (1 Cor 12:22–25).

The rebellion of our first parents against God results in a loss of physical innocence. Instead of knowing everything, as they had hoped, they now know something that they had not previously experienced: they know that they are naked and feel ashamed of their nakedness (Gen 3:7). Something is wrong, terribly wrong, with them and their bodies. They are no longer as they know they should be. In their shame they have lost face with each other and with God. They become aware of their all-too-naked, exposed bodies, which they now no longer wear with pride. Since they are now no longer happy and at home in their bodies, they dissociate themselves as persons from them. For self-protection they cover themselves and hide their genitalia with a makeshift loincloth made from fig leaves (3:7). Most tellingly, they hide themselves from God because they realize that despite their dress, they are still naked in his eyes (3:8).

When God confronts them and calls them to account for their stupidity, he does not strip them bare and shame them by exposing them to public disdain. Instead, he treats them and their bodies with dignity and compassion. In an act of mercy that foreshadows his redemption, he makes even better clothes for them from the skins of animals—clothes that cover their whole body rather than just their genitalia (3:21). He covers their shame and recovers their modesty; he respects their sexuality and their need for sexual self-protection; he shields them from the intrusive, critical gaze of others. He respects their privacy and protects them from the worst social consequences of their sin. They therefore can interact sexually in privacy and safety with their spouse and give themselves bodily to each other willingly and lovingly in sexual intercourse, even in their exile from the garden. They can engage relatively safely with others in society because their inner selves, with their guilt and shame, thoughts and feelings, passions and desires, are hidden from public view. But their shame remains because their guilt remains. It goes with them and with all their descendants as they live uneasily with dressed bodies east of Eden. They dress for fear of exposure and rejection; they dress to present themselves in the best light to others and gain their approval.

## THE EXILED BODY

The original state of the human body created by God in his image is changed by its tragic fall into sin. This new state of being is the result of a rather mysterious encounter. An unannounced, unidentified snake, a speaking serpent, instigates it. That wily creature is the mouthpiece of Satan, the enemy of humanity and of marriage as God's good gift to human beings (Rev 12:9). He targets the man through his wife. But why her? Why does he set out to dislocate their one-flesh relationship from their life with God? How could that be of any threat to him?

The explanation that makes most sense to me is given in the Wisdom of Solomon.[8] There, in 2:23–24, we read:

> God created man for incorruption,
> and made him in the image of his own eternal nature,
> but through the devil's envy death entered the world,
> and those who are belong to him experience it.[9]

---

8. The Wisdom of Solomon belongs to the apocryphal books of the Old Testament. They consist of those books which were originally included in the Septuagint, the Greek translation of the Old Testament, but later excluded from the Hebrew Bible as unauthorized for use in public worship. In his translation of the Bible, Luther places them between the two testaments so that they could be used devotionally by believers for their personal instruction and edification.

9. RSV Catholic Edition translation. Paul alludes to this passage in Rom 5:12. See also Luther's reference to it in LW 29:134 and 42:151.

The devil, the arch-angel who rebelled against God with other angelic spirits, envied our parents because he had not been given bodily life.[10] Even though Adam and Eve were not eternal super-spirits like Satan and his cronies, God had created their bodies in his image and given them the power to procreate, a power that Satan did not have. Compared to him and all the other spirits, they were such inferior, dependent creatures. Why should God lavish such honor and love on them? Why should he choose them to create new spirits physically through sexual intercourse? His envy of them bred contempt for them and what he considered to be their disgusting physical sexuality.

In *The Screwtape Letters*, C. S. Lewis depicts demonic disgust at their physicality in graphic terms.[11] There Screwtape, a high-ranking evil spirit, describes the man that his underling is meant to attack as "this thing of earth and slime" (151), "this thing begotten in a bed" (159). He dismisses men and women as "disgusting human vermin" (17), "mere animals" (143), "hairless bipeds" (74), whom God had made as "loathsome little replicas of Himself" (45). The contempt of this demon stands in sharp contrast with God's high regard for them and their sexual bodies.

So, the devil sets out to subvert Adam and Eve's union with God and pervert their intimacy with each other. He addresses the woman and asks her whether God had, meanly and demeaningly, forbidden her and her husband to eat fruit from the trees in the garden. When she tells him that God had only prohibited them to eat from one tree because its fruit would be deadly for them, he casts doubt on God's word that warned against its consumption. He contradicts God's warning and assures her that they most

10. In "Afternoon Sermon on the Feast of Christ's Birth" (December 25, 1544), WA 49:632.29–39, Luther says that the Qur'an is right in its claim that Satan fell because he refused to bow down and adore the man made in God's image.

11. C. S. Lewis, *The Screwtape Letters*, (London and Glasgow: Collins, 1942).

certainly would not die from eating its fruit. Instead, they would have an even better life with more perfect knowledge, because they would become divine like God; they would not just be people in his image and under him, but equal to him and no longer dependent on him. They would become their own gods with super-minds that would enable them to know everything. With their super-minds they would transcend the limitations of their bodies. The key to attaining that state was to consume the forbidden fruit.

Their rebellion against God has an immediate negative effect on their bodily union with each other. They no longer act as one flesh and are unhappy to be naked with each other. Reckless Eve acts as an independent agent apart from Adam and God by listening to the serpent and giving some of the forbidden fruit to her feckless husband for him to eat. When confronted by God, Adam blames his wife for what he himself had done and blames God for giving her to him. She, in turn, blames the serpent. Thus, the devil gets a foothold in their marriage, in order to disorder it and estrange them from each other and God. They fall out with each other and with God.

This is a full-frontal attack on the whole person, the body with its appetite for enjoyable food, the mind with its quest for more knowledge, and the soul with its trust in God and his word. So, when Adam and Eve follow the serpent's advice, they sin with their whole being in body, mind, and soul. Since they rebel against God with their whole person, their whole self is corrupted by that original sin, the first sin that is the seed of all subsequent sins. It may be called "person-sin," because it involves the whole person rather than just the body and its deeds.[12] Sadly, the man and the woman do not become like God at all. Instead, they cease to reflect God's image, because they turn away from him. Just as an object no longer has light if it is hidden away from the sun, so they no longer have the spiritual life that comes from him and is with him. And

---

12. See the citation of Luther in the Formula of Concord: Epitome, 1.20, BoC (490) and its Solid Declaration, 1.6, BoC (533).

that scars and mars their whole being. Nothing in them is quite as it should be. They become diminished persons in body, mind, and spirit that are no longer perfectly attuned to God.

Even though this act of rebellion revolves around the eating of fruit from a tree, it is not basically a physical offense. It is a spiritual offense that involves the soul and all its highest powers. Like the body, both the soul and the mind are polluted and corrupted. The soul is no longer holy and righteous before God (Rom 3:9–20; Eph 4:24). No longer attuned to God's word, the mind becomes a "mind of flesh" (Col 2:18) that is hostile to God and insubordinate to his law (Rom 8:7). Yet it is the body that suffers the most obvious penalty. It is now doomed to die (Gen 3:19). That begins immediately and escalates gradually as the body weakens, suffers, sickens, ages, and wears out. The devil makes life in the body hard for Adam and Eve (3:15); he terrorizes them and their descendants by the threat of death (Heb 2:13). The woman experiences trouble in childbearing and pain in childbirth; even her sexual desire for her husband is distorted by a perverse desire for sexual domination (3:16). The man has to work hard to make a living, because the ground no longer cooperates productively with him (3:17–19). But worst of all, God himself banishes them from the garden and shuts the gate to the tree of life. They live in exile apart from intimate, life-giving contact with him (3:23–24).

By its banishment from God's presence, the body is diminished and doomed to die. Much of its beauty and splendor is lost. The body that was once fully alive becomes a "body of death" (Rom 7:24), a "mortal body" (Rom 8:11). The body that was once righteous becomes as "body of sin" (Rom 6:6), "sinful flesh" (Rom 8:3). The body that was highly honored is now brought low (Phil 3:21). Yet, though beset by death, some of its former glory still appears, for a short while, when people are healthy and young. But it does not last and cannot last. It is like the beauty of wildflowers that blossom for a day before they fade ever so quickly away (Ps 103:15–16; Isa 40:6–7).

So begins the cycle of human life since the fall, the cycle of diminished bodily life under the shadow of sin and death, the cycle of the generations portrayed in the genealogies of Genesis. This cycle of life in the body begins with birth and ends with death. By its relentless recurrence, the human body becomes a "body of flesh" (Col 2:11), a body that has turned in on itself away from God in pursuit of its own comfort and survival. Practically speaking, its god is its belly (Phil 3:19). Even though it is kept alive by the living God, it sets its mind on earthly things. It lives an earth-bound life, like an eagle shut up in a cage. Consequently, it is no longer spiritually alive but becomes spiritually dead in trespasses and sin (Eph 2:1). It does not have the abundant, heavenly life that comes from God and is found only in him.

## A GOOD LIFE IN GOD'S GOOD WORLD

It would be untruthful and misleading to paint a completely dismal picture of life in the body after the fall. To be sure, it is severely disrupted and curtailed by disorder and trouble, evil and injustice, sickness and infirmity, sin and death. But bodily life is not all bad, because the body that God has made is still good, even if it is no longer perfectly good. Although sin and death overshadow it at every turn, and every good thing is matched by something bad—birth with death, health with sickness, happiness with sorrow—God still maintains the conditions for a good life on earth. By his word he gives us a nuanced vision of a good life in the body, a good life in a good world that provides us with ample evidence of his goodness (Acts 14:17).

Thus, life is still relatively good for people who now live outside the garden. God does not abandon the descendants of Adam and Eve because they reject him. They do not die right away as might be expected. Though God does curtail sin and punish wickedness, to protect the world and its inhabitants, he does not write them off. He does not give up on them but is still unobtrusively involved with them. He keeps them alive and protects their right to life, even if they, like Cain, are murderers (Gen 4:13–15). He works indirectly and discreetly through what he has made to take good care of them. So, for example, he uses sexual intercourse to create children and parents to provide for them. He works through his ordinances in the order of creation to create new life and nourish it. Through his law he curbs sin and maintains civic righteousness. He upholds all things by the power of his word (Heb 1:3). That includes his gift of life and our right to life.

In his discussion on the marriage of priests in the *Apology of the Augsburg Confession*, Philipp Melanchthon claims that our natural, human rights are established by God's ordinances in creation.[13] His ordinances are the decrees that institute and maintain right order in the world. Thus, natural rights are built into the natural order of the created world. Natural law supersedes civil law. Since that is so, human regulations, such as those that establish so-called same-sex marriage, cannot abolish any natural right, such as the union of a man and woman in conjugal marriage. Only God can override or change our natural rights. He concludes: "a natural right truly is a divine right, because it is an order divinely stamped upon nature."

By his decrees recorded in Genesis 1 and elsewhere, God still orders the world for human life and continues to maintain human life (Heb 1:3). By his powerful utterances in Genesis 1:3, 6, 9, he creates and maintains the cosmic and terrestrial order that is needed for life to flourish on earth. By his decree in Genesis 1:11, the earth still produces vegetation. By his word of blessing to Adam and Eve in 1:20a, which is repeated for Noah and his sons in 9:1, 7 and for Jacob in 35:9–11, he still enables them and their descendants to procreate. By his mandate for Adam and Eve in 1:20b, he commissions and empowers them to keep ruling over the earth as coworkers with him. By his mandate in 1:29, he still provides food for them from the plants and trees, just as later in 9:3–4 he gives them the meat of the animals to eat.

These creative decrees once spoken at the beginning are still in force; they remain the living word of God. They are performative

---

13. The Apology of the Augsburg Confession, 23.8, BoC (249).

utterances that do what they say. So, if God should no longer say, "Let there be light," the whole cosmos would become dark and chaotic, formless and void, unfit for life and growth. Through them God maintains the conditions for physical life on earth and keeps us physically alive. They create and uphold the good order for human life and for the reception of God's earthly blessings. Since they sustain God's good order in creation, the order for the transmission of his blessings, they, traditionally, are called divine ordinances. Melanchthon rightly notes:

> The Word of God formed human nature in such a way that it may be fruitful not only at the beginning of creation but as long as this physical [bodily] nature of ours exists. Likewise, the earth became fruitful by this Word [Gen 1:11]: 'Let the earth put forth vegetation; plants yielding seed.'[14] Because of this ordinance, the earth commenced to produce plants not only in the beginning, but yearly the fields are clothed as long as this natural order exists.[15]

The same pattern continues both before and after the fall. By his declaration in 2:18, the Lord God establishes and maintains the conjugal union of husband and wife in marriage. In response to Noah's burnt offering after the flood in 8:21–22, the Lord decrees that even though the human heart is still evil from youth to old age, he will maintain the right order for human life on earth, with the agricultural cycle of seedtime and harvest, the meteorological cycle of hot and cold weather, the seasonal cycle of summer and winter, and the work cycle of day and night. By his decree in Genesis 9:6, he protects human life from murder by sanctioning limited, proportionate retribution; by his covenant in Genesis 9:8–16 with Noah and all his descendants, including us, he declares that he will never again destroy animal and human life on earth with another flood. All these divine performative utterances remain in force

---

14. See also Luther's remarks in *Lectures on Genesis Chapters 1–5*, LW 1:75–76.

15. Apology of the Augsburg Confession, 23.8, BoC (249).

after the fall until the end of the world. Through them he maintains bodily life on earth. They establish and maintain our natural right to life. Governments do not give us that right, nor can they abolish it. Instead, those who are in government are required to respect and uphold God's ordinances by their laws, policies, and actions. If they fail to protect the God-given right to life in their jurisdiction, they abandon their most fundamental responsibility.

God also defends human life in the body through his law, the natural law that is summarized by the seven commandments in the second table of the Decalogue. He protects the good gifts that he provides for humankind and the good order by which he delivers them to all people on earth—parents and family, physical life and good health, sexual intercourse and marriage, money and property, justice and a good reputation, the household as an economic unit with its persons and assets. By his law he curbs social disorder and maintains the communal, civic order that is necessary for a good human life on earth. He also establishes governments to enforce his law for the common good of all humankind and defend the rights of all their citizens (Rom 13:1–7).

Even though the descendants of Adam turn away from God and spurn him, he still offers a relatively good, bodily life to them in the order of creation. If they are law-abiding, clean-living, moral people who respect God's order for the world and human society, they enjoy his earthly blessings. The promise attached to the fourth commandment applies to them; it will be well with them and they will live long on the earth (Deut 5:16). They will have good lives with good families, good marriages, and good communities. They will be able to do good work to provide for their families, care for the people around them, and look after the natural world that sustains them. They will be able to enjoy food and drink and all the other good things that God so richly provides for their enjoyment in their bodily life (1 Tim 6:17), for he does not just provide them with their livelihood but also gives them the ability to produce wealth (Deut 8:18) and the capacity to enjoy the fruit of their work (Eccl 5:19; 6:2).

But all that depends on their respect for the right order by which God delivers these temporal blessings to them and other people through both the natural world and good government. In his explanation to the first commandment, Luther tells us how that happens:

> Although much that is good comes to us from human beings, nevertheless, anything received according to his command and ordinance in fact comes from God. Our parents and our authorities—as well as everyone who is a neighbor—have received the command to do us all kinds of good. So we receive our blessings not from them, but from God through them. Creatures are only the hands, channels, and means through which God bestows all blessings. For example, he gives the mother breasts and milk for her infant or gives grain and all sorts of fruits for sustenance—things that no creature could produce by itself. No one, therefore, should presume to take or give anything unless God has commanded it. ... Therefore, we should not spurn even this way of receiving such things through God's creatures, nor are we through arrogance to seek other methods and ways than God has commanded. For that would not be receiving them from God, but seeking them from ourselves.[16]

So the enjoyment of life in the body depends on respect for the ordered way by which God delivers his blessings to us. Nothing could be more dangerous and destructive than setting up other ways to gain perceived material benefits for ourselves in defiance of God's good order for their delivery.

All good things come from God; they are anonymous gifts from him. His hidden hand is at work everywhere and always in every human life. There is no life in the body apart from him. With him is life. Apart from him, there is only death. He provides us with the necessities of life, just as he gives us life and keeps us alive. Thus,

---

16. The Large Catechism, 1.26, BoC (389).

Jesus reminds us in Matthew 5:45 that God the Father "makes his sun rise on the evil and on the good, and sends rain on the just and on the unjust." Then in 6:25–29 he adds that the heavenly Father, who provides all people with food to eat and clothes to wear, also determines the length of their physical lives. We acknowledge all that when we ask God, in the fourth petition of the Lord's Prayer, to give us and all people our daily bread. In his Small Catechism, Luther lists what is included in the gift of daily bread:

> Everything included in the necessities and nourishment for our bodies, such as food, drink, clothing, shoes, house, farm, fields, livestock, money, property, an upright spouse, upright children, upright members of the household, upright and faithful rulers, good government, good weather, peace, health, decency, honor, good friends, faithful neighbors, and the like.[17]

All that and much more comes from God the Father.

So Jesus does not paint a picture of a miserable life in the body as it ekes out a mere existence in a vale of tears. He gives us the warm vision of family life in the house of a loving generous Father who anonymously lavishes his gifts equally on all his children, whether they are good or bad. Prodigal sons and daughters are not excluded from a good life on God's earthly estate. But that does not make them good people, for since the fall nobody is completely good any longer (Mark 10:18); no one is righteous and holy in God's sight except Jesus.

I can think of no better summary of how God treats the body that he has created in his image than Luther's explanation of the first article of the Apostles' Creed:

> I believe that God has created me together with all that exists. God has given me and still preserves my body and soul: eyes, ears, and all my limbs and senses; reason and

---

17. The Small Catechism, 3.14, BoC (357).

all mental faculties. In addition, God daily and abundantly provides shoes and clothing, food and drink, house and farm, spouse and children, fields, livestock, and all property—along with all the necessities and nourishment for this body and life. God protects me against all danger and shields and preserves me from all evil. And all this is done out of pure, fatherly, and divine goodness and mercy, without any merit or worthiness of mine at all. For all this I owe it to God to thank and praise, serve and obey him. This is most certainly true.[18]

## HOW THIS IS DONE: OUR VOCATION IN THE ORDER OF CREATION

God's creation of human bodies and care for them is not a theory but a reality that governs what we actually do and what we can potentially do every day of our lives. He sets the terms for our daily reception from him and our daily interaction with him, for in him we live and move and have our being (Acts 17:28). He allots us our bodies with their abilities and capacities, their location in families and societies, their work and their rest from work, necessities for their survival and luxuries for their enjoyment, their lifespan and the seasons in their lifecycle.[19] Our task is to recognize what he is doing with our bodies at each stage of our lives and work together with him. How well we harmonize with him and his activity in the order of creation shapes the story of our bodies for good and ill—for good if we cooperate with him as our Creator, for ill if we defy him by attempting to reconstruct our own bodily existence.

Since God is our Creator, he relieves us of the stressful burden of making do for ourselves, as if we were our own creators. Because we receive our bodies and the life-support system from him, they serve us best when we adjust to his provision for them and

---

18. The Small Catechism, 2.1, BoC (354–55).

19. See the notion of our lot in life by God's allotment of these to us in Eccl 2:10; 3:22; 5:18, 19; 9:9.

cooperate with him. We fit in best with what God wishes to accomplish with our bodies in the order of creation by exercising the duty of caring for them, serving God with them, having children if we can, and devoting them to him in thanksgiving, prayer, and praise.

## Duty of Care for the Body

Because God values our bodies so highly and takes such good care of them, we, most obviously, need to take good care of them. They are given by him; they are cherished by him; they belong to him. The life of every human body is a gift from God. By creating humanity in his image, he gives the right to life of every human being at every stage of life from conception to death and in every condition of our human existence. By that most basic human right, which God protects with the fifth commandment, he obligates us to respect the life of every human body. It rules out murder, abortion, euthanasia, suicide, and any other violation of human bodies. Yet it also goes well beyond that. In his explanation of the fifth commandment, Luther reminds us that we should not hurt or harm our neighbor in his bodily life, but help and support him in every bodily need.[20]

Now more than any time in recent history, the church needs to preach and teach and confess that God has created the human body and still cares for it in every possible way. We do not own it, nor can we do as we please with it. It is a gift from God that is not to be abused by mistreating it, but it is to be used as he instructs us in the Ten Commandments. This needs to be taught to counter the common view that the body can be reconstructed to make it do what we desire and be what we want it to be, the view that we are our own gods who create our own bodily lives. So, instead of enjoying our allotted, physical life with its God-given order and beneficial limits, we imagine that we can free ourselves and our minds from the limitations of the body with cosmetic surgery and sexual reassignment, hallucinogenic drugs and pornography,

---

20. The Small Catechism, 1.10, BoC (352).

technology, and other similar measures. We therefore need to learn that God has given each of us a particular body, with all its limits and finite abilities, to enhance our physical enjoyment rather than diminish it.

We owe a duty of care for our own bodies as a gift from God. We are to look after them in many different ways. Here are just a few. We take good care of them by attention to diet and exercise, hygiene and health, work and rest, a regular routine, and good habits. We look after them properly by avoiding physical abuse and overindulgence, physical sloth and overwork, physical indiscipline and rigidity. Our duty of care for them also involves learning what we can from scientists who study them and tell us how they work. But, most of all, we take good care of our bodies by respecting the God-given order for them in the natural world, in society, and in the family and in marriage, for through these orders God provides for our bodies and uses them to provide bodily care for the people around us. They keep us physically fit, well adjusted, and healthy.

We also exercise the duty of care for our bodies by our respect for both the ecological order of the natural physical world that supports us and the ecological order of the social-moral world that sustains us. Both provide us with what we need for a good life in the body. By fitting in with that ordered, ordering environment, and in keeping with it and its requirements, we cooperate with God our Creator and receive his blessings in our bodily existence on earth. That applies both to God-fearing believers who are obedient to God's law, and upright unbelievers who live moral lives according to what they know to be right, for, as Jesus reminds us, our heavenly Father "makes his sun rise on the evil and on the good, and sends his rain on the just and on the unjust" (Matt 5:45).

### Working with God

Our bodies were designed to work with others and with God here on earth. They were made to be receptive and active: receptive in obtaining life from God and active in working with God to promote life here on earth. Each body has received different characteristics and abilities because each body has something different to do. Thus, my male body qualifies me to work as a husband to my wife, a father to my children, and a grandfather to my grandchildren. Unlike me, the body of a single woman qualifies her to serve as a female relative, a female friend, and a female caregiver to others regardless of their marital status and without sexual complications. We all have different vocations according to our location in the world and in our society. My location as a man is in my marriage and my family in the city of Adelaide, Australia. That is where God has appointed me to work with him in caring for my wife, children, and grandchildren. He employs me to work with him in that location with those people.

He employs people to work with him in the whole of society. He uses farmers and bakers to provide bread for people to eat. He uses men and women to create new human beings and to nurture and educate them. So goes the whole of the economic order of our society. Each person has some task to do for the economy of our nation and every nation on earth. Broadly speaking, God employs people to work with him in three main industries: primary industry, such as farming and mining, which produce useful things from the natural world; secondary industry, such as manufacturing and trade, which make new products from natural material and distribute them; and tertiary industry, like education and health care, which provide services for society. In all these workplaces, God employs people to provide the necessities and luxuries that support and enrich life in the body for people on earth.

All people work for God, whether they know it or not, even when they do not do exactly what he wants them to do. He is their employer who supervises and overrules all that they do, so that they work with him for the common good of humanity. Christians differ from unbelievers by acknowledging God as their employer. They therefore seek to please him by obeying his commandments, which show them how they can work well with God and in harmony with his work in the world. They can also seek his help and guidance and power to work with him by praying to him, for since he is the Creator, he wants to help and empower them to serve as good stewards of his creation. That is his mandate for them as persons who have been created in his image. They have the mandate to use their bodies to work with him on earth.

## The Privilege of Procreation

Procreation goes hand in hand with God's creation of us as male and female persons. As our Creator, God commissions human beings to be fruitful and multiply (Gen 1:28). In this way, he shares some of his own life-giving power with them. Like the commission to care for the earth and rule over the animals on it, he gives this mandate to humanity as a whole. It is not exercised individually by each person but by married couples as they are blessed by him. By sexual intercourse and bearing children, they work with God in his creation of new people, preserving human life on earth. By procreation and the nurture of children they serve God physically. So, a married couple who can have children but deliberately refuses to do so commits an unnatural, life-denying act of defiance that rejects the blessings God wishes to bestow on them and the whole human race. On the other hand, by choosing to have children, Christians, most obviously and counterculturally, confess their faith in God as the Creator of humankind and so contradict the prevalent secular notion that we are not creatures but our own creators. They acknowledge God as their Creator and put their trust in his providence.

## Thanksgiving

Our proper response to God's creation of our bodies and provision for them is thanksgiving. Our bodies are God's good gift to us. He also gives us everything that nourishes and supports, sustains and protects, and delights and enriches them. Everything is freely and generously given to all people, even though they do not deserve such lavish bounty. He gives them everything for their enjoyment (1 Tim 6:17). That should evoke spontaneous, grateful thanksgiving. Yet it seldom happens, apart from those whom he has redeemed (Rom 1:21). And even they too often forget him and his benefits (Ps 103:1–5). We who are God's people need to be quite deliberate in our practice of thanksgiving. The simplest way to do that is by saying grace before and after our daily meals. By those prayers we acknowledge that God the Father provides us with our daily bread and receive it with thanksgiving. Nothing else is more appropriate than that! Nothing else is better for our bodies and more countercultural than that! Nothing else does more for our full enjoyment of bodily life than that! As we thank God the Father for our daily bread and every other good and perfect gift, we come to appreciate them and become more aware of God's hand in our physical lives and in the world around us. Thanksgiving attunes us and our bodies to God's daily provision for us. With it comes the priceless gift of contentment (1 Tim 6:6–8; Heb 13:5; cf. Eccl 5:19).

## Prayer for Our Bodily Livelihood

Since God gives us our daily bread to nourish and sustain our bodies, we can ask him to provide it for us and all people. Daily bread calls for daily prayer. Just as our bodies need daily nourishment, so they are meant to engage in daily prayer. Jesus himself teaches us this in the Lord's Prayer. In the fourth, central petition he invites us to join with him in his prayer for our daily bread, the bread that our bodies need for their survival. This includes everything that we need to nourish and sustain our bodies. We have dependent bodies that are only able to work and produce goods if they keep on receiving nourishment. Our physical life is dependent on our reception from God. When we pray for our daily bread, our bodies do what they were meant to do. They receive from God. By that prayerful stance they take their proper, receptive place in the order of creation.

## Full-Bodied Praise

The human body was not just made to work with God in the administration of his earthly estate; it was made in his image to adore and praise and glorify him as its Creator. It was designed to promote God and advertise his goodness. Since God has created us with our bodies, the credit for them belongs to him. They do what they are meant to do by speaking of him and his goodness to the people on earth. That's why we have bodies with lungs that breathe, tongues that speak, and voices that sing. Our bodies, which are animated by the breath of life that comes from God, are meant to praise God in word and deed. That is the message of the Psalter, which ends with this decree and this response to it in Psalm 150:6: "Let everything that has breath praise the LORD! Praise the LORD!"

The biblical vision of the created body culminates in praise of God its Creator. For example, Psalm 8 celebrates the wonder of human creation in God's image for physical life on earth in a jubilant hymn of praise. It praises God for his unreasonable interest in humanity. In amazement at the place of human beings in their cosmic context, it asks God this astonished question in verse 4:

> What is man that you are mindful of him,
> and the son of man (*adam*) that you care for him?

In answer to that question, the psalm celebrates the cosmic location and supernatural status of all people on earth. It locates them under the angels in the heavenly realm and over the animals in the earthly realm; it also affirms that God confers some of his royal glory and honor on people so that they can serve as God's vice-regents by exercising dominion over the animals on earth, a task that applies equally to Adam as to all his descendants. Yet because of revolt against their heavenly Overlord, that mandate, as the author of Hebrews notes, is left undone (2:5–18). It remains unfulfilled until the incarnation of God's Son and his work of redemption as the Son of Man.

### AFFIRMING OUR COMMON IDENTITY

The notion of identity has become a key topic of debate in much of the Western world. It has become an urgent issue because many people have been so dislocated that they are no longer certain about themselves and their place in the world. Since they feel that they can no longer be truly identified by their parentage, their family, and their place in society, they need to identify themselves in some other way, such as by their race, their class, their politics, or, now rather forcefully, by their sexuality. To secure a certain identity for themselves, they assume a kind of tribal identity that includes them in the company of others who identify as they do and excludes those who do not share the same identity. The divisiveness of this stance creates many problems for them and for all of society. It further fractures an already-fractured social order. Sadly, the fixation on one aspect of identity by some people may serve to diminish and dehumanize them and all of society.

The traditional notion of identity is much more helpful and much more fruitful, because it is based on what is given and yet open in orientation. In this view, we do not have a single identity but have many different layers of identity, which do not exclude each other but make for personal uniqueness and social enrichment. Each layer of identity shows a different, characteristic aspect of a person. Take my passport as an example. It not only identifies me by the personal names that my parents gave me and by the surname I inherited from my father, but also by my date and place of birth, as well as my nationality. It locates me in that physical context. Other identifications include my parentage, my sex, and my marital status. All of these are inherited apart from my marital status, which was a matter of choice. Besides these, there are also many other layers of identity, such as my ethnicity, my religious affiliation, and my occupation. Taken together, this rich mix makes me the unique, rather odd person that I am. None of these excludes any other identity or all of them.

A problem has arisen for us because many people now seem to seek their identity in only one aspect of themselves and reject other people who have a different identity or one that seems to negate theirs. This is where the biblical teaching on our common creation in God's image is so true and helpful. Underneath the other layers of identity, we all share the same common human identity as people who have been made in God's image. Whether we acknowledge it or not, we all share the same humanity, an innate identity that is granted in our conception that cannot be taken away from us. No one, or nothing, can unperson us and cancel our human identity. That foundational identity does not threaten the other layers of identity; instead, it confirms them all by giving each its proper due in its proper place in the hierarchy of identity. So I maintain most passionately that we, at present, need to acknowledge, affirm, and build on the common identity that we have with all other people as we negotiate the antagonisms of politics, the cross-currents of culture wars, and the conflicts of identity. We all have so much to gain from each other, and, most of all, from people who differ from us.

In the human body of Jesus, we see the excellence of God the Creator mirrored for us. By his body he discloses the glory of God the Father and the glory of humanity. With his human body he undoes the damage done by our rebellion against God and restores God's good order on earth. Nothing on earth is more wonderful and beautiful than that. So we quite rightly say: "O Lord, our Lord, how majestic is your name in all the earth!"

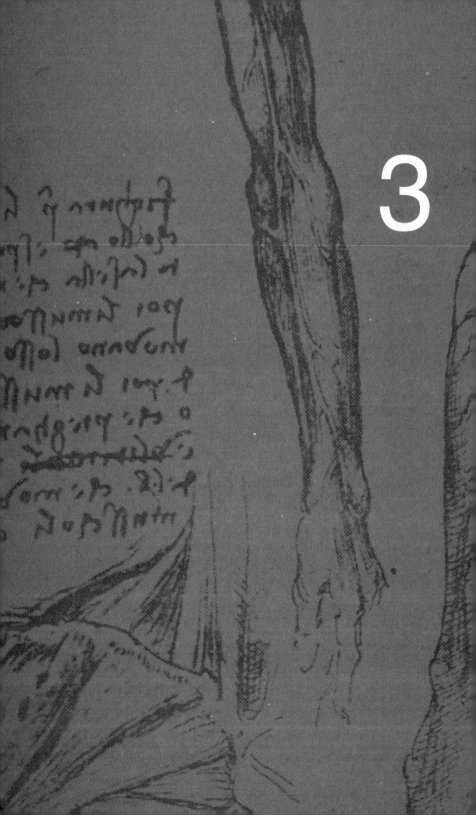

3

# THE REDEEMED BODY

Our Lord ... was in truth physically in the flesh of the line of David, Son of God by the will and power of God; truly born of a virgin, baptized by John so that all righteousness might be fulfilled by him; truly nailed for us in the flesh under Pontius Pilate and Herod the governor, from the fruit of which we are, from his God-blessed suffering, so that he might through his resurrection raise up a standard throughout the ages for his holy and faithful people, whether among the Jews or among the Gentiles, in the one body of his church ... even after the resurrection he was in the flesh. And when he came to those who were with Peter he said to them, "Take me and handle me, and see that I am not a disembodied phantom." Then they immediately touched him and believed, being blended with his flesh and spirit ... and after the resurrection he ate and drank with them as a fleshly person even though he was spiritually united with the Father.

*—Ignatius*

**S**urveys tell us that very few people are at all happy with their bodies. While it is easy to understand why some people may be dissatisfied with their bodies, it is rather odd that so many healthy, attractive people should be so unhappy with their physical appearance. In fact, most women and many men would like to have a different body than the one they now have. Their obsessive concern for their bodies all too often generates an unhealthy disdain for them. At best, it alienates them from their bodies, so that they are no longer at home in them; at worst, they dissociate themselves mentally and emotionally from them, because they do not wish to be identified by them. The most extreme instance of this is what is now called gender dysphoria, the perceived sensation that the sexual identity of a person does not match the sex of the body.

There are, of course, many reasons for body dissatisfaction, particularly among teenagers. The most obvious reason is the desire to stand out, attract attention, and gain the approval of others. Add to that the pressure from media to match the ideal appearance of airbrushed models, film stars, and celebrities. Consequently, people try to remake themselves in the image of these ideal people.

But it goes deeper than that. All too often, people are dissatisfied with their bodies because they are dissatisfied with themselves. They feel that they are unacceptable people, unworthy of approval and acceptance and love. That self-dissatisfaction for failure to be what they would like to be is projected on their physical appearance and misplaced on their imperfect bodies as the cause of their inadequacy. Which is all too easy to do. They don't need to look very hard at their bodies to discover some blemish, because no matter how good we may look, we all have flaws. Even film stars have pimples and wrinkles, spots and scars.

People who are unhappy with their appearance often try to change how they look. They opt for two common kinds of a bodily transformation. On the one hand, they dress up. They cover up their body with the fig leaves of fashionable clothing and decorate it with beautiful jewelry. They improve its appearance with makeup, hairdos, and tattoos. They mask its natural smell with deodorants and perfume. All that is, of course, rather harmless. On the other hand, some people decide to have cosmetic plastic surgery, not to correct deformities such as a cleft palate, but to improve their appearance. They undergo a physical makeover in order to become more sexually attractive or to appear younger than they actually are. Yet no matter how good these kinds of makeover may make them feel, these operations can't change them as persons. They don't make them beautiful people; they merely disguise their self-dissatisfaction.

Popular psychology is less superficial in its attempt to deal with our alienation from our bodies and our dissatisfaction with them. It advises a mental makeover with a simple kind of cognitive therapy. It assumes that our dissatisfaction with ourselves and our bodies comes from an unhealthy, negative attitude to them, our critical assessment of them and lack of appreciation of them. So the solution to body dissatisfaction is to convince ourselves that we are attractive, beautiful, and acceptable. By reprogramming our minds with positive thinking, we can ease our uneasy relationship with our bodies. We can learn to love our bodies just as they are. In the light of our self-approbation and self-appreciation, they will then flourish and blossom, like a well-watered flower in the warm sun. But this, too, does not work, at least not in the long run, because it makes us even more obsessed with ourselves and our appearance. It masks the deeper reasons for our alienation from our bodies by treating the symptoms of the malady rather than the malady itself.

The story of our primeval parents and their fall from grace in Genesis 3 touches on the spiritual reasons for our alienation from our bodies. We are ashamed of our bodies and cover them up because we have an uneasy, guilty conscience. We are afraid that God will see how bad we are in our hearts, with our evil thoughts, disordered desires, and perverted imagination, and so justly reject us. We therefore cover up our bodies in order to hide our guilt and inner ugliness from him. Consequently, we are not just alienated from God and each other, but also from our own bodies. We project our failure onto them and dissociate them from us, like a child who blames its bad hand for stealing forbidden cookies from a jar. Our bodies become something apart from us. Our guilty conscience makes us unhappy with our bodies as the mistaken source of our discontentment and distress. We are embarrassed by them because we are ashamed of ourselves.

Thus, the widespread, deep-seated human sense of alienation from the body is not neurotic, nor even mistaken. It has real spiritual causes and cannot just be treated cosmetically or superficially; it requires a real spiritual solution. That is clearly taught by God in his word. He tells us that even though our spiritual ugliness is wrongly projected from the soul to the body, both need to be completely recreated and renewed from the inside out. We require a total change, the radical transformation of the whole person that begins with the conscience and involves our whole being. We all need to start from scratch by being born again in a heavenly way (John 3:3, 5). And that is what God the Father provides for through his incarnate Son. Jesus redeems the body, transforms the mind, and creates a new self (Rom 12:1–2; Eph 4:20–24; Titus 3:4–7). He gives us a clear conscience by forgiving us and offering himself to us as our righteousness (1 Cor 1:30; 2 Cor 5:21). We can therefore dress up with him (Rom 13:14; Gal 3:27). Like a magic cloak that transforms its wearer, he gives us a new self with a new mind and new body.

## GOD'S EMBODIED SON

God our Creator regards the human body so highly that he chose to take on a human body to rescue humankind from bodily corruption and spiritual ruin. From his birth to his ascension, Jesus engaged with people in a bodily way, speaking to them, touching them, helping them, freeing them from unclean spirits, and healing them. He did not just associate with them physically in order to identify himself physically with them; he engaged with them physically to redeem them body-and-soul for life with God the Father.

That is why the Gospels frequently tell how Jesus touched people with his hands to help them. He touched an unclean leper to cleanse him (Matt 8:3). He touched Peter's mother-in-law to heal her fever (Matt 8:15) as well as the severed ear of a disciple to reattach it (Luke 22:50–51). He touched the eyes of blind people to give them sight (Matt 9:29; 20:34) as well as the tongue and ears of a mute man to restore his speech (Mark 7:33). He touched the coffin of the widow's son in Nain to resuscitate him (Luke 7:14) and took a dead girl and an exorcised boy by their hands to revive them (Matt 9:25; Mark 9:27). No wonder, then, that sick people came to Jesus to touch him and his clothing (Mark 3:10; Matt 9:20–21; 14:36). Jesus related to people bodily to give them bodily help. His human hand offered divine help to people in need.

Yet every miracle that Jesus performed was a sign, a foretaste, and a pledge of their bodily resurrection from the dead. Only then would their ears no longer be deaf, their eyes no longer be blind, their tongues no longer mute, their limbs no longer crippled, and their bodies no longer disabled by the devil (Isa 35:5–6; Luke 7:21–22). Jesus sacrificed himself bodily by his physical death on the cross in order to pardon and heal them, to purify and sanctify them for eternal life with God the Father (Heb 10:5–14). He was put to death in the flesh in order to make them fully alive by the Holy Spirit (1 Pet 3:18). That was the chief purpose of his incarnation.

St. Peter explains that great achievement in this way (1 Pet 2:24): "He himself bore our sins in his body on the tree, that we might die to sin and live to righteousness. By his wounds you have been healed." We are healed by his bodily death and resurrection, his physical death for our sins and his physical resurrection for our justification. Our healing comes at the cost of his death. God sent his own Son in the likeness of sinful human flesh as an offering for sin to condemn sin in the flesh, fulfill God's law for us bodily, and empower us to walk with our bodies on our journey through life according to his Spirit rather than according to our sinful human flesh (Rom 8:3–4). He took on our sin bodily in order to share his righteousness bodily with us; he took on our death physically to share his life with us; he took on our mortal flesh to give us his Holy Spirit through his immortal body. As God's incarnate Son, he is both our sanctification and justification (1 Cor 1:30).

The incarnation of God's Son shows the utter weakness and helplessness of fallen humanity (Rom 5:6–10). It was corrupted by sin, disabled by the devil, and disempowered by death. But since God loved it so much, he sent his Son to live a human life in the body in order to rescue humanity from sin, death, and the devil. Thus, in the Nicene Creed we confess that he came down from heaven and was incarnate for us and for our salvation. He was embodied for us so that we might have salvation already now as we live in the body here on earth.

God's Son became flesh for us.[1] He was manifest in the flesh (1 Tim 3:16). Just as the Lord God once disclosed his glory, his gracious presence, to his people in a cloud that both revealed him and concealed him, God's Son now discloses his glory in his human body. His body has now become the place for theophany, the place where God shows his glory to all people, in order to give them access to his grace. Through his human body Jesus shares his own divine life with us; through his human face, as

---

1. In LW 22:111, Luther quite rightly notes, "In Scriptural usage the word 'flesh' embraces both body and soul, for without the soul the body is dead."

in a mirror, he shows us the face of God the Father; through his human mouth and limbs he speaks the Father's word to us, both by what he says and by what he does. With his human hands he delivers the Father's gifts to us. He resides with us bodily so that we can receive God's grace and truth. He is the bodily theophany of the Father (Heb 1:3); by seeing him, we see the Father (John 14:9). In short, he makes God the Father known to us safely in physical human terms.[2] St. John sums up the great mystery of his embodiment for us simply and directly: "And the Word became flesh and dwelt among us, and we have seen his glory, glory as of the only Son from the Father, full of grace and truth. ... For from his fullness we have all received grace upon grace" (John 1:14, 16). Through his Son, God the Father shows himself to us in a human way for us to perceive him with our five senses.[3]

Our vision of God through the incarnation is incomplete and of little use to us unless we see that Jesus remains an embodied man even after his ascension. He retains his human body, which now transcends all time and space, in order to interact with us in our bodies. As we confess in the Athanasian Creed, he takes our humanity into God. He takes his resurrected body into his fellowship and life with God the Father in order to bridge heaven and earth for us. The author of Hebrews shows us how these two aspects of his incarnation are combined for us.[4] After arguing that Jesus tasted death for everyone in order to bring God's many sons to glory, he draws this summary conclusion in 2:14–15:

---

2. The Letter of Barnabas, an early Christian sermon from about AD 130, gives this explanation for the incarnation (5.9–10): "And when he chose his own apostles who were to preach his gospel, even though they were most lawless and utterly sinful, in order to demonstrate that he had not come to call the righteous but sinners, he showed himself to be the Son of God. For if he had not come in the flesh, how could men have looked on him and been saved, when as they look at the sun ... they cannot gaze at its rays?"

3. Thus, Luther makes this bold assertion: "God in His divine wisdom arranges to manifest Himself to human beings by some definite and visible form which can be seen with the eyes and touched with the hands, in short, within the scope of the five senses" (*Lectures on Genesis: Chapters 15–20*, LW 3:109).

4. For what follows, see John W. Kleinig, *Hebrews,* Concordia Commentary (Saint Louis: Concordia, 2017), 128–44.

"Since therefore the children share in flesh and blood, he himself likewise partook of the same things, that through death he might destroy the one who has the power of death, that is, the devil, and deliver all those who through fear of death were subject to lifelong slavery." Like the members of a human family that have the same genetic traits and the same physical characteristics, Jesus shares the blood and flesh of Adam's descendants. That includes us; he is our human brother. Yet he does not just identify himself with us physically by his incarnation; he shares our human flesh and blood, so that he can share his flesh and blood with us. He becomes one of Adam's children like us so that we can become children of God through him. By sharing our blood and flesh in his bodily life on earth, he breaks the hold of the devil over us and disempowers him for us; by sharing his blood and flesh with us, he now frees us from enslavement by the devil through the fear of bodily death, the fear of death that comes from a guilty conscience and the fear of condemnation by God when we die.

The author of Hebrews goes on to explain how God's incarnate Son frees us from the crippling fear of death in 2:17: "Therefore he had to be made like his brothers in every respect, so that he might become a merciful and faithful high priest in the service of God, to make propitiation for the sins of the people." Here, "propitiation" refers to the result of Christ's death as a sacrifice by which he deals with our sin and gives us access to God's grace. As our exalted high priest, Jesus now pardons us sinners and reconciles us with God the Father. He is our human representative with God. He represents us in the presence of his Father; he brings God's grace and mercy bodily to us and brings us with our bodies to God the Father. Since he provides us with forgiveness and the remission of sins from his heavenly Father, he frees us from the three terrible tyrants that spoil life in the body for us: sin that gives us a bad conscience and makes us afraid of God's rejection of us, the devil who enslaves us through our fear of death and eternal punishment, and death itself, which intimidates us and robs us of life long before we actually die.

## OUR COMMON LIFE

The four Gospels initiate us into the mystery of the incarnation and our involvement in it. In them we see how Jesus shared our whole human lifecycle in the body from birth to death, in order to bring us with our bodies back to God the Father. We see how he was conceived by the Holy Spirit and born with a human body like ours through the Virgin Mary. We see how he grew up like us as a boy in a human family. We see how in mature manhood he was baptized with water for us by John the Baptist to take on our sin and give us his righteousness. We see how he was tempted like us, without yielding to it as we do. We see how he spoke the Father's word and did the Father's work for us and for all people. We see how he suffered physically for us, died a physical death for us, and was raised bodily to life for us. We see how he showed himself bodily to his disciples after his resurrection and ascended bodily into heaven to take our humanity with him into his eternal relationship as Son with God the Father. So, through him as human and divine, we can now participate in the eternal life of the triune God with our whole being: body and mind, soul and spirit.

The Gospels show us the life of Jesus in the body. They tell us the story of Jesus in order to give us a picture of Jesus as God's incarnate Son. This, as Luther notes, is in keeping with the whole of the Bible, for "from the beginning God set forth his word in pictures."[5] Then he adds that clearest of all pictures is God's image, Jesus. The Gospels paint a picture of him as a man with a human body, the man in whose image we were made. Through faith in him and his word we receive an accurate picture of God the Father; he shows us the heart of God in word and deed. Yet it does not stop there. We also see ourselves remade, re-imaged in Jesus. As we see ourselves in Jesus, we see ourselves as God the Father sees us. Thus, says Luther, when God observes our faith and Christ in us

---

5. See Wedding Sermon (October 26, 1528), WA 27:386.14–15.

through faith in him, God says, "Here is my image! This is how I intended Adam to be when I created him."[6]

The author of Hebrews teaches that Jesus made purification for the pollution of human sins by his human life and human death (1:3). He went through our whole lifecycle from birth to death in order to purify and sanctify our whole life in the body for eternal life with God. He cleanses our bodies from sin with his word so that they can share in his holiness. In a sermon on the second article of the Apostles' Creed, Luther depicts this vividly for us:

[Christ] made it all pure in His body so that through Him what belongs to the old birth and this life does not harm us. Rather, it is considered to be as pure as His [birth and life] because I am clothed in His birth and life through Baptism and faith so that everything I do is also pleasing to God and is called a holy walking, standing, eating, drinking, sleeping, and staying awake, etc. Everything must become nothing but holiness in every Christian, even though he still lives in the flesh and is indeed impure in and of himself. However, through faith he is altogether pure. Thus it is a holiness of someone else and yet our own, so that God does not wish to consider everything that we do in this life to be impure in and of itself, but that everything should be holy, precious, and pleasing through this Child who makes the whole world holy through His life. ... If you wish to boast of a holy object, why do you not praise the holy object that Jesus Christ, God's Son, has touched with His own body? What does He touch? My living and dying; my walking, standing; my suffering, misfortune, and trials—all of which He experienced, bore, and passed through.[7]

6. See the sermon on Matthew 8:5–13 (June 18, 1534), WA 37: 453.1–2

7. A Sermon about Jesus Christ (April 16–17, 1533), LW 57:121, 126. See also The Sermon on the Mount, LW 21:34.

Jesus makes all aspects of life in the body pure and holy for us. Through baptism he clothes us with his body. Through faith in him our bodily life is as pure and holy as his. So when God looks at us he sees nothing unclean or unholy in us and our bodies. What could be better than that!

## THE NEW TEMPLE

In the Old Testament, the temple was God's earthly residence, the place where he dwelt with his people on earth. There he appeared to them in his glory in the morning and evening service at the temple to bless them (Exod 29:42–46). There he met with the assembled congregation in order to make himself known to them. There he cleansed them from their sins and shared his holiness with them. There they petitioned him for his help and presented their offerings to him. There they ate holy food and drank holy wine in his presence as his honored guests. There they had access to God and his generous provision for them in the divine service.[8] Like Jacob's stairway, the temple was the gate of heaven for them.

St. John makes an amazing claim in 2:21. It comes at the end of his report that Jesus cleared all the money changers from the outer courts of the temple. When challenged to demonstrate his authority for this act, he gave this cryptic response: "Destroy this temple, and I will raise it in three days." He thereby alluded to a promise in Zechariah 6:12–13 that when the Messiah came, he as king would build a new temple in order to serve in it as high priest. St. John explains that Jesus was speaking about the temple of his body. His crucified and resurrected human body would be the temple in the new age. There he would officiate as high priest in his Father's house and Father's presence. Thus, his resurrected body is now the dwelling place of the living God, the place where the triune God interacts with his people on earth. This is where

---

8. This is the name for the regular weekly service that includes the celebration of the Lord's Supper. Lutherans prefer to use this term for the service of worship because it refers to God's service of us as well as our service of him.

God is to be found. This is where we meet with God. But what a strange place it is! It is both physical and spiritual, earthly and heavenly, visible and invisible.

St. Paul explains how the resurrected body of Jesus now functions as the temple of God. In Colossians 1:19–22 he claims that the fullness of God now dwells in Jesus as in a temple. There he is both the victim and the priest. As victim he sacrificed his body and blood, so that by his body and blood he was able to reconcile the world to himself and make peace with its inhabitants by atoning for sin. As the priest he now presents those who are at peace with God the Father and free from accusation as his holy offering to his Father. Thus, through the temple of his body, Jesus brings God's pardon and peace to the congregation so that he can bring them back to God, holy and blameless and free from sin.

Later, in Colossians 2:9, Paul declares that the fullness of deity dwells bodily in Christ. This is an amazing assertion! We have access to the triune God in the human body of Jesus. All of God's gifts are given to us through his body. His body is our spiritual treasury; it is full of more divine, hidden treasure than we could ever measure. The whole fullness of heaven is crammed there in that body. All of God's heavenly gifts are available to us on earth in the glorified body of Jesus—and nowhere else than there! You can't have God's Son apart from his body. You can't have the Holy Spirit apart from his body. You can't have God the Father apart from his body. Through his body, all baptized believers have been full-filled (Col 2:10); just as everything that belongs to God belongs to Jesus, so everything that belongs to Jesus belongs to them. God's fullness is their fullness. They have access to the ruler of the universe and all his resources. Best of all, they have been freed from sin and raised to eternal life together with Jesus. By faith they participate in the divine life of the Holy Trinity. They share in the fellowship of the Son with the Father by the Holy Spirit. Their life is hidden with Christ in God (Col 3:3). They live and move and have their being in that hidden, heavenly dimension, even as they still live in the body here on earth.

As the temple of the living God, Christ's body reaches out to include the church, the assembly of all the saints in heaven and earth as well as each local congregation. Since the bodies of all baptized believers are incorporated into Christ and united with his body, they are living stones in his temple (1 Pet 2:4–5). They are joined to his body as the foundation stone (1 Cor 3:10–11; cf. Col 2:7), chief cornerstone (Eph 2:20; 1 Pet 2:6), or capstone (Matt 21:42; 1 Pet 2:7) of the temple. The picture varies to make the same point. United with Jesus, they are part of the supernatural temple that he is building on earth. Each congregation is the place where the triune God dwells with his people on earth and attends to them (1 Cor 3:16–17; 2 Cor 6:16; see also Ign Eph 9.1). There they have access to God the Father though his Son by the Holy Spirit (Eph 2:18–22). As a physical community of faith, each congregation manifests God and his love bodily on earth. There is so much of him that no single person can show him adequately; he needs a whole community of different people, each with their different characteristics, all taken together, and each making a unique contribution, to embody him properly and exhibit him bodily on earth (Eph 4:15–16). So each congregation is a bodily outpost of heaven on earth. In each congregation, the resurrected body of Jesus is the bridge between heaven and earth. In each congregation, his flesh is the new and living way into the Father's presence (Heb 10:19–20).

## THE BODY LANGUAGE OF JESUS

At his ascension into heaven, Jesus withdrew himself from the sight of his disciples without separating himself bodily from them. In fact, he promised that he would be with them always, to the end of the world (Matt 28:20); he promised that he would not leave them like orphans abandoned by their parents, but would come and manifest himself to them in a new way through his word and his Holy Spirit (John 14:18–26). After his ascension, he continued his ministry in word and deed in the church on earth (Acts 1:1–2). To be sure, he was no longer visibly present with them (Acts 1:9); his body was transposed, like an object from space and time into a sixth dimension, and transformed, like a grub into a butterfly, so that it was no longer subject to the limitations of time and space. The spatial world does not contain him; he, as it were, contains it, for he ascended to fill all things with his presence.

By his physical ascension to the right hand of his heavenly Father, his human body with his human nature is no longer limited by time and space as it once was but is present wherever he wills to be (Eph 4:8–10). When the Bible maintains that Jesus now sits at the right hand of his Father, it does not refer to his spatial location, like me in the room where I now sit, but to his enthronement as co-ruler with him and his royal position, status, and power.[9] He can therefore make himself available to many different people in different places at the same time. His local ministry thereby becomes universal in its scope and range.[10] He can reach out to make contact with me in Australia at the same time as he reaches out to people in Africa and Asia and the Americas and all over the world.

In the present age of the church, his contact with his disciples is both physical and spiritual. Jesus uses God's word as a physical

---

9. See Luther's exposition of this teaching in "This Is My Body" (1527), LW 37:55–66.

10. See the helpful discussion of this in The Formula of Concord: Solid Declaration, 7.91–105, BoC 609–11. There the authors refer to Luther's distinction between three modes of presence—the perceptible, circumscribed, spatial mode of presence, like water in a bottle; the imperceptible, uncircumscribed, spatially pervasive mode of presence, like the sound of music or the sight of light in the air; the divine, heavenly mode of presence, which cannot be measured or comprehended because it transcends time and space, but by which Jesus measures and comprehends all creatures because they are all completely permeable and present to him who is one person with God in both his divinity and humanity. It is not as if the glorified body of Jesus is extended and located everywhere in creation, but that his divinity is now so closely united with his human nature that it, in this third mode of presence, is available wherever he chooses to grant people bodily access to him and his gifts through it.

means to give them his Holy Spirit, the Spirit that creates faith and revives them, the Spirit that purifies them and makes them holy, the Spirit that transforms them and makes them more and more like Jesus. That is hard for us to comprehend because we think of words as immaterial entities, like our thoughts, even when they are written on paper, rather than physical sounds that are made by human mouths and heard by human ears. They are, in fact, just as physical as all our other actions, because they are spoken by people physically, with the air from their lungs, and are heard physically by sound waves through the air. Speech is just as much a bodily act as eating and drinking, standing and sitting, walking and running.

To be sure, we use words to communicate with each other. Yet that is always done with the body. The body does not just use words to say what we want it to say; it accompanies and clarifies what we say by our body language, the language of gesture and posture, tone of voice and physical expression, action and reaction. In fact, body language determines the power of spoken words; it is an essential part of effective, affective communication. This applies most of all to personal communication; by the body language that accompanies our speaking, we show others what we think and how we feel, what they mean to us, and how we regard them; it helps us to see and understand what someone is saying. And all that happens bodily rather than abstractly! Verbal speech and conversation cannot exist apart from the body.

Since we depend on body language for human communication, God's Son uses body language to communicate with us. He is, in fact, the only expert in body language. In his earthly ministry he never wrote a book but went about preaching and teaching. His spoken words were always accompanied by his actions and his bodily presence. He often linked what he said with the touch of his hands. But most of all, he communicated the Father's grace and mercy, compassion and love, by his sacrificial, bodily death on the cross. Yet he never acted, nor did he suffer, without speaking.

His acts and suffering were always accompanied by his words, for they enacted what he was saying; they told what he was giving. Thus, he healed people with his spoken word. He spoke salvation to people on earth by his words from the cross. That spoken word was powerful and effective because it was filled with the Holy Spirit. His words were the bodily means by which he communicated the Holy Spirit and the gifts of the Spirit to people on earth.

Yet he did not just speak the Father's word to us; he embodied God's word—he was the incarnate word of God (John 1:1–2, 14). His whole bodily life on earth, his physical death, and his burial enacted God's word for us. He translated God's speech into a human life with all its troubles in order to reestablish God's conversation with us in every circumstance and condition of life in the body here on earth.

In John 6:63 Jesus says, "The words I have spoken to you are Spirit and life." That short sentence summarizes the connection of the Holy Spirit with the words that Jesus speaks. By his word Jesus speaks his Spirit to us and breathes his Spirit into us. The association of "spirit" with spoken words was obvious to all Hebrew and Greek speakers in the ancient world. For them, "spirit" meant "life-breath," the "life-power" that was evident in breathing. Speaking used breath to form words and to carry them into the ears of the hearer. So breath and speaking went together. The power of a person's speech depended on the vitality of the person that was conveyed by the words that were spoken. So, too, with Jesus! The risen Lord Jesus spoke his Spirit to his apostles when he commissioned them (John 20:22). And he still speaks the Spirit to us, the Spirit who speaks the word of God to us (Heb 3:7; 10:15–17; Rev 2:7, 11, 17, 29; 3:6, 13, 22). Since his words are filled with the Spirit, they do what they say. His words are effective and powerful (1 Thess 2:13; Heb 4:12). When Jesus speaks, the Spirit acts through his words. The performative power of his words depends on the Holy Spirit that energizes them. When he speaks, he speaks with the Holy Spirit; his words convey the Spirit.

That is a central teaching of Luther and the Lutheran Church in the Book of Concord.[11] The Augsburg Confession teaches that since the Holy Spirit is given and received through the word of God,[12] God has appointed ministers to teach the gospel and to administer the sacraments as the means by which "the Holy Spirit is given, who effects faith where and when it pleases God in those who hear the gospel."[13] That word is "the external word," "the embodied word"[14] that is heard in the reading of the Scriptures, spoken in the absolution, proclaimed in the sermon, sung in the liturgy, and enacted in baptism and in the Lord's Supper.[15] The word of God is the means of grace because it is the means of the Spirit. It conveys the Spirit to the faithful people of God as they hear it, believe in it, and receive it. Through it, God's incarnate Son stays physically in touch with us and keeps us physically in touch with himself.

Normally we depend on our physical sight and touch to stay in physical contact with each other. Yet even then, we depend mainly on speech for personal contact with others. Apart from the words that we speak and hear, we do not know each other. They disclose the mind and heart of other people to us. Things are both different and yet similar with Jesus. Unlike our contact with other people, we cannot see the bodily presence of the risen Lord Jesus with

---

11. For the bestowal and work of the Spirit through the word, see the Augsburg Confession 5:1–4; 18:3; 28:8; the Apology of the Augsburg Confession 4.135; 12.44; 24.58, 59, 70; the Smalcald Articles 3.3.3.3–13; LC 2.38, 42, 58; the Formula of Concord: Epitome 2.1,4, 13, 19; 12.22; Formula of Concord: Solid Declaration 2.5, 38, 48, 52, 54, 55, 56, 65; 3.16; 11.29, 33, 39, 40, 41, 76, 77; 12.30.

12. 18, 3, BoC (51).

13. 5.2, Latin text, BoC (41).

14. 5.4, BoC (41) and (40). In the German text, "the external word" is translated by this memorable phrase.

15. Luther explains what is meant by "the external word" most fully in the Smalcald Articles 3. 3–13, BoC 322–23. It is the opposite of "the internal word" that is received by the false prophets who believed that they had God speaking his words in them. In contrast to their unmediated spiritual inspiration, Luther taught that normally the Spirit was mediated through the external word, the embodied word. By the use of this term he refers to the written words of the sacred Scriptures that are preached and heard in public worship, the words that are spoken in the Absolution and enacted in the Lord's Supper, the words that are meditated on and assimilated in daily devotions.

our physical eyes, nor can we touch him visibly with our physical hands. Rather, like our contact with other people, we depend on his spoken word to stay in touch with him. Through his word he shows himself to us and communicates his bodily presence to us; through his word we see what he is doing for us and giving to us; through his word we see how he regards us and how he loves us. His words are windows into his heart and mind as well as into the heart and mind of God the Father.

Our ears, says Luther, are our Christian organs.[16] We are like some blind people who actually "see" with their ears. By clicking with their tongues or by using a pair of clickers, they use sound to "see" what is around them, like bats do in the darkness. They have trained their minds to see what they hear. Some do that with such amazing clarity that they have an accurate, three-dimensional picture of their physical surroundings and the location of their own bodies in that place. In fact, I heard one such person who had lost his sight claim that he could now see more clearly, without peripheral visual distractions, than when he still had his physical sight. The Holy Spirit trains us to likewise see with our ears, ears that hear God's voice. We see how Jesus interacts with us bodily through his word. We see with the eyes of our hearts, hearts that hear the gospel and are enlightened by the Holy Spirit (Eph 1:18). God's word gives us the vision by which we see Jesus with us and us with Jesus. Thus Luther remarks, "I do not have vision because I can see, but because I have vision I see."[17]

### LITURGICAL BODY CARE

We who live this side of Easter often envy the disciples, because they were able to interact with Jesus in a physical way during the three years that they spent together with him. We imagine that we would be much more blessed than we now are if only we, like Thomas, could actually see him with our human eyes and touch

---

16. See Luther, *Lectures on Hebrews*, LW 29:224.

17. Luther, *First Psalm Lectures: Psalms 76–126*, LW 11:174.

him with our human hands. Yet Jesus himself said, "Blessed are those who have not seen [me] and yet have believed" (John 20:29). In other words, we who live this side of Easter are better off than they, because Jesus is now much more available and accessible to us than ever in his earthly ministry. Let me state this as sharply and paradoxically as I can: Jesus deals with us more physically and spiritually now than before his ascension. Here is how Luther explains that reality:

> [Jesus] did not want to give us His divinity unconcealed; this was impossible. For God said (Exod 33:20), "Man shall not see Me and live." Therefore it was necessary for God to hide, cover, and conceal Himself, thus enabling us to touch and apprehend Him. He must disguise Himself in flesh and blood, in the Word, in the external ministry, in Baptism, in the Sacrament and Lord's Supper, where He gives us His body in the bread and His blood in the wine, to eat and drink. He must conceal Himself in forms to which He adds His Word, in order that we may recognize Him. ... God is not to be sought or found outside the Person born of Mary, the Person endowed with real flesh and blood, and cruci-fied. God is to be apprehended and found in the flesh and blood of Christ solely by faith.[18]

God's Son, who had hidden his divinity in human flesh and blood during his life in the body, now hides himself even more fully as God and man in his word and the holy sacraments, so that we can now have safe access to God the Father through his flesh and blood.

The exalted Lord Jesus continues his ministry of word and deed in the church (Acts 1:1–2). There he deals with us bodily and spir-itually through physical means, the means by which he gives us access to the grace of God the Father and makes the Spirit available to us. He deals with us through his embodied word—the spoken word that is preached and taught with a human mouth; the saving

---

18. Luther, *Sermons on the Gospel of St. John: Chapters 6–8*, LW 23:123.

word that is heard and received with human ears; the living word that is enacted with human hands for people with human bodies in baptism and delivered with human hands into human mouths in the Lord's Supper. Here is how Luther describes Christ's physical engagement with us:

> God has given us Baptism, the Sacrament of the Altar, and Absolution to bring Christ very close to us, so that we can have him not only in our heart but also on our tongue, so that we can feel Him, grasp Him, and touch Him. … He wants to come to you, plant Himself before your very eyes, press Himself into your hands, and say, "Just listen to Me and take hold of Me, give Me eye and ear; there you have Baptism and the Sacrament of the Altar. Open your mouth, let Me place My hand on your head. I give you this water which I sprinkle over your head."[19]

All of this means that Jesus cares for us and our bodies most certainly and tangibly in the divine service of worship. There he engages with us bodily through the pastor as his appointed spokesman and anointed agent. There by faith we can receive and perceive him with our five senses.

Jesus cares for us bodily in three main ways in the congregation of God's holy people: in baptism, in the word, and in the Lord's Supper. There he joins us in body and soul with himself in baptism. There he addresses us physically and spiritually through his spoken word to us. There he gives his body and blood to us, physically and spiritually in the Lord's Supper, for liberation from sin, protection from the devil, salvation from death, and participation in the divine life of the triune God.

### Baptism

From a human point of view, the act of baptism quite obviously involves the human body. The officiant marks our body with the

---

19. Luther, *Sermons on the Gospel of St. John: Chapters 1–4*, LW 22:420–21.

sign of the cross as with a brand, pours water over it, and lays his hand on our head for blessing. Yet the involvement of the human body goes much further and far deeper than that. In this enactment, the risen Lord Jesus reclaims our whole life in the body for himself from that day onward and for all eternity. In baptism the risen Lord Jesus washes us with the water that purifies us and makes us completely clean (Eph 5:25). He does not just sprinkle our hearts with his Spirit in order to give us a clean conscience; he washes our bodies so that they, too, are fit for life with him and his heavenly Father (Heb 10:22). That washing regenerates us completely and makes us new people with a new identity, a new way of life, and a new inheritance (Titus 3:3–7; cf. 1 Pet 1:3, 23). Through Baptism our sinful bodies were put to death with Jesus in his physical death and buried with him in his grave, so that, dead to sin, we could share in his resurrected life on our journey with the body here on earth (Rom 6:3–11).

Through baptism Jesus unites us physically with himself, like a husband with his wife in marriage (Eph 5:25). By his bodily union with us, we not only become one flesh with him (Eph 5:31–32) but also one spirit with him (1 Cor 6:17). His body is ours, our body his. He dwells with us bodily here on earth so that we have a common life with him in heaven. He shares our bodily lives so that he can share with us his Holy Spirit and everything else that belongs to him.[20] Through Baptism we become part of a new heavenly community on earth; by our union with his body we are joined with all the other members of his body (1 Cor 12:12–13). Best of all, since our bodies are united with the body of Jesus, they share in the hope of eternal life with God the Father (Rom 6:5). Luther sums up that hope well in his Large Catechism:

---

20. See Luther's summary in the Large Catechism, 4.41, BoC (461): "In baptism, therefore, every Christian has enough to study and practice all his or her life. Christians always enough to do to believe firmly what baptism promises and brings—victory over death and the devil, forgiveness of sins, God's grace, the entire Christ, and the Holy Spirit with all his gifts."

Because the water and the Word together constitute one baptism, both body and soul shall be saved and live forever; the soul through the Word which it believes, the body because it is united with the soul and apprehends baptism in the only way it can. No greater jewel, therefore, can adorn our body and soul than baptism, for through it we become completely holy and blessed, which no other kind of life and no work on earth can acquire.[21]

## The Spoken Word

The four Gospels show us how Jesus did everything with his spoken word. He preached and taught God's word. He healed people with a word (Luke 7:7), drove out demons with a word (Matt 8:16), stilled the storm with a word (Mark 4:29), and gave life to dead people through his word (Mark 5:41; Luke 7:14). Jesus still speaks the life-giving word of God to us in the divine service of worship (Heb 4:12). He speaks it physically to us through the voice of a pastor as his mouthpiece. That word is powerful and effective; it does what it says. It does not just tell us how to live; it gives us eternal life. It does not just tell us what is wrong with us; it rights what is wrong about us. Through his spoken word, the word of the law that diagnoses our sickness and the word of the gospel that heals us, Jesus operates on us, like a skillful surgeon, spiritually, personally, and physically. He addresses us through the readings from the Bible and the sermon of the pastor. He also addresses us through words that are spoken as we receive his body and blood; he addresses us through the spoken absolution and the spoken benediction. All of these engage us bodily through our ears and eyes; all of these affect us personally because they engage us bodily.

Take, for example, the spoken absolution. The guilt of our sin does not just stain our conscience; it saps our physical vitality. Thus David laments in Psalm 32:3–4:

---

21. The Large Catechism, 4.46, BoC (462).

When I kept silent, my bones wasted away
> through my groaning all day long.
For day and night your hand was heavy upon me;
> my strength was dried up as by the heat of summer.[22]

Hence the word of absolution that frees us from the guilt of sin also revives the body, even as it relieves the soul. Just as Jesus healed people with God's word, he still heals his disciples in their souls, minds, and bodies. Hence St. Paul encourages the young pastor Timothy to teach "the sound words of our Lord Jesus" (1 Tim 6:3), which he himself had modeled for him (2 Tim 1:13); he also speaks about the need for instruction in "sound doctrine," "healthy, healing teaching" that distinguishes between law and gospel (1 Tim 1:10; 2 Tim 4:3; Titus 1:9). That teaching is sound and healthy because it heals the whole person and promotes the spiritual health of both the soul and the body.

The spoken word comes externally from the mouth of a speaker through the ears of its hearers and into their souls. There in turn it has its effect on the body through their souls and minds. Thus, the whole person is addressed and reformed by God's word. Faith, says Luther, is attached and bound to an external word as its object: "Yes, it must be external so that it can be perceived and grasped by the senses and thus brought into the heart, just as the entire Gospel is an external, oral proclamation."[23] In a sermon on John 14:45, Luther gives this vivid description of our physical, verbal encounter with God through his incarnate Son:

> He [God] did not bid you soar heavenward on your own and gape to see what God is doing in heaven with the angels. No, this is His command (Matt. 17:5): "This is My beloved Son; listen to Him. There I descend to you on earth so that you can see, hear, and touch Me. There and nowhere else is the place for those to encounter and find Me who desire

---

22. See also Ps 31:9–10 and 38:3–4.

23. The Large Catechism, 4.30, BoC (460).

Me and would like to be delivered from sin and be saved." We should quickly assent and say, "God himself says this, and I will follow Him and give ear to no other word or message; nor do I want to know anything else about God. For as St. Paul declares (Col. 2:9), in His Person "dwells the whole fullness of Deity bodily"; and there is no God apart from Him where I could come to Him or find Him. ... Now whenever one hears this Man's Word and sees His work, there one surely hears and sees God's Word and work.[24]

## The Lord's Supper

The risen Lord Jesus interacts with us bodily in Holy Communion. There he gives us his own living body and blood to eat and drink. There Christ "is present ... according to and with his assumed human nature, according to which he is our brother and we are flesh of his flesh and bone of his bone."[25] There, says Paul in 1 Corinthians 10:16–17, we are all united with each other as members of his body, because we have all participated in his body, just as we have all eaten from the same loaf of bread. His body, given to us as our holy Spirit-filled food (1 Cor 10:3), draws us together in a holy community that is both physical and spiritual. His flesh and blood are life-giving; they convey his own supernatural life to us with our mortal bodies (John 6:48–58). Like a mother with a baby in her womb, Jesus nourishes us with his body and blood. Or, to change the picture, Jesus transfuses his lifeblood from his body into ours.

We also receive his body and blood for our healing from sin. Paul assumes this in 1 Corinthians 11:22–30, where he teaches that the desecration of Christ's body and blood affects the body in three negative ways. Depending on its severity, it results in infirmity, sickness, or even death. If so, then, conversely, the faithful reception of Christ's body and blood results in strength, health,

---

24. Luther, *Sermons on the Gospel of St. John: Chapters 14–16*, LW 24:65–66.

25. Formula of Concord. Solid Declaration 8.78, BoC (631).

and vitality. In that regard Luther makes this impassioned appeal about the Lord's Supper:

> We must never regard the sacrament as a harmful thing from which we should flee, but as a pure, wholesome, soothing medicine that aids us and gives life to both soul and body. For where the soul is healed, the body is helped as well.[26]

Christ's body and blood do not just benefit us for our life on earth; they give us access to heaven itself as we live on earth. In Hebrews 10:19–21, we are taught that just as the flesh of Jesus is "the new and living way" into God's presence, so his blood makes us fit for safe entry by that way into the heavenly sanctuary in the divine service of worship. Christ's body and blood work together to usher us into that most holy place.[27] Jesus prepares our hearts and our bodies to enter the heavenly realm by washing us with the pure water of baptism and sprinkling us with his blood, the blood that purifies our conscience, so that we can serve the living God (Heb 9:13–14). By our participation in Holy Communion, Jesus shares his own holiness with us through his most holy body and blood; he makes our souls and bodies holy with his body (Heb 10:10) and his blood (Heb 10:29; 13:12).

The body of Jesus is our spiritual food just as his blood is spiritual drink (1 Cor 10:3–4). St. Paul calls it spiritual food and drink because it conveys the Holy Spirit to us in Holy Communion. That makes it food with a difference. Normally, we assimilate food into our bodies, so that it becomes part of us. But by this food the Holy Spirit assimilates us into the body of Christ. We are changed

---

26. The Large Catechism, 5.68, BoC (474). Luther borrows this picture from the Letter of Ignatius to the Ephesians 20.2, with his description of the Lord's Supper as "the medicine of immortality, the antidote against death, to make us live forever in Christ."

27. Luther gives this memorable explanation in LW 35:66: "Thus, the sacrament is for us a ford, a bridge, a door, a ship, and a stretcher by which and in which we pass from this world into eternal life."

into his likeness. Here is how Luther describes its transformative effect on us:

> Now if Christ's flesh is distinguished from all [other] flesh and is solely and pre-eminently spiritual flesh, born not of flesh but of the Spirit, then it is also spiritual food. If it is a spiritual food, it is eternal food which cannot perish. ... Perishable food is transformed into the body which eats it; this food, however, transforms the person who eats it into itself, and makes him like itself, spiritual, alive, and eternal. ... His flesh is ... a food of an entirely different kind from perishable food ... it is a spiritual flesh and does not let itself be transformed, but transforms those who eat it, and it gives them the Spirit. ... It is as if a wolf devoured a sheep and the sheep were so powerful a food that it transformed the wolf and turned him into a sheep. So when we eat Christ's flesh physically and spiritually, the food is so powerful that it transforms us into itself and out of fleshly, sinful, mortal men makes us spiritual, holy, living men. This we are already, though in a hidden manner in faith and hope; this fact is not yet manifest, but we shall experience it on the Last Day.[28]

## The Holy Congregation

The risen Lord Jesus engages with us bodily through the proclamation and enactment of his word by pastors in the divine service. Yet that is not the only way that he interacts with us bodily. He meets with us through the congregation as a whole and each of its members individually. In fact, Jesus surprises us by declaring that we receive him and his heavenly Father by receiving little children as fellow disciples (Mark 9:36–37). The whole congregation is his body, and each baptized person is a part of his body. It is his physical agency; he does his work through this body and each person

---

28. Luther, "This is My Body (1527)," LW 37:99–101.

in it, just as we use our bodies and each of its members to do our work. Through the congregation he helps me out. Through the congregation he helps me to hear his word and receive his body and blood, confess my sins and receive the absolution, confess my faith and praise his heavenly Father, and present my offerings of money, thanksgiving, and intercessory prayer. Through the congregation he shares my troubles and temptations, my pain and my sorrow, my successes and my failures, my joys and my achievements (1 Cor 12:26). Through the members of the congregation, who each have their own vocation and their own spiritual gifts (Rom 12:3–8), he shows the Father's love to me physically (Eph 4:15–16) and cares for me bodily (1 Cor 12:14–25). Thus, Jesus provides body care for us in the church so that he can provide body care to others through us in the church.

## EMBODIED FAITH

Since the Western world in which we live prizes abstract thought and virtual reality rather than actual facts and concrete realities, we all too readily reduce the Christian faith to religious ideas that can be cobbled together in a doctrinal system or a religious philosophy of life. To be sure, our cognitive understanding is part of our faith. But only a small part! For faith does not depend on our understanding, nor can it be limited to it. It is much more than mere assent to religious ideas and principles; it has to do with facts, such as the life of Jesus and his dealings with us, our actual personal association with him, and our way of life as his disciples. There is nothing abstract or notional about that! Faith, and the life of faith, involves our whole selves, body and soul and spirit. It is always embodied faith, just as we are always embodied souls.

In his commentary on Galatians, Luther speaks at some length about "incarnate faith."[29] By his use of this evocative phrase he means that God never deals with us in a disembodied way. While we may distinguish, and must distinguish, between the faith in our

---

29. *Lectures on Galatians: Chapters 1–4* (1535), LW 26:261–67.

hearts and the works that we do with the body, they cannot be separated. Both are part and parcel of our life in Christ. Faith in Christ always issues in bodily acts, like any emotion in its physical display; the bodily acts of Christians always depend on faith in Christ, like sight on the light of the sun. Living faith, actual confidence in Christ, is always active in love and good works (Gal 5:6; Jas 2:14–26). Through faith Christ activates and energizes the body of the believer, just as the spirit animates the body (Jas 2:26). Our works, the things that we do with our bodies, are always carried out by God and in God (John 3:21); he produces them in us through his Holy Spirit. The works of faith that we do together with him are his works that he does together with us in our bodies.

We see how our faith in Christ is embodied and enacted, most accurately, by what happens in the service of worship. From a human point of view, the whole service is a human, bodily enactment in word and deed; everything is done by the assembled congregation. Yet, from God's point of view, it is a divine enactment in which he is at work with his faithful people through his physically spoken and enacted word. He is at work in a two-way interaction with the congregation. First, there is his sacramental descent, in which God the Father gives us his Spirit and every other heavenly blessing through his incarnate Son by the means of grace. Then, corresponding with that, there is the sacrificial ascent of the incarnate Son, who offers us and our gifts back to the Father through his Spirit. The triune God is equally at work in both our reception and action; God the Father, Son, and Holy Spirit are just as much at work in the faithful sacrificial enactment by which we serve him as in the faithful sacramental enactment by which he serves us. Both equally involve the body together with the soul, the first in its faithful reception of gifts from God and the second in its faithful presentation of offerings to God.

In Romans 12:1–2 St. Paul makes this surprising and puzzling appeal: surprising because he speaks of worship with our bodies and puzzling because he couples bodily worship with mental renewal. He says:

> I appeal to you, therefore, brothers, by the mercies of God, to present your bodies as a living sacrifice, holy and well-pleasing to God, which is your service of the word. Do not be conformed to this world but be transformed by the renewal of your mind, so that by testing you may discern what is the will of God, what is good and well-pleasing and perfect.[30]

I need to explain five parts of my translation of these verses. First, the term "sacrifice" alludes to the bodies of the male lambs that were offered to God in the daily services at the temple. In contrast to their dead bodies offered to atone for sin, Christians were to offer their living bodies to God as thank offerings to him for his atoning sacrifice. The bodies of the lambs were made holy because they were offered to God on the altar of the temple. Our bodies are made holy by being offered to God. Like the lambs, our bodies are well-pleasing to him because they are offered as God himself has instructed in his word.

Second, Paul equates the offering of our living bodies with our service of God, our worship of him.

Third, Paul uses an unusual adjective to describe our service, an adjective that is commonly translated as "spiritual" in the sense of "immaterial" (which makes little sense when used in connection with our bodies!) or "reasonable" because of its association with the renewal of our minds in the following verse. However, this adjective (Greek *logikos*) is derived from the term for a word or speech (Greek *logos*). Like the mention of the pure milk of the word in 1 Peter 2:2 (KJV; NKJV), it has to do with words, God's words spoken by human beings. Our bodily service, which involves us as speakers rather than as dumb animals, depends on our proclamation and enactment of God's word. Thus, in the first

---

30. Here I give my own translation.

century in Greek-speaking Jewish synagogues, "the service of the word" described the presentation of verbal thanksgiving to God as a well-pleasing sacrifice.[31]

Fourth, the passive form of the imperative "be transformed" alludes to God's activity by giving us his Holy Spirit to renew us (see also Eph 4:23; Titus 3:5). Paul therefore appeals to us to let God transform us and rely on his Spirit to renew us.

Fifth, the phrase "by the mercies of God" emphasizes that we not only offer our bodies as a living sacrifice in response to God's merciful treatment of us, but also depend on his merciful empowerment to do so. Jesus presents us with our bodies to God the Father (Eph 5:26; Col 1:22).

In Romans 12:1–2, which introduces words of encouragement in the last part of the letter, St. Paul focuses on the role of the body in the service of worship. Since Christ has redeemed our bodies, they belong to him and are meant to be used in his service. Paul therefore urges us to present our bodies as an offering to God the Father, just as Jesus offered his body to the Father in his human life and human death and now offers it to us in Holy Communion to free our bodies from sin, death, and the devil. Since Jesus makes them holy through his word and Holy Spirit, they are "holy and well-pleasing" sacrifices to God. We offer our living bodies as an act of worship both in the divine service and in the whole of our lives. We entrust them to him and put them at his disposal. Our bodies are our main, lifelong gift to him in response to the gift of his Son to us, just as my body is my lifelong gift to my wife.

Yet our bodily self-offering is only one side of our service. It involves our whole selves, our minds as well as our bodies. So, after encouraging us to present our bodies to God, St. Paul urges us to offer our minds, with our thinking and feeling, our imagining and desiring, our planning and deciding, to God for him to change and renew by his word and Holy Spirit. As we are transformed by God himself, our minds are attuned to the mind of Christ, so that

---

31. See Ps 50:14–15, 23; 69:30; 116:17.

we begin to think and feel and act as he does. Guided by God's word and enlightened by his Spirit, we examine what happens to us and test our experiences to see how he is at work in our lives, carrying out his good and gracious will for us; from experience we also discern what he wants to do with us and us to do for him (see Eph 5:8–10). We discover what pleases him and how to please him day by day in our bodily journey on earth. Our experience of him in that bodily arena transforms us for "good and well-pleasing and perfect" service of him. Thus, we have a kind of circuit in which we offer our bodies and minds to God in the divine service, so that we can serve him better in our bodily dealings with others in our daily lives and be thereby equipped for our fuller participation with our bodies in the service of worship.

## BODILY SERVICE

We participate with our bodies in our worship of God. The author of Hebrews tells us that through the flesh of Jesus our great high priest we have access to the heavenly sanctuary (10:19–23). Since our hearts have been sprinkled clean from a bad conscience by the blood of Jesus, and our bodies have been washed with the pure water of baptism, we can now approach God the Father with our bodies as well as our hearts. Through Jesus, we therefore now have bodily access to God's heavenly presence by our involvement in corporate worship. Without our bodies we have no access to him. We are not pure spirits or mere souls who "have" bodies. In a real sense we "are" spiritual bodies. Our bodies therefore play an important part in our worship. In fact, the whole worship service revolves around a holy meal with physical eating and drinking and spoken conversation.

In corporate worship, pastors serve God and the congregation with their bodies. With their bodies they stand on holy ground before God the Father and minister in his presence together with Jesus and the angels. With their bodies they represent Christ and act on his behalf in the ministry of the gospel. With their eyes they regard the congregation as God's beloved sons and daughters.

With their mouths they speak God's word to the assembled congregation in many different ways. With their hands they baptize people, place the sign of the cross on people, invite them to pray, receive the offering of the congregation for presentation to God, distribute the body and blood of Jesus, and convey God's blessing to people by placing them on their heads.

In corporate worship, all the members of the congregation also serve God with their bodies. They are joined to Jesus and adopted as children of his heavenly Father by having their bodies washed in baptism. They enter God's presence and assemble there with their human bodies. They hear God's word with attentive ears. Like Simeon, they see Jesus and his salvation with human eyes in the Holy Supper (Luke 2:25–32); they see him with enlightened eyes in the faces of his ministers;[32] they behold the glory of the Lord, with unveiled faces, as they hear the gospel of Jesus, the gospel that shows him to them (2 Cor 3:18). They confess their faith in Jesus with a human mouth (Rom 10:9–10). They praise him with human lips (Heb 13:15; see also Zech 3:9–10); they confess their sins, present their offerings, and pray for others and themselves with human lips. In some present-day congregations, they, like the first Christians, even greet each other with a holy kiss on the cheek, the kiss of love and peace (Rom 16:16; 1 Cor 16:20; 2 Cor 13:12; 1 Thess 5:26; 1 Pet 5:14). They receive the body and blood of Jesus with human hands and human mouths; they lift up holy hands in prayer (Ps 28:2; 1 Tim 2:8) and praise (Ps 134:2). They stand on their legs to hear the gospel and walk forward with them to receive the sacrament; they stand to pray and kneel to receive Christ's body and blood. They sing the Lord's song in

---

32. Luther gives us this vivid description of that visual involvement with God in the service of public worship: "Thus, apostles and pastors are nothing but channels through which Christ leads and transmits His Gospel from the Father to us. Therefore, wherever you hear the Gospel properly taught or see a person baptized, wherever you see someone administer or receive the Sacrament, or wherever you witness someone absolving another, there you may say without hesitation: 'Today I beheld God's Word and work. Yes, I saw and heard God Himself preaching and baptizing.' To be sure, the tongue, the voice, the hands, are those of a human being; but the Word and the ministry are really those of Divine Majesty Himself" (Luther, *Sermons on the Gospel of St. John: Chapters 14–16*, LW 24:67).

wholehearted, full-bodied praise with one voice in bodily unison with each other (Ps 84:2; Rom 15:5–6).

They therefore offer their bodies as living sacrifices to God the Father through Jesus by the power of the Holy Spirit. They come to Jesus, the living cornerstone of God's temple, in order to be built up with him as "a spiritual [Spirit-filled] house, to be a holy priesthood, to offer spiritual [Spirit-produced] sacrifices [well-pleasing] to God through Jesus" (1 Pet 2:5).

Besides our bodies, we present two other physical offerings to God.[33] On the one hand, we present money and other goods as gifts of mercy in the divine service as our sacrifice of praise, our thank offering to God (Heb 13:16b). These offerings are sanctified by the word of God and prayer (1 Tim 4:5); they are placed on the altar or beside it to show that they now belong to God. By these gifts of mercy, we provide for the work of the church, the livelihood of pastors and church workers, and the needs of disadvantaged and impoverished people (Matt 6:2–4; Acts 2:44–45; 6:1–6; 1 John 3:16–18).

On the other hand, we intercede for the church, the world, and all people in need in prayers for the church, and put ourselves at God's disposal to help out people in trouble with deeds of mercy (Heb 13:16a). Jesus himself lists some of these deeds in Matthew 25:31–46: providing food and drink for impoverished people, offering hospitality to homeless strangers, clothing those who have no clothes, caring for the sick and the dying, and visiting people in prison.[34] This list is suggestive rather than exhaustive. Elsewhere, care for orphans and widows is also mentioned, as in James 1:27. They all have to do with bodily needs. Both our gifts of mercy and deeds of mercy are our spiritual sacrifices to God, bodily offerings produced by his Holy Spirit.

---

33. See John W. Kleinig, *Hebrews*, Concordia Commentary (Saint Louis: Concordia, 2017), 688–89, 710–11, 715.

34. See also 1 Tim 5:9–10.

Our bodily participation in corporate worship is a vital part of our life in Christ. It is so important for us because our bodies are destined for life with God. Jesus became incarnate for us in order to redeem our bodies for their present, hidden involvement by faith in eternal life with God as well as for their future resurrection from the dead for eternal life with him in heaven, where we shall see him face to face (Rev 22:4).

## HOLY BODIES

How then, in the light of Christ's redemption of our bodies, does God the Father regard our bodies? How does he see them? With that question we have come to the heart of this book, so let me answer it as simply and plainly as I can. He regards them as holy, just as holy as the human body of Jesus, for he does not consider us apart from Jesus, nor does he consider Jesus as our head apart from us. That, I admit, is a stunning assertion with far-reaching consequences. It seems too good to be true. Yet, since it is what God himself tells us in his word, it must be true. And wonderful! If we truly believe that truth, it cannot but change the way that we view and treat our bodies.

To make sense of that truth, we must begin with the holiness of Jesus. He is "the Holy One of God" (Mark 1:24; John 6:69), the only man who is inherently and completely holy. Everyone else and everything else that is holy derives its holiness from him. As God's only Son, he shares in the holiness of his holy Father and shares the Father's holiness with us. In fact, he became incarnate in order to share God's holiness with us—and to share it bodily, by his human conception and birth, his human baptism and ministry, his human suffering and death, his human resurrection and ascension! He consecrated his human body by his sacrificial death in order to consecrate our human bodies (John 17:19). So now, as our high priest, he prays for our sanctification through him and his proclamation of God's word (John 17:17); as our human brother who shares our flesh and blood, he sanctifies us (Heb 2:11).

Thus, the risen Lord Jesus is "our sanctification," our one and only source of holiness (1 Cor 1:30). Together with his holy Father, he calls us to be saints and makes us saints, holy people with the same status as the angels who stand before God in heaven and share perfectly in his holiness (1 Cor 1:2). Yet, even so, we are not holy in ourselves but only in Christ (Phil 1:1; 4:31); we are sanctified in him (1 Cor 1:2) and through our faith in him (Acts 26:18). He shares his holiness with us; we receive our holiness from him, like light from the sun. Since we are now holy in his sight (Col 1:22), we are also holy in the sight of God the Father (Eph 1:5). When the Father looks at us as we are in his holy Son, he sees that we are just as holy as his Son. He admires us as he admires his Son. What's more, like human fathers who instruct and discipline their children to be good members of the family, God the Father instructs us in the school of the church and disciplines us in the training arena of bodily life, so that we can share ever more fully in his holiness (Heb 12:10). His goal is to sanctify us completely, with our whole spirit and soul and body, for eternal life with him (1 Thess 5:23). That is an ongoing, lifelong operation for him. Since he is faithful in keeping his promises, we can be sure that he will accomplish it (1 Thess 5:24).

We do not make and keep ourselves holy; God the Father does that through his Son and the Holy Spirit who sanctifies us (1 Cor 6:11; 2 Thess 2:13). He sanctifies us through the means of grace, his holy things through which we receive his Holy Spirit. He therefore makes us holy through his holy word (John 17:17; 1 Tim 4:5; 1 Pet 1:2); he makes us holy through holy baptism (1 Cor 6:11; Eph 5:25–27); he makes us holy through Christ's body and blood in Holy Communion (Heb 10:10, 29; 13:12; cf. 1 Pet 1:2). These divinely instituted means of sanctification are available to us in the divine service. We, therefore, are made and kept holy by our obedient participation in it and our faithful meditation on God's word.[35]

---

35. For a fuller treatment of this, see John W. Kleinig, "Worship and the Way of Holiness." *Logia* 16/1 (2007): 5–8.

St. Paul explains what that means for us and our bodies in four passages: 2 Corinthians 6:14–7:1; 1 Corinthians 6:19–20; Romans 6:11–23; and Ephesians 5:25–27. The first two deal with the purpose of our sanctification, the third deals with our bodily involvement in sanctification, and the fourth with the goal of our sanctification.

In 2 Corinthians 6:14–7:1, Paul urges the Christians in Corinth to avoid taking part in pagan religious activities. Paraphrasing three promises from the Old Testament that Jesus has fulfilled, he tells them that they must separate themselves from everything that is unclean to God, everything that pollutes them and so desecrates their holiness. The reason for this is that they are "the temple of the living God," his earthly sanctuary (6:16). Since they are his holy temple, God dwells in their midst and travels with them as community in their journey on earth, just as he had done with the Israelites in the tabernacle on their journey to the promised land. Yet they are not just his holy temple, a temple made from human bodies; Paul, by applying God's instruction in Isaiah 52:11 for the exiled priests to the whole congregation, implies that they also serve as his holy priests in that temple. What is more, they are God's sons and daughters, who serve him as his royal priests; they officiate in God's house with God's Son, the high priest in charge of God's temple. Since they have been appointed as holy priests to serve in God's holy temple, Paul urges them to join with him in purifying themselves from every kind of defilement, everything that desecrates their holiness and hampers their participation in God's holiness (6:17). That involves their flesh, that is, their bodies, as well as their spirit, for they go hand in hand both in defilement and in purification from defilement (7:1). What affects the body also affects the spirit, and vice versa! They purify themselves by their faithful participation in corporate worship though confession and absolution, attention to God's word as law and gospel, and prayerful reception of the Lord's Supper. By their ongoing, corporate involvement in the service of worship, they bring "holiness to completion in the fear of God" (7:1). Their communal sanctification in God's temple as holy priests is an ongoing process, the process by which they detach themselves from impurity in order to share more and more fully in God's holiness.

In 1 Corinthians 6:19–20, St. Paul explores the purpose of our sanctification from personal rather than a congregational point of view. Jesus, he says, has ransomed our bodies at the cost of his own death; he has freed them from sin and death. So our bodies now no longer belong to us; they belong to Jesus. He claims them for himself in baptism; he shares his own body and his own life with them in Holy Communion. He thereby consecrates each body with his Holy Spirit as God's temple, God's residence, the place where God's glory dwells as it had once dwelt first in the tabernacle and then in the temple. By his focus on the body as God's temple, Paul compares it with the shrines that pagan priests used to transport the idols of their gods in procession around a town. The body of each Christian is a mobile shrine that takes the triune God out and about in the world; it discloses God and conveys his blessings to other people. Just as God's hidden glory had filled the tabernacle and the temple, so God's hidden glory now fills the body of each Christian as a shrine; his glory is now manifest in their bodies, just as it had been manifest in the tabernacle (Exod 29:42; 40:34–35; Lev 9:6, 23–24) and the temple (1 Kgs 8:11; 2 Chr 5:11–14; 7:1). They therefore are to glorify God with their bodies. That is their theophanic, glory-manifesting, God-showing vocation! Created as they are in God's image and recreated in Christ's image, their bodies are holy shrines that God uses to disclose himself to other people in their social context.

In Romans 6:11–23, St. Paul explains how God involves us in our ongoing sanctification. Since we have died to sin with Christ and been raised to life with God in baptism, we are called to avoid any relapse into slavery—slavery to lawless desire, sin, impurity, and death. That is a matter of life and death for us, life with God and death apart from God. Here Paul uses sacrificial imagery to explore those two alternatives by contrasting the presentation of our bodies either to sin with its destructive tyranny, like the sacrifice of an animal as a victim for death to devour, or to God with his life-giving righteousness, like the offering of priests in his life-giving service. On the one hand, unbelievers recklessly "sacrifice" their bodies in the lawless pursuit of what they desire. In their quest for a fuller, richer, happier, freer life, they hand over the members of their bodies with each limb and organ to worse and worse impurity (6:19). That sacrifice leads to ever-increasing, shameful defilement of their bodies. The final, eventual result of bodily self-pollution is death. Ironically, by seeking a life of freedom apart from God, they become enslaved and destroyed by death (6:16, 23). On the other hand, we Christians, now freed from sin (6:18), brought from death to life (6:11), and alive to God in Christ Jesus (6:13), are urged to "offer" ourselves with our body and all its members, including our sexual organs, to God in living, life-giving, transformational service (6:13, 19). Since we cannot keep ourselves pure and holy by ourselves and our own efforts, we rely on God to do it for us.

That self-offering in worship and prayer leads to a life of righteousness, rich in all good works, and ongoing sanctification (6:19, 22). The final outcome is eternal life with God (6:23). That purifying, sanctifying transformation does not happen automatically without our consent and cooperation. It requires our wholehearted, willing, receptive obedience, the obedient entrusting of ourselves with our bodies to God for him to sanctify them for eternal life with him (6:16, 17). He does it for us; we go along with him in what he is doing.

Paul describes the goal of bodily sanctification vividly for us with the use of nuptial imagery in Ephesians 5:25–27. Contrary to usual Jewish custom, here Jesus, the heavenly bridegroom, prepares his bride for her wedding by bathing, dressing, and adorning her.[36] In baptism, Jesus does all this for his bride. He cleanses the

---

36. For this and what follows, see Thomas M. Winger, *Ephesians,* Concordia Commentary (Saint Louis: Concordia, 2015), 612–14. The Greek adjective *endoxos,* which is translated "radiant" in the NIV and "in splendor" in the ESV, means "glorious," "filled with glory." In this case it is the glory of the risen Lord Jesus.

congregation and all its members to prepare them for himself, so that he can consummate his union with them by sharing himself and his holiness with them. By dressing her up in his holiness, he makes his bride perfect and fit for life with him. He makes her beautiful and parades her before himself in radiant splendor. He adorns her with his own splendor, so that she stands in his light and shares in his glory.[37] Better than any plastic surgeon, he rids her of everything that is ugly and unpresentable in her—every spot, every wrinkle, and every blemish. He does that for all baptized believers, not just at the resurrection, but already now by his nuptial transformation of us. A holy, beautiful, perfect bride: that is how we actually look to him, not in make-believe but in truth! That is how he regards our bodies! That, too, is how we are to regard our own bodies, because they are united with Christ's own body and so share in his holiness and glory! That is the result of his spiritual transformation, his wonderful re-creation of us!

### HOW THIS IS DONE: OUR HOLY CALLING

Picture a married man and woman who have deliberately chosen not to consummate their marriage physically, even though they have no physical or emotional incapacity that disqualifies them from sexual cohabitation. They love each other dearly and are committed to each other in a mental and emotional personal relationship. Yet they have decided not to live together, engage in sexual intercourse, and have children. The wear and tear of bodily association and interaction is not for them. In fact, they dislike it and disown it because it is too demanding and complicated for them physically. It suits them to stay in touch with each other electronically, via cell phone and the internet. They opt for a virtual marriage, which is, in truth, no marriage. They miss out on the real benefits of marriage.

Many people who claim to be Christians are a bit like this. They say that they are spiritual but not religious. They don't want to have

---

37. See Ps 45:13 and Ezek 16:8–14; Rev 19:7–8; 21:2.

anything to do with the church and other Christians. They regard the regular service for worship as unspiritual, ritual mumbo jumbo. They look for nothing more from Jesus than a disembodied spiritual or emotional relationship with him. Like that virtual couple who refuse to cohabitate, they miss out on most of what Christ provides. Let me put the issue as bluntly and provocatively as I can: faith in Jesus requires bodily cohabitation and interaction with him. It's that or nothing! It is an embodied faith in God's embodied Son that entails four kinds of bodily interaction with him.

### Going to Church

Bodily interaction with Jesus most obviously entails regular and faithful involvement in the service of worship. Faithful attendance involves the body in the ways that Christ has established for us through his word. By faith we are united, body and soul, with the body of Jesus in baptism. In faith we assemble with our fellow Christians for the bodily enactment of the divine service. In faith we confess our sins to God and receive his word of pardon; we hear God's word and confess our faith in the triune God; we present our gifts to him as our thank offering and pray for ourselves and others; we receive the body and blood of Jesus and God's benediction. All that is done with the body and for the body. It cannot happen apart from our human bodies. A virtual service via television or radio or the internet will not do! A virtual service is just that! Though it may be better devotionally than nothing in some circumstances—like the prohibition of assembly in an epidemic—it is, at best, a partial, somewhat discarnate substitute for our real personal interaction with God and each other. It may communicate some aspects of the service, like the depiction of our family in a photograph or a home movie, but that virtual portrayal of worship remains a pale copy of what it really is. We need to participate physically in public worship with our bodies. By our faithful, bodily participation in congregational worship, we receive God's incarnate Son and all the blessings of his incarnation; we receive grace upon grace from him who dwells among us (John 1:14, 16).

## Celebrating the Incarnation

For us to receive the incarnate Son and his blessings, the full mystery of the incarnation—with his descent from the Father to bring God bodily to us and his ascent to the Father to bring us bodily to himself—must be preached, taught, confessed, and believed. That is summed up for us in the second article of the Apostles' Creed and the Nicene Creed and presented to us in the year of the church with all its full range of celebrations. A disembodied Christ, no matter how fashionable, will not do; a partial incarnation is of little or no use to us. No matter how unfashionable some articles of faith may be, such as his virgin birth or his physical resurrection, we need the whole incarnate Son of God with his whole incarnation—his bodily conception and birth, his bodily baptism and ministry, his bodily death and burial and descent into hell,[38] his bodily resurrection and ascension, his bodily reign together with his Father and bodily reappearance to judge the living and the dead. But we can't stop there! All that is for the salvation of our bodies and souls! As a result of his incarnation he is now bodily present with us as God and man in the service of worship in order to pardon and redeem us, purify and sanctify us, body and soul for life with God the Father. Whenever and wherever we gather in his name, that gospel must be proclaimed in all its parts for us to believe and receive the salvation that Christ has won for us and now delivers to us here on earth with his holy word and sacraments.

God's word shows us his incarnate Son from two points of view: a heavenly and earthly point of view. These two perspectives are complementary. By faith we now see his full divinity available to us in his human body here on earth in the church (Col 2:9) and his human body taken up into his divine life with God the Father in heaven (Col 3:1; Heb 2:9; 3:1; 12:2). By faith we also see him in his humanity as our man with God and God's man with us. We see his flesh as the way by which God comes to us on earth (Col

---

38. For a discussion of this rather unpopular teaching, see Matthew Y. Emerson, *"He Descended to the Dead": An Evangelical Theology of Holy Saturday* (Downers Grove, IL: IVP Academic, 2019).

2:9–10) as well as the way by which we come to God in heaven (Heb 10:19–22). We now see him as our high priest who ushers us bodily into the Father's presence (Heb 7:25) and brings the Father's gifts to us for our life in the body here on earth (Heb 13:20–21). We see ourselves and our bodies in him and with him in the Father's presence (Eph 1:3–4; 2:4–7), as well as him with us and in us here on earth (Eph 3:14–19). In short: we do well to see ourselves as Jesus sees us, with pure and holy bodies that are being reconfigured for eternal life with God in heaven. By faith we are privileged to live heavenly lives on earth and earthly lives in heaven at each moment and each stage of our bodily journey with Jesus.

### Receiving Medicine for Body and Soul

God's incarnate Son Jesus presents his glorified and glorifying body and blood to us in Holy Communion. We therefore need to put our faith in his promises and come to his Holy Supper with our human bodies to receive him and all his gifts for us. In faith we can ask him to redeem our bodies and souls from the devil and to free them from the ravages of sin; we can also ask him to purify and sanctify us in body and soul for life with God the Father and obedient service of him. In faith we can receive spiritual life and health for ourselves in body and soul; we can also receive spiritual empowerment and protection for our bodies and souls in our whole life on earth. Thus, Luther encourages Christians to use the sacrament of Holy Communion as "a pure, wholesome, soothing medicine" for body and soul as well as an "antidote against the poison" of sin in them. He then concludes, "For here in the sacrament you receive from Christ's lips the forgiveness of sins, which contains and conveys God's grace and Spirit with all his gifts, protection, defense, and power against death and the devil and all evils."[39]

---

39. The Large Catechism, 5.68, 70, BoC (474).

## Doing Holy Work

Jesus purifies and sanctifies our bodies so we can work with him here on earth (Titus 2:14; 2 Tim 2:21). Just as Jesus did the work of God the Father in his life on earth, so we do the work of God together with Jesus. We work with him in our station in life, whether it be in our family, our society, or our congregation. There in that location, we serve the Father together with Jesus by interceding for those whom God has placed in our care and by showing God's love to them.[40] We do the work of God as holy priests; we do holy work when we believe in his holy word and ask him to bless us, our work, and the people that we encounter in our daily work. Holy work is the prayerful work of a believer. Thus, we pray the Lord's Prayer as our daily prayer of consecration. In it we pray for the hallowing of God's name by our faith in his word and the coming of his kingdom by our reception of the Holy Spirit, so that we may lead godly lives according to it. Because we are sanctified by the word of God and prayer in the divine service and our daily devotions, we can do holy work in obedience to God and his holy word. From a human point of view, we do these good works[41] in obedience to God's law; from a divine point of view, we do God's works by faith in the gospel of Jesus and the power of his Holy Spirit.[42] Our good works do not make us holy; God's Spirit-inspiring, Spirit-giving word makes us and our works holy. There are, indeed, two kinds of holy work: the prayerful work of faith, which makes us holy because we hear God's word and receive Christ's holy body and blood, and the active work of obedience to God's word that we do because we have been made holy. Only holy people can do holy work. This is how Luther explains the role of God's word in doing this:

---

40. Luther teaches this by the juxtaposition of Rom 13:9 and 1 Tim 2:1 at the end of the Household Chart in the Small Catechism 7.14, BoC (367). Even though we have different callings according to our places in the social order, we have a common, holy priestly vocation to exercise love and intercede for others.

41. See Matt 5:16; Eph 2:10; 1 Tim 3:1; 5:10, 25; 6:18; Titus 2:7, 14; 3:8, 14; Heb 10:24; 1 Pet 2:12.

42. See John 6:28, 29; 1 Thess 1:3; 2 Thess 1:11.

God's Word is the true holy object above all holy objects. ... God's Word is the treasure that makes everything holy. By it all the saints have themselves been made holy. At whatever time God's Word is taught, preached, heard, read, or pondered, there the person, the day, and the work is hallowed, not on account of the external work but on account of the Word that makes us all saints. Accordingly, I constantly repeat that all our life and work must be based on God's Word if they are to be God-pleasing or holy.[43]

A television set does not invent what it shows. By itself it can produce nothing and show nothing. It needs to receive the programs that are transmitted to it before it can show anything to its viewers. What's more, both its reception and transmission depend on empowerment by electricity. It is the same with us. Our spiritual transmission depends on our reception of it. And both of these depend on our enlightenment and empowerment by the Holy Spirit.

There are then two sides to a Christian life in the body. On the one hand, there is the receptive life in which God the Father gives us his Holy Spirit and every other spiritual gift to us through Jesus. On the other hand, there is the transmitted life in which we do the holy work that God gives us to do while it is day. Both belong together. Both involve our bodies. Both are the fruit of the incarnation and our faith in God's incarnate Son. We can only pass on God's gifts as we receive them bodily. We can only work with God as he energizes us bodily. We can only show God as he is on display in our bodies.

---

43. The Large Catechism, 1.91–92, BoC (399).

# 4

# THE SPIRITUAL BODY

In Christ a part of our flesh and blood, that is, our human nature, sits in heaven above at the right hand of God. ... It is an unspeakably great glory and honor for mankind to have been raised so high by Him, not merely to heaven among the holy angels and archangels, who are certainly great and excellent princes and lords, but to the level of direct equality with God himself. How could the High Majesty become humbler than by honoring this sorry flesh and blood and exalting it through His divine honor and majesty? He descends to the level of our nature and becomes a member of the human race! It is an honor which no angel in heaven shares.

—*Martin Luther*

In Luke 7:11–17, the evangelist paints a vivid and instructive picture for us. It is instructive because it shows the eventual outcome of life in the body from two points of view, the first apart from Jesus and the other with him.

On the one hand, we have a funeral procession led by an unnamed mother whose only son has died. She walks with his corpse and its bearers from her home in the town of Nain to the cemetery outside the town. We see the procession as it is about to pass out through the town gate. She is surrounded by a crowd of townspeople who share her grief and go with her on that painful journey. With the death of her son she has lost everything that counts for her. She has had two devastating deaths, first the death of her husband and now the death of her only son. Her future looks grim and gray. From now on she awaits her own death and the death of her family with her. She and all the other mourners will eventually go the same way through the same gate to the same place as her son. So here then we have a funeral procession in which the dying carry a dead man to be buried, before they, too, are carried by other people to the same place of death. A sad picture indeed of the end of life in the body here on earth apart from Jesus!

On the other hand, we also have another counter-procession that reverses that dismal funeral procession. It is led by Jesus, who has come to visit that place. He heads another group that consists of his disciples and an even larger crowd of people. In a dramatic intervention, he stops the funeral procession as it is about to pass out through the gate of the town; he turns it around so that it does not leave the town and reach the cemetery. He does four things to reverse the funeral procession. First, he is filled with compassion for the bereaved mother and tells her, without giving any reason for his command, that she now no longer has any cause to weep. Then he touches the unclean corpse of her son with his holy hands to remove its death with his own living body and give it life from his own body. Then strangely, he addresses the corpse of the young man as if he were merely asleep, commands him to arise, and restores him to life. Finally, he gives the son, now once again able to speak, back to his astonished mother. Their conversation, once terminated by his death, is now miraculously restored.

With that reunion the funeral procession is turned into a triumphal victory procession. The people in it now no longer lament but instead glorify God for sending Jesus to free that young man from the fierce grip of death and for giving him back to his mother. They praise him for comforting his mother by reviving her son, just as God had done through the prophet Elijah for the widow of Zarephath (1 Kgs 17:17–24). Though taken away from his mother by a premature death, the young man was brought back from death to a new life with his mother. The course of both their lives was completely reversed. It was Jesus who brought about that great reversal. His visit to that town ended the reign of death over that family.

In the light of that story we may view the outcome of life in the body in two ways from two different points of view. The view from those two perspectives depends on whether we see the course of life apart from Jesus or together with him.

Apart from Jesus, life on earth in the body ends in death. After death there is nothing to envisage for the body except its complete disintegration. So human life in the body passes by under the dark shadow of death toward its final, inevitable termination. Even though we may keep pretending that we will never die, we can do nothing to escape our own death. The best diet and the healthiest lifestyle may prolong it a little, but they can't stop it from happening. All too quickly we reach our own death (Ps 90:5–10). That is the fixed, inexorable course of life in the body!

As if that were not bad enough, we do not just eventually taste the bitterness of death when we die; we begin to die long before we actually die. In fact, as the Lord God had warned Adam that he would die as soon as he ate the fruit of the forbidden tree (Gen 2:17), so we begin dying as soon as we start to live. Throughout our life on earth, death reaches out to rob us of life in many different ways. Each knockback and setback, accident and injury, sickness and infirmity, hurtful act and painful experience, grief and sorrow, loss and bereavement, is a little death. Even though we may be filled with physical vitality when we are young, we lose it gradually. Life winds down and peters out for us as we age; our bodies wear out, weaken, and decay well before we die. So bit by bit, life is taken away from us, until we have nothing left of it. We may ignore the onset of death and pretend it is not happening, but that changes nothing. Physical life in the body ends in physical death, which overshadows the whole of life on earth.

But that is not the final outcome of life in the body together with Jesus. Seen from his point of view, the death of a believer is not a period but a semicolon. With him the course of an earthly life passes through the gate of death to eternal life with God the Father. And that happens already now as soon as we hear God's word and believe in Jesus as God's Son (John 3:16, 36; 5:25; 1 John 5:12). Through faith in God's Son we pass from a lesser life to a greater life, from ever-diminishing life to super-abundant life, from temporal life on earth to eternal life in heaven. We proceed through death to life. We die with Jesus in order to live with him and his heavenly Father. That reversal begins with our rebirth in baptism (Titus 3:5–7; 1 Pet 1:3, 23). But it is not complete on the day of its enactment. It includes the whole of our life in the body as baptized people and culminates in our actual, physical death. Throughout our entire life and in each day, Jesus brings us through death to ever-fuller participation in his undying life.

So from faith's point of view, the course of life in the body ends in life rather than death. In fact, our spiritual life began with death, for even though we were physically alive, we were born spiritually dead without any ability to fear, love, and trust in the living God, dead in our transgressions and sins (Eph 2:1, 5; Col 2:13). From the moment of our conception, we were all disconnected from the source of life, like a branch cut from a vine, and so not yet enlivened by the life-giving Holy Spirit. We were all spiritual zombies until the risen Lord Jesus gave us eternal life through a new birth by water and his life-giving Spirit (John 3:5; Col 3:11–13; Titus 3:4–7; 1 Pet 1:3). Thus, eternal life begins for us already now in our bodily existence, for by faith we now share in the divine life of Jesus. What's more, we become more and more alive spiritually as we age physically. Our physical strength is taken away from us so that we come to rely more and more on the Holy Spirit. Best of all, we get death behind us before we die, so that when we die physically, we have nothing but life before us (John 5:25). In contrast with the greater, total death of our baptism by our immersion in the death of Jesus, our physical death is, in fact, a little death that brings that death to completion.

Yet that does not abolish the agony of physical death. It is just as bitter and painful and tragic with Jesus as it is apart from him. There is nothing good about death for us. It remains our last, worst enemy (1 Cor 15:26). As he was dying from cancer, a friend of mine, a pastor in the prime of life, put it well when he said, "Dying comes hard!" So, too, the pain of bereavement for those who have been left behind. Yet despite that, Jesus takes away "the sting of death" (1 Cor 15:55–56) by traveling with us through the valley of the shadow of death (Ps 23:4). He accompanies us in our frightful, painful journey through death and comforts us with the promise of our bodily resurrection together with him. He keeps us safe from all the powers of darkness. With him as our companion, the pangs of death are like the pain of a baby as it is delivered from its mother's womb to a fuller life in this world.

We live in a society that covers up the horror of death and sugarcoats its agony by speaking well of it. Thus, many leading thinkers regard dying as a natural process that should be welcomed and affirmed as something good. Some of them go even further than that! Whereas our ancestors spoke about the blessed death of those who died with faith in Christ, these teachers now advocate voluntary euthanasia by suicide as the best way of dying. It is, they say, a good death, because it avoids the pain of dying and embraces physical death as natural transition into nothingness, or a natural reunion with the cosmic order, like a drop of water that is absorbed back into the ocean.

But such a death is not a good death. In fact, the death of Jesus is the only good human death, not for him but for us. It is good for us because by it Jesus overcame death for us. His victory over death becomes our victory. Death does not defeat us. Rather, Jesus reverses the apparent outcome of life in the body by leading us through death into his Father's house. He turns our funeral procession into a victory procession together with him. As we travel through life, we wait eagerly for the redemption of our bodies and eternal life with God as his adopted children (Rom 8:23).

## OUR HOPE OF FULL EMBODIMENT

People commonly view their bodies as a temporary, earthly home for their souls. If all goes well, they become more and more at home in them as time passes, like the houses that they inhabit. Like their homes, their bodies locate them in time and space. Their bodies give them their station, their unique place in the natural, social, and domestic context that sustains and nourishes them in their life on earth. Apart from their bodies and their given bodily habitat, they cannot live and thrive. Their bodies locate them here on earth and make them the people that they are. So, since they are at home in their bodies, they leave that home when they die. They take up residence somewhere else, or, as some falsely believe, nowhere at all. If they belong to Jesus, they take up residence with him and his body.

People also view their bodies as a set of clothes that they, happily or unhappily, wear for as long as they live, and then, gladly or sadly, take off when they die. In that they are not completely wrong. That is indeed how it appears from a human point of view. Yet that is not the full story. Yes, we do slough off our sinful, mortal bodies when we die. But we don't put them off like dirty clothes in order to free our souls from our bodies, as if they were a burden or perhaps even a prison for our souls. Instead, we who trust in Jesus put off our bodies like worn out, shabby clothes in order to put on our best dress, a new, perfect body over us. Yet, strictly speaking, we don't do that; Christ does it for us. He dresses us with himself and his own body.

Yet that total revival does not just happen when we die a physical death. Jesus began to do it for us and with us when we were baptized. In baptism he took off our old self, the old Adam, and dressed us up with a new self, a new Adam (Col 2:11–12; 3:9–10). In fact, he clothed us with his whole self, like a large overcoat or royal robes, so that we now share his identity and status and inheritance as God's Son (Gal 3:27). He covers for us. To illustrate this amazing transformation, Paul compares Baptism to the ancient Jewish rite of circumcision. Whereas the person who circumcised a young man cut off the foreskin of his penis with his human hands in order to make a boy part of God's people, Jesus circumcises members of both sexes with his divine hands by completely removing the whole "body of flesh," our sinful nature in his death (Col 2:11). We who were once dead in sin were made alive and raised from the dead as new persons with a new self and a new way of life (Col 2:12–13). So by that renewal, God the master surgeon does not just give us a heart transplant but a body transplant. We become a new creation in Christ (2 Cor 5:17).

The transformation that began with the rite of Baptism continues for as long as we live here on earth. It is not just a passing intervention at one point in our lives; it is an ongoing process by which Jesus gradually undresses us until we are completely dressed and fully re-embodied in him. Thus, St. Paul urges the Christians in Rome "to put on the Lord Jesus Christ" (Rom 13:14). He also instructs the Christians in Ephesus to put off their old selves, the old Adam, which has been mortally corrupted by deceitful physical and mental desires, in order to be made a new people with a new spirit and new mentality, and to put on the new self, the new Adam, created to be like God in true righteousness and holiness (Eph 4:22–24). They therefore do not bring about their own transformation; they go along with Jesus and rely on him to transform them. He recreates them in his image gradually by undressing them of their vices and dressing them up in his virtues, so that they can represent him better and display him more fully (Col 3:8–15).

The disciples of Jesus do not just reflect his character, his nature as God's Son; they are also called to be like him in how they act and in what they do. Thus, they go along with Jesus by dressing up for life in a new day, God's eternal day; they copy him by putting off "the deeds of darkness" like dirty clothing and by putting on the protective "armor of light" that Jesus provides for them in their daily battle against the powers of darkness (Rom 13:12; 1 Thess 5:8). Since they belong to Jesus, who lives with them and helps them, they are also now able to put off all their destructive vices by asking him to remove them and put on all his constructive virtues, which they receive from him in prayer. They can put off the deadly, life-destroying vices of their own sinful flesh, such as anger and bad temper, malice and slander, envy and deceit, hypocrisy and obscenity (Col 3:8; 1 Pet 2:1), and put on the lively, life-promoting virtues of Christ, such as compassion and kindness, humility and meekness, patience and forbearance, generosity and love (Col 3:12–14). That is their new, visible dress, the beautiful clothes that Christ supplies! That is the bridal apparel that equips them for life with him as their heavenly bridegroom (Rev 19:7–8)!

Paul describes the goal of our revival vividly in 2 Corinthians 5:1–7. He pictures our present earthly body as a temporary, destructible tent and compares it with Christ's heavenly body as the eternal, indestructible, God-built residence for our resurrected bodies. He says:

For we know that if the tent that is our earthly home is
    destroyed,
we have a building from God,
a house not made with hands, eternal in the heavens.
For in this tent we groan, longing to put on our heavenly
    dwelling,
if indeed by putting it on we may not be found naked.
For while we are still in this tent, we groan, being burdened—
not that we would be unclothed,
but that we would be further clothed,
so that what is mortal may be swallowed up by life.
He who has prepared this very thing is God,
who has given us the Spirit as a guarantee.
So we are always of good courage.
We know that while we are at home in the body
we are away from the Lord,
for we walk by faith, not by sight.

We are not destined to become discarnate souls, naked wraiths, disembodied ghosts, when we die. Nothing could be worse than that! Instead, we long to overcome all that now oppresses and distresses us in our bodies by becoming even more fully embodied. That is what God has promised us and prepared for us by the incarnation of his Son! That is our hope, the hope that fills us with good courage! God provides us with a new place of residence like a new set of clothes, a heavenly dwelling that Jesus himself has built for us with his own body. That is our true home. There we will at last be at home with him and each other. We can be sure of that, because we have received the Holy Spirit as the guarantee for our life with Jesus there in that place.

Meanwhile, like the Israelites who groaned under the burden of their oppression by Pharaoh and his slave drivers (Exod 2:13–14), we groan because we are burdened by sin, death, and the devil for as long as we live in the body. We long for freedom from our bondage to decay; we long to be further clothed and fully dressed rather than unclothed and naked. When our bodies are raised from death, we hope to take up residence with Jesus in that heavenly place, where we will be even more fully and perfectly embodied than we now are. There we will not be less alive than we are now; we will be much more alive than we ever were here on earth. Our bodies will share in the eternal life of the Holy Trinity. And we will be at home with God the Father and the Holy Spirit because we will be at home with Jesus.

People in the ancient world commonly pictured death as a greedy monster that lived in the sea or the watery underworld. When they died, they fancied that they were swallowed up as by the waters of the sea; they were overwhelmed and engulfed by death. Death drove the breath of life from their bodies. Death was envisaged as a hungry, flesh-eating monster with a large mouth and even larger belly. In an amazing reversal of that normal pattern, Jesus himself fulfills the prophecy of death's death in Isaiah 25:7. By his death, Jesus not only swallows up death, that awful life-gobbler, but also promises to swallow up all that is mortal in us by his life. Our bodies will finally be overwhelmed and engulfed by life rather than death.

But all that is now hidden from our human eyes, which see no visible evidence of that victory over death, even though our transformation has already begun. As we continue to live in the body, we live by faith rather than sight. We live in the hope of our full embodiment.

### WELCOME JUDGMENT

Innocent people welcome judgment. They welcome it because they have a clear conscience; they know that they will be vindicated by any just judge. They have nothing to fear from any right court of law.

But that does not apply to us or any other human being with the risen Lord Jesus as our Judge. None of us is innocent; none is righteous in God's sight (Rom 3:9–18). We have all rebelled against

God and gone astray from his way in our life in the body. We all have a bad conscience about what we have done and what we are; we are all failures by God's standards. Already in our conscience we experience God's righteous judgment as he charges us with rebellion against him, discloses our sin, exposes our guilt, and sentences us to death. Paul puts this bluntly in Romans 6:23 when he says, "The wages of sin is death." That's the temporal and eternal consequence of our sin, the inevitable penalty of our rebellion against God, the source of life. We live, as it were, on death row. We live as people who have been sentenced to death. Even if we pretend that this is not so, the day of death will surely come for us, that fearful day when God the Judge confronts us in his final judgment of us (Heb 9:27; see also Rom 14:10–12). By rights we should expect nothing but condemnation to eternal death from him then (Rom 3:19–20, 23).

Yet that is not the destiny of those who belong to Jesus. Even though the wages of sin is death, Paul adds, "the free gift of God is eternal life in Christ Jesus our Lord" (Rom 6:23). God the Father has sent his Son to take up our sin in his own body and suffer the penalty for it physically on our behalf. Even though he was without sin, God charged him with our sin and condemned him to death as a sin offering for us (Rom 8:3; 2 Cor 5:21); because he was without sin, God also raised him with his body, in order to give us his purity, righteousness, and innocence (Rom 4:24–25). So instead of being put to death, we receive forgiveness of sins through Jesus (Luke 24:47). He speaks his Father's word of pardon to sinners here on earth. He does not just pardon the evil deeds that they have done but also frees them from the sinful state of mistrust of God and rebellion against him. He speaks God's word of grace to those who are guilty of rebellion against their Creator and under the sentence of eternal death from him for their rejection of him as their life-giver. That welcome word of pardon is God's final judgment which they hear already now, long before they stand before his tribunal at the end of the world. This means that "there is now no condemnation for those who are in Christ Jesus" (Rom 8:1). Neither now, nor when they die!

By his incarnate life, death, resurrection, and ascension, Jesus has become the Judge of the living and the dead (Acts 10:42; 2 Cor 5:10; 2 Tim 4:1). God the Father has entrusted all judgment to him as the Son of Man, our man with God (John 5:19–27). He is now our gracious, life-giving Judge. That changes the prospect of judgment for us so completely that we need now no longer dread it but may welcome it instead. We may welcome it because through it he now fixes us up and sets things right for us. By his judgment he sets things right in two ways. On the one hand, Jesus judges us by justifying us through the gospel and making us well-pleasing to God the Father. We thereby gain the full approval of our heavenly Father. On the other hand, Jesus judges our works by God's law, which shows us which works are well pleasing to him, and then rewards us accordingly. We thereby gain the reward from him for our labor.

As the Judge of all people, Jesus determines their eternal destiny either by speaking his word of absolution, which assures them of his approval, or by withholding it, so that they remain under condemnation. He pronounces God's final sentence on all sinners, whether it be to eternal life or eternal death. That sentence depends on whether they believe in Jesus as their Savior or reject him (John 3:36; 1 John 5:12). Since we trust in Jesus, his word of forgiveness opens the door to his Father's house, admits us to his royal presence, and gives us access to his grace. That welcome life-sentence assures us that God the Father is just as pleased with us as he is with his own dear Son. We who hear the word of Jesus and believe him no longer face the awful prospect of condemnation at the last judgment, because we have already passed from death to life with God the Father before we actually die physically (John 5:24). Consequently, we can approach the Father with the full assurance of faith and serve him with a good conscience (Heb 9:14; 10:22); we can "serve him without fear, in holiness and righteousness before him all our days" (Luke 1:74–75). We are, says Luther rather memorably, "more than halfway out of death in Christ."[1]

As our Judge, Jesus also assesses what we have done. In 2 Corinthians 5:10, St. Paul explains why he always aims to please the Lord Jesus with these words: "For we must all appear before the judgment seat of Christ, so that each one may receive what is due for what has been done in the body, whether good or evil." Here Paul does not consider how we gain salvation but how we gain recompense for our faithful service of Christ. In the former instance, we picture ourselves on trial in God's court of law in a criminal case in which we hope for acquittal or pardon. In this instance, we picture ourselves as plaintiffs in a civil tribunal in which we hope for vindication and fair compensation for our work. In this tribunal, the Lord Jesus is both our employer and our judge. Yet we do not appeal to him for fair payment for what we have done in our own right; he assesses our performance to judge what he has accomplished through us with our work in the body.

On the one hand, Jesus rejects every evil work and dissociates it from us. He rids us of each evil deed, partially in this life and fully at death, so that we can stand before him blameless in his final appraisal of us. That process of purification is completed with our physical death rather than after death. Thus in 1 Corinthians 3:11–15, Paul depicts death as an ordeal by fire, a purging fire, like a smelter, that tests what we have done and burns up everything that is not fit for eternity. Yet even if all our shoddy work is rejected, we, his coworkers, will still be saved through the purifying fire of God's final judgment. And that is good news for us, because it means that we will not be stuck forever with the bad things that we have done.

On the other hand, our Lord Jesus gives his approval of everything that is good and rewards us for our faithful service (1 Cor 3:14; 2 Cor 5:10). By his judgment he brings us into the light, so that it may be clearly seen that our works have been carried out in God and together with him (John 3:21). We, however, seldom

---

1. Luther, *Commentary on 1 Corinthians 15* (1532), LW 28:111.

see our reward, our payment for faithful service in this life. That comes only with the final appraisal. Our reward will be that we will receive our master's approval with his commendation, "Well done, good and faithful servant. ... Enter into the joy of your master" (Matt 25:21). Yet even though we will only receive our full reward in eternity, the Ten Commandments show us the good works that please God and tell us how we can work with Jesus here on earth. We can be sure that these good works will last for eternity, because they are Christ's works through us. What's more, the Holy Spirit assures us of that with this blessing in Revelation 14:13: "Blessed are the dead who die in the Lord from now on. Yes ... they will rest from their labor, for their deeds will follow them."

So we welcome Christ's judgment of us and our works. We welcome it because he thereby undoes what is evil in us and in the world around us. We do not dread his judgment because we know its outcome for us; we know that only good can come from it for our life in the body. Like the psalmist who asks the Lord to judge him (Ps 7:8; 26:1; 35:24; 43:1), we can therefore gladly welcome his judgment.

## LATENT TRANSFORMATION

We have been given a paradoxical state of life in the body: the life that we now live in the flesh by faith in the Son of God who gave himself to death on our behalf, the life of people who have been crucified with Christ so that they now have him living in them (Gal 2:20). We no longer have life in ourselves but receive life from him and in him. This is how Paul describes that state of life in 2 Corinthians 4:8–11, 16–18:

> We are afflicted in every way, but not crushed; perplexed, but not driven to despair; persecuted, but not forsaken; struck down, but not destroyed; always carrying in the body the death of Jesus, so that the life of Jesus may also be manifested in our bodies. For we who live are always being given over to death for Jesus' sake, so that the life of

Jesus also may be manifested in our mortal flesh. ... So we do not lose heart. Though our outer self is wasting away, our inner self is being renewed day by day. For this light momentary affliction is preparing for us an eternal weight of glory beyond all comparison, as we look not to things that are seen but to things that are unseen. For the things that are seen are transient, but the things that are unseen are eternal.

God created Adam and Eve in his image, so that they would be able to manifest him and his glory in their bodies. Because they and all their descendants have sinned and fall short of God's glory (Rom 3:23), God sent his Son to manifest his life-giving glory bodily in his human life, death, and resurrection. Through Jesus, God now manifests his glory in the bodies of those who preach the gospel and of those who hear what they preach. But he does that in a way that confounds all expectations. He does not display his glory through their extraordinary, superhuman physical vitality. Rather, he hands them over to death with Jesus in order to manifest the life of Jesus in their bodies. So as their bodies share in the death of Jesus, they also manifest the life of Jesus in their mortal flesh. As the light of bodily life grows ever dimmer, the light of his spiritual life shines ever brighter.

From a human point of view, our outer humanity, our old human self, is gradually destroyed as our bodies visibly age and come ever closer to death. We are undone by all the things that oppress and distress us, the things that hurt and harm us, the afflictions by which the Holy Spirit puts our sinful selves to death and conforms us to Christ in his suffering. But from God's point of view, the gradual, visible destruction of our bodies masks a hidden, opposite process of inner transformation that pervades us ever more completely as we go along on our journey to eternity. Day by day, God creates a new inner self, a new eternal person in our dying bodies, so that we can share ever more fully in the life and glory of Jesus. Amazingly, he uses our afflictions to transform us from the inside out and prepare us to receive his glory. He thereby increases our capacity for eternal life.

Paul paints an amazing picture of that latent transformation. He compares our mortal bodies to earthly containers that are far too small to receive their eternal contents. The weight of Christ's life, the immense pressure of his incomparable, mind-boggling, hidden glory that pervades them, presses out in them and threatens to break them apart, like a wineskin filled with fermenting wine. It is too much for them to take in completely. But it does not break them. Instead, it stretches, enlarges, and transforms them, so that, as they are renewed, they are able to participate ever more fully in his abundant life. They also receive a clearer vision of their present lives as they shift their focus away from what is transient and unseen to what is eternal and unseen. They see their lives "hidden with Christ in God" (Col 3:3).

## BECOMING LIKE JESUS

When people get married, they no longer live by themselves but begin to live bodily with each other. They share a common physical life in their cohabitation. At least that is what is meant to happen in a proper marriage. Their convivial life involves them in a reciprocal interaction. On the one hand, they each share their whole physical life with their spouse. Their life story, written on their bodies and in their minds, is combined with the life story of their spouse. And that includes their whole past with all its liabilities and assets. On the other hand, they also each share in the whole physical life of their spouse with all its liabilities and assets. The events in that person's life become entwined with their own lives. Yet it does not cease to be their story but becomes part of a bigger story, the story of their life together, the story of their married life.

Two things happen through their physical communion with each other. They have a common life with shared experiences that affect them both. They share common joys, such as the birth of children and holidays; they also share common troubles, like bereavements and financial hardships. They are also transformed physically, mentally, and personally by their participation in each other's lives. Their shared experiences change them. Through the successes and failures of their relationship, they learn to support and complement each other, so that they fit together better and work together more productively; they not only become more alike in some ways but also develop their own unique personalities in contrast to each other.

Something like that happens in our life with Christ. Like a good marriage, our union and communion with him in body and soul involves us in a reciprocal, lifelong process of adjustment. Yet, unlike any marriage, it is not an equal, symmetrical interaction, because Jesus leads the way in both sides of the relationship. It is an asymmetrical interaction in which he remains the active agent while we remain receptive correspondents. He adjusts himself to us, so that he can adjust us to himself in it; he accommodates himself to us physically in order to accommodate us physically to himself and his heavenly Father.

Our common life with Jesus depends on his incarnation. The Son, who shares a common life with God the Father in heaven, became one of us here on earth, so that he could share our whole human lifecycle on earth from the womb to the tomb (Gal 4:4–5). God sent him into the "likeness" of our sinful human flesh to be a sin offering for us and put an end to the tyranny of sin in the flesh for us (Rom 8:3). He was born in our human "likeness" and died as we do (Phil 2:6–8). He "became like" us in every respect as our flesh-and-blood brother, so that, tempted as we are and beset by all human weaknesses, he could become our sympathetic high priest (Heb 2:17; 4:5). Nothing that we experience and suffer during our life in the body is alien to him. He stands on common human ground with us.

Jesus has conformed himself to us so that he can now conform us to himself. As we travel through life with him, he adjusts us to himself, so that we can share more and more fully in his life with God the Father. He became like us so that we can be like him. That is God's purpose for us as creatures made in his image and marred by sin. From all eternity, God the Father "predestined us to be conformed to the image of his Son" (Rom 8:30). That has always been his goal, his destination for us. Our destiny is to share in the sonship of God's Son. We have been called to share a common life with Jesus here on earth and forever with him in heaven.

In Romans 6:3–8, St. Paul describes how God conforms us to Jesus by uniting us with him and his bodily death and resurrection. He says:

> Do you not know that all of us who have been baptized into Christ Jesus have been baptized into his death? We were *buried* therefore *with him* by baptism into his death, in order that, just as Christ was raised from death by the glory of God the Father, we too might walk in newness of life. For if we have been *planted*[2] *with him* in a death like his, we shall certainly be *planted with him* in a resurrection like his. We know that our old self [man] was *crucified with him* in order that the body of sin might be brought to nothing, so that we would no longer be enslaved to sin. For one who has died [with Christ] stands justified[3] from sin. Now if we have *died with Christ*, we believe that we will also *live with him*.[4]

Through baptism, we who have been united with Jesus share in his destiny. Grafted in him, we have been transplanted into his death and resurrection. This vivid image is taken from horticulture. It describes the process of cutting a twig from an old root stock and planting it into a new root stock so that it can grow as a living branch together with all the other branches in a new fruit-bearing tree.[5] Here God is pictured as a gardener, and the risen

---

2. Or grafted. The ESV has "united" here and in the second half of the sentence.

3. Or acquitted. The ESV has "set free." See Michael P. Middendorf, *Romans 1–8*, Concordia Commentary (St. Louis: Concordia, 2013), 466–67

4. Translation and emphases from the author.

5. Paul's use of this analogy reverses what usually happens. The twig that is grafted into a healthy stock determines the characteristics of the branches that spring from it and the fruit that they bear.

Lord Jesus as a vigorous tree. Since we were sickly branches on a dying family tree of Adam, God cuts us off from it and grafts us into a new Adam, his Son Jesus. We now share a new common life with him as we are nourished by him and grow together with him. We become more and more like him as we share in his earthly journey in the body. He transforms our lowly, mortal bodies so that they become like his glorious, immortal body (Phil 3:21).

In baptism we are conformed into the image of Jesus by sharing in his death, burial, and resurrection. We share in his death through our baptismal union with the risen Lord Jesus (Rom 6:3, 5, 8; Phil 3:10; 2 Tim 2:11). Our former sinful self, the old Adam, is put to death for its sin together with him; we are, as it were, crucified with him (Rom 6:6–7; Gal 2:9). The old life of the sinning and sinned-against body, with all its guilt and shame, ends then and there. The reign of sin is over for us because God the heavenly Judge has declared us righteous and acquitted us of sin by putting us to death together with Jesus. Our slavery to sin has ended.

Through baptism we also share in the burial of Jesus (Rom 6:4; Col 2:12). We have been buried with him. Our old self, the old Adam with its sinful body and even more sinful mind, has been interred in that sacramental burial. In God's sight it is dead and done for, even if we may still try to revive it.

Since we have been baptized into Christ, we now, most wonderfully, share with him in the resurrection of his body from the dead. We have been raised to eternal life together with him (Eph 2:6; Col 2:12; 3:1); we have been made alive together with him (Eph 2:6; Col 2:13). As we live in the body, we now no longer have life in ourselves, but we live by faith in him as he lives in us, the faith that he himself gives us (Gal 2:20). By faith we already now live with him in the presence of the Father (Rom 6:8; Col 3:1–3; 2 Tim 2:11). He transforms us by his life-giving Spirit as we walk with him on the new way of life that he provides for us; he gives life to our mortal bodies through his Spirit that dwells in us (Rom 6:4; 8:10–11). Yet that new life is provisional and incomplete; it anticipates and provides a foretaste of our eternal life with God the Father after our bodies have been raised from the dead.

The goal of our bodily union with Jesus is our glorification together with him. As coheirs with God's Son, we share in his earthly sufferings in order to share in his heavenly glory (Rom 8:17). By his suffering he shares in our lowly status as sinners and meager inheritance as the children of Adam so that he can save us from our sorry state and share his royal status and rich inheritance with us (Rom 8:18, 28–30; 1 Pet 1:3–5). He wants us to reign with him in glory (2 Tim 2:2; Rev 5:10; 20:5). Amazingly, we begin to do that already now in this life, because we have been enthroned with Jesus at the right hand of God the Father in the heavenly realm (Eph 2:6). As his royal courtiers and members of his royal family, we administer his grace prayerfully by doing the good works that God has prepared for us to do together with Jesus; we are God's "workmanship," his work of art that he has created to display himself and his goodness to the world around us (Eph 2:10). That's how highly God honors our bodies and the deeds that they do in his service!

### FULLY DRESSED

Since we belong to the risen Lord Jesus, we may now view our bodies in the light of their resurrection from the dead. That mystery changes everything for us. It turns a dark, dismal picture of our earthly life into a bright, joyful sight. Yet it remains a mystery, because it is hidden from our natural sight. The mystery of our resurrection from the dead has to do with what no human eye has ever seen, no human ear has ever heard, and no human mind has ever imagined (1 Cor 2:6–12). It is disclosed to us in faith through God's word and the Holy Spirit who enlightens us.

Unlike us, the Bible does not usually speak about the resurrection from "the dead" but about the resurrection of "corpses." Nevertheless, both terms are commonly misunderstood as the reconstitution of our present bodies with all their present characteristics, their revival and resuscitation in their earthly form.

Yet the resurrection of the body differs radically from the resuscitation of a dead person, such as the daughter of Jairus in Mark
5:35–43, the widow's son in Luke 7:11–17, or Lazarus in John 11:1–
44. Restored to their former state of life, they were doomed to die
again. But, unlike them with their dead bodies, the resurrection of
the body has to do with its transformation into a new state of being,
like the change of a grub into a butterfly, or a lump of carbon into
a diamond. Jesus himself best exemplifies that transformation by
his appearances to his disciples after his resurrection. Even though
his body was no longer subject to the limitations of time, space,
and matter, he appeared to them visibly in a locked room, walked
with them, stood in their midst, spoke with them, ate with them,
and allowed them to touch him. There was nothing ghostly about
him (Luke 24:37–39).

Jesus describes the result of that transformation in his controversy with the Sadducees about the resurrection of the body. In
Luke 20:36, he asserts that when people are raised from the dead,
they will be like the angels as sons of God; they will have the same
fraternal status and relationship with God the Father as Jesus and
will be immortal creatures like the angels. They will be the same
persons as previously, but with a changed body.

Contrary to common belief, we will not be raised as disembodied souls. That would be a ghastly prospect, for our survival
as ghosts would be even worse than the worst kind of human life
on earth. An existence as a ghost is no life at all, for ghosts are the
living dead, diminished entities, homeless souls that haunt the
realm of the living without enjoying life at all. We will also not be
raised with exactly the same bodies that we have here on earth.
That, too, would be horrible prospect, for we would be stuck with
our present damaged bodies and be burdened by all their infirmi-
ties and disabilities. Rather, we will be raised from the dead with
splendid bodies that have been completely changed. Even our scars,
if they remain with us, like the scars of Jesus (Luke 24:40; John
20:20, 27), will be transfigured and transformed. Jesus will remake
us; he will "transform our lowly [bodies] to be like his glorious

body" (Phil 3:21). Yet they will not be alien to us. They will still be recognizable as our bodies—even more recognizable than now, for our resurrected bodies will provide a perfect match for our redeemed souls. We will recognize ourselves and each other as the people we once were before we died. Only then will we be fully at home with ourselves in our bodies and with others in their bodies.

That, of course, is hard for us to envisage. It goes beyond anything that we have ever experienced. It evades the grasp of our earthbound, human minds, which understandably dismiss it as wishful thinking, a wild flight of sheer fantasy. So, like Paul's skeptical critic in 1 Corinthians 15:35, we cannot help but ask, "How are the dead raised? With what kind of body do they come?" Paul answers that question at some length in 1 Corinthians 15:36–57. There he describes our transformation from three different points of view: our resurrection with spiritual bodies (15:37–44a), our recreation in Christ's image as heavenly people (15:44b–49), and our victory over death by being clothed with his immortality (15:50–57).

Paul answers the second question about the nature of our resurrected bodies first with this explanation in 15:36–44a:

> You foolish person! What you sow is not made alive unless it dies. And what you sow is not the body that is to be, but a bare kernel, perhaps of wheat or some other grain. But God gives it a body as he has chosen, and to each kind of seed its own body. For not all flesh is the same, but there is one kind [of flesh] for humans, another for animals, another for birds, and another for fish. There are heavenly bodies and earthly bodies, but the glory of the heavenly [body] is of one kind, and the glory of the earthly [body] is another. There is one glory of the sun, and another glory of the moon, and another glory of the stars; for star differs from star in glory. So it is with the resurrection from the dead. It is sown in corruption; it is raised in incorruption. It is sown in dishonor; it is raised in glory. It is sown in weakness; it is raised in power. It is sown a natural body; it is raised a spiritual body.

Our present bodies will not be raised to eternal life with God by being taken straight into heaven, like Enoch or Elijah. They must die before God makes them live again. Only after they have died will they be raised to life by God, who will give each of us the new body that he has chosen for us. Here Paul uses a simple analogy, taken from what Jesus said about his own death in John 12:24, to help us to envisage this. Our present bodies are like seeds of wheat or some other kind of grain, seeds with dormant life in them. Our resurrected bodies will be like the living, growing plants of wheat that are produced from them. Both the seed and the plant are the same kind of wheat; they have the same nature, the same genetic code. Yet the "body" of the plant is quite different from the "body" of its seed. So we will be the same persons but with different bodies.

Two further analogies help us to imagine how our resurrected bodies will differ from our present bodies. On the one hand, Paul reminds us that there are various kinds of "flesh" here on earth, each with its own state of life and mode of being. Thus, despite all their similarities, the "flesh" of a human person differs from the "flesh" of an animal, just as the "flesh" of an animal differs from the "flesh" of birds and fish. By implication, the "flesh" of our resurrected bodies will also differ from the "flesh" of our natural bodies; it will have a different state of life with another mode of being. On the other hand, not only do heavenly bodies have greater glory than all earthly bodies; they also differ from each other in their radiance and glory, their degree of luminosity. Thus, the sun has brighter light than the moon, and the moon has brighter light than the stars, which, in turn, vary in brightness. So too, by implication, our resurrected heavenly bodies will have greater glory than our present earthly bodies, each with its own kind of glory and own degree of glory. That then will be a cause of delight and joy rather than envy and jealousy, as is now the case with people who are much more attractive than we are. Our glory will be their glory, just as Christ's glory is ours.

Our heavenly bodies will differ from our earthly bodies in four ways. No longer subject to corruption and decay in a dying world, they will be entirely incorruptible and imperishable. No longer dark and unpresentable and degraded by sin, they will be bright and beautiful and glorious in their radiance. No longer physically weak and spiritually infirm from the threat of death, they will be healed and empowered by the Holy Spirit. No longer natural bodies that are animated with the same kind of vitality as the animals, they will be wholly enlivened and pervaded by the Holy Spirit. Our resurrected bodies will differ from our natural bodies because they will be completely animated by God's Spirit. They will be spiritual bodies. Luther gives this eloquent explanation of what is meant by a spiritual body:

> When it is called a spiritual body, this does not imply that it no longer has physical life or flesh and blood. No, then it could not be called true body. But when it is called a spiritual body, this means that it will have life and yet not be a body that eats, sleeps, digests, but a body that is nourished and preserved spiritually by God and has life entirely in Him. ... It will be a completely spiritual existence, or life, of the whole person, covering both body and soul. It will issue from the Spirit and will come immediately from or through God, so that we will be illumined by Him and know Him not only with regard to the soul, but our whole body will be pervaded.[6]

After considering the kind of bodies that God will provide for each of us at the resurrection, Paul explains how they will be raised as spiritual bodies in 15:44b–49:

> If there is a natural body, there is also a spiritual body. Thus it is written, "The first Adam became a living soul"[7]; the last Adam became a life-giving spirit. But it is not the spiritual that is first but the natural, and then the spiritual. The first man was from the earth, a man of dust; the second man

---

6. Luther, *Commentary on 1 Corinthians 15* (1532), LW 28:189–90.

7. The ESV has "living being."

is from heaven. As was the man of dust, so also are those who are of the dust, and as is the man of heaven, so also are those who are of heaven. Just as we have worn[8] the image of the man of dust, so shall we also wear[9] the image of the man of heaven.

Here the focus shifts from our bodies to Jesus as the second Adam, our man from heaven. The argument proceeds by analogy between Adam and Jesus. It is an argument by contrast rather than just similarity. Adam was created as a living soul. He was a life-receiving person with a natural body that was animated with the same life-power, the same vitality as the animals. By nature he was "a man of dust" because he had been formed from the dust of the earth and was doomed to return to dust when he died. He is the prototype of those who have natural, human bodies. Like him, we earthlings are people of dust. Since Adam's image is imprinted on us, we share in his life. Like him, our life is marked by corruption, shame, and weakness. We "wear" his image like a dirty, shabby, worn-out set of clothes in our life on earth.

In contrast with him, Jesus is our second Adam, the prototype of people with spiritual bodies. He is "the man from heaven." By virtue of his bodily life, death, and resurrection, he has become "a life-giving spirit." He animates people with his own divine, spiritual life. Like him, we are heavenly people, even though we have come from earth and not from heaven. Because we have been recreated in his image, we, like him, have a spiritual body. So just as we "have worn" the image of Adam with our natural bodies, which share in his corruption, shame, and weakness, so we will also "wear" the image of Jesus, the man from heaven, with our spiritual bodies, which will share in his incorruption, power, and glory. Our bodies will wear his image as their new dress for our full enjoyment of eternal life in heaven.

---

8. The ESV has "borne."
9. The ESV has "bear."

After telling us how God will give us spiritual bodies at the resurrection, Paul draws together the threads of his argument in 15:50–56 by depicting their transformation in three scenes: the final awakening of sleeping people, dressing them up for life in a new day, and celebrating their victory over their final enemy, death.

> I tell you this, brothers; flesh and blood cannot inherit the kingdom of heaven, nor does corruption inherit incorruption. Behold! I tell you a mystery. We shall not all sleep, but we shall all be changed, in a moment, in the twinkling of an eye, at the last trumpet. For the trumpet will sound and the dead will be raised[10] incorruptible,[11] and we shall be changed. For this corruptible [body] must be clothed with incorruption, and this mortal [body] must be clothed with immortality.[12] When this corruptible [body] is clothed with incorruption, and this mortal [body] is clothed with immortality,[13] then shall come to pass the saying that is written:
>
> > "Death is swallowed up in victory."
> > "O death, where is your victory?
> >  O death, where is your sting?"
>
> The sting of death is sin, and the power of sin is the law. But thanks be to God, who gives us the victory through our Lord Jesus Christ.

Here those who have died are compared with people who are so fast asleep that they need to be woken and dressed up in their best clothes for a day of celebration (see also 1 Cor 15:6, 18, 20, 51; 1 Thess 5:6–7). According to Luther, their sleep is far deeper than

---

10. Or "roused" and therefore "awakened."

11. The ESV has "imperishable."

12. The ESV has: "For this perishable body must put on the imperishable, and this mortal body must put on immortality."

13. The ESV has, "When the perishable puts on the imperishable, and the mortal puts on immortality."

the best earthly sleep because they no longer remember what has happened to them in their life on earth.[14] Yet at the same time, their souls are more awake to God and the angels than they ever were when they were alive here on earth. As they sleep in Christ, they glimpse and overhear what is happening in heaven. But they have yet to enter what they now foresee and overhear.

The natural body must be changed before it can enter into its royal inheritance. It cannot inherit eternal life with God in heaven dressed in its corrupted, mortal state. So God undresses it by putting it to sleep in death. Then he wakes it up from the sleep of death and clothes it with the robes it needs for life with him in heaven, the robes of incorruption and immortality. He clothes it with the same royal, priestly robe that his victorious Son wears as he celebrates his victory over death (Rev 1:13). By clothing the resurrected body with incorruption and immortality, he transforms it and frees it from the grip of death through Jesus Christ. They thereby share in Christ's victory over death. He not only conquers death for them; he swallows up death by overwhelming it with life. By clothing the resurrected body with Christ's incorruption and immortality, God gives believers the victory through the Lord Jesus Christ, the victor over sin and death.

So, even though death conquers our natural bodies, the spiritual body that God provides for us will completely vanquish death at our resurrection from the dead. Then we will have eyes to see him face to face, ears to hear his voice clearly without distortion, lips to glorify him in harmony with the angels, and bodies to adore him perfectly. Then the heavenly promise in Revelation 21:4 will be fulfilled: "Death shall be no more, neither shall there be mourning, nor crying, nor pain anymore, for the former things have passed away."

---

14. Luther, *Lectures on Genesis: Chapters 21–25*, LW 4:313.

### A SPLENDID SIGHT!

Our bodies are destined for the glory of eternal life with Christ. There they will be seen in all their proper splendor. There we will radiate the glory of Jesus as they stand with him in the presence of God the Father. There we will collectively be the lovely bride of Jesus—his holy church—beautifully dressed for him as our husband (Rev 22:2, 10–11; cf. Ps 45:10–14). There we will see God face to face together with the angels and all the saints (Rev 22:4). Then we will no longer have to worry about how we look, because we will be perfect in his sight, just as Jesus had commanded and promised in Matthew 5:48. This is how C. S. Lewis describes our future appearance after a lifelong transformation:

> If we let Him—for we can prevent him if we choose—He will make the feeblest and filthiest of us into a god or goddess, a dazzling, radiant, immortal creature, pulsating all through with such energy and joy and wisdom and love as we cannot now imagine, a bright stainless mirror which reflects back to God perfectly (though of course on a smaller scale) his boundless power and delight and goodness. The process will be long and in parts painful; but that is what we are in for. Nothing less. He meant what he said.[15]

Yet despite the promise of that splendid sight, we, like babies in the womb, do not yet really know what we will be like. But we do know that when Jesus does appear on the last day to claim us as his bride, we will be like him (1 John 3:2). When we finally see him as he is in all his glory, we will reflect him perfectly in body and soul. Then we will also see him in each other and ourselves in him.

Until then, we walk by faith rather than physical sight (2 Cor 5:7). As long as we live in the body here on earth, we do not yet see the risen Lord Jesus as he now is, nor do we yet see ourselves fully remade in his image. We do not perceive our gradual inner

15. Lewis, *Mere Christianity*, 172.

transformation by him and his Holy Spirit. Our life remains hidden from our physical eyes until Christ appears. Only then will we appear with him in glory (Col 3:4).

Yet neither his glory nor our glory is entirely concealed from us. It is disclosed to us through the proclamation of the gospel, just as the glory of God was reflected in the face of Moses as he spoke God's law to the Israelites (Exod 34:29–35; 2 Cor 3:7–15). The hearing of the gospel enlightens the eyes of our hearts so that we see the glorious face of Jesus as he speaks to us in his word (2 Cor 4:5–6). As we listen to him, we behold his hidden glory; as we behold his glory, we ourselves are "transformed into his image from one degree of glory to another" (2 Cor 3:18). His light shines in us and illumines us as we hear him speaking to us.

In Ephesians 5:25–27 and Colossians 1:21–22, St. Paul tells us how Jesus and his heavenly Father now see us. These astonishing passages show us how we who have been baptized and believe in Jesus now appear in God's sight. They tell us how he regards us since we belong to Jesus. In doing so, they give us a glimpse of our future beauty and splendor.

In Ephesians 5:25–27, Paul describes how Christ transforms us through baptism. What he says about the church applies to all Christians individually and as a community. Christ loved us so much that he sacrificed himself for us, in order to cleanse us from all impurity and make us holy. He did all that so that he could "present the church to himself in glory,[16] without spot or wrinkle or any such thing, that she might be holy and without blemish" (Eph 5:27). Here Paul compares our baptism to the preparation of Jewish bride for her wedding. Usually a bride prepared herself for her wedding by bathing her body, dressing it in a beautiful gown, and decorating it with expensive jewelry. In this she was helped by her attendants. Then, after she had been properly prepared, she presented herself to her groom and his attendants in the

---

16. The ESV has "in splendor."

marriage ceremony. But in Christ's marriage to his bride, she does not prepare herself and present herself to him. Rather, Christ first prepares his bride by washing, dressing, and adorning her. Then he presents her to himself. He does all this to honor her because he loves her and wants her to feel lovely. He makes her beautiful and shows her how much he admires her.

Well, how does Jesus prepare his bride for her union with him? He transforms her completely. On the one hand, he deals with all that is unsightly about her. He covers up all her unpresentable features with his purity and righteousness; he removes every spot and wrinkle and blemish from her body. On the other hand, he also adorns her with his own holiness and glory. He makes her holy by sharing his own holiness with her. He makes her glorious by filling her with his glory.

Why does he present her to himself? He does not station her before his face in order to assess her critically, appraise her appearance, and judge whether she is fit to be his bride. He presents her to himself to show his full approval of her, his great delight in her, and his unqualified appreciation of her beauty. Just as he has made her righteous by declaring her righteous, so he makes her beautiful by declaring her beautiful. Like the lover in the Song of Songs 4:1, he says to her, "Behold, you are beautiful, my love." As he parades her before himself, he looks on her with loving admiration. She is perfect in his eyes. He enjoys the sight of her and wants her to enjoy his love. That's how Jesus regards her and us. He delights in the sight of us. He is happy to see us. He does not just look at us, but he actually sees us; he does not just see us, but he really admires us; he does not just admire us, but he pays close attention to us; he does not just attend to us, but he lavishes his love on us. Like the royal bride in Ps 45:10–13, he, amazingly, desires our beauty, dressed as we are in the royal robes of heavenly glory.

In Colossians 1:21–22, Paul adds another dimension to our presentation by Jesus. Here the picture changes from his presentation of us to himself as his bride to his presentation of us as an offering to God. He says:

And you, who once were alienated and hostile in mind, doing evil deeds, he [Jesus] has now reconciled in his body of flesh by his death, in order to present you holy and blameless and above reproach[17] in his sight.[18]

Here Jesus is compared with the Jewish high priest, and his body is regarded as an offering that was presented to reconcile people with God. As our high priest, Jesus has sacrificed his body for us by his death on the cross in order to now reconcile us with God the Father by his body and blood (Col 1:20, 22). Since we are now reconciled with God, Jesus presents us as his perfect, well-pleasing offering to God. He presents us in God's sight for his full approval and gracious acceptance of us. Thus we are now holy in God's sight because Jesus shares his own holiness with us; we are now without blemish in his sight because Jesus has removed our sin; we are now above reproach in his sight, people who have done nothing to deserve accusation and condemnation, because Jesus has pardoned us and cleansed us with his blood. Jesus now shows us together with himself to God the Father in anticipation of our final appearance before him with our resurrected bodies (2 Cor 4:14).

Yet as we now live in the body, we do not see ourselves fully from all angles, because we cannot see ourselves as we are in Christ. Only God sees us as we are and as we will be when we are raised from the dead. What's more, he tells us how he sees us in his word. And that dazzles and amazes us (1 Cor 2:9–10). It fills us with good hope and unutterable joy (1 Pet 1:8). Jesus sees us as his holy, glorious bride. We are a splendid sight in his eyes. He never ceases to admire us. In fact, Jesus is so pleased with us and proud of us as his lovely bride that he presents us to his heavenly Father for his unqualified appreciation of us. So his Father shares his admiration of us. He sees us as we are in his Son, unblemished

---

17. That is, they are without accusation and condemnation.
18. The ESV has "before him." This refers to God the Father.

and blameless, holy and perfect. We are a splendid sight to them both. A great sight for holy eyes!

## HOW THIS IS DONE: OUR HEAVENLY ORIENTATION

In 1 Corinthians 15:58, Paul ends his rhapsodic chapter on the resurrection of the body with these sober words of encouragement: "Therefore, my beloved brothers, be steadfast, immovable, always abounding in the work of the Lord, knowing that in the Lord your labor is not in vain." Here he teaches us that our belief in this fundamental Christian doctrine affects us practically in two ways. First, it provides us with a sure, eternal foundation for our life in the body here on earth and governs what we do with our bodies. In an unstable and chaotic world where people feel that their lives and work have accomplished little or nothing of lasting worth, we have the stability that enables us to achieve what is of lasting worth, because we have been appointed to do the Lord's work by working together with him. We have an unshakable, secure rock on which to build our lives. Second, with that sure and certain foundation we can be sure that no task that we undertake in his service, in the world, the church, our families, or our congregations, will be in vain, because we are not working for time but for eternity. The resurrection of our bodies reorients our whole existence by providing us with an eternal destination.

There are six practices in this present life that build on this reality of the resurrection of bodies and the glory yet to come: joyful thanksgiving, hopeful proclamation, daily dying and rising with Jesus, funerals that actually celebrate the resurrection, the remembrance of those who have died, and modest dress.

### Easter Jubilation

While Paul concludes his teaching on the resurrection of the body with a call to engage in thanksgiving in 1 Corinthians 15:57, Peter begins his first letter with ardent praise for our involvement in Christ's resurrection in 1 Peter 1:3–8. The good news of our bodily resurrection calls for physical jubilation. Our miraculous rebirth through the resurrection of Jesus has given us a living hope, the life-giving hope of our salvation and our eternal inheritance with Jesus. That hope fills us with inexpressible and glorious joy—joy that gives us a foretaste of heavenly glory. That sets the right note for us already now in this life! It calls for thanksgiving during the fifty days of rejoicing from Easter to Pentecost and on every Sunday. It calls for festive thanksgiving whenever we celebrate the death of death in Holy Communion. It calls for songs of praise and musical celebration that express what cannot be otherwise expressed. But, most of all, it calls for daily, lifelong jubilation, full-bodied, wholehearted rejoicing that anticipates and echoes the joy of eternal life with God in heaven.

### Easter Proclamation

The resurrection of Jesus calls for faithful proclamation that associates his resurrection with our resurrection, and vice versa. The resurrection of Jesus must be preached for us to participate in it and benefit from it. It provides no benefit for us unless it is proclaimed to us. Preaching the gospel does not just tell us that Jesus has abolished death, but it actually brings his life and immortality to light in us (1 Tim 1:10). Through the gospel, the risen Lord Jesus offers to those who hear and believe its message his life-giving Spirit, the Spirit who produces faith in the gospel, awakens them to spiritual life with Christ, and empowers them to live faithful, heavenly lives on earth. Thus, the preaching of the resurrection does not just offer the hope of eternal life after death; it actually raises people from spiritual death here and now. It awakens them to communal life with Jesus by its effective appeal, such as this from Ephesians 5:14: "Awake, O sleeper, and arise from the dead, and Christ will shine on you."

The preaching of the resurrection, in turn, evokes our vocal confession of faith in Jesus as Lord. Our confession of faith in the risen Lord Jesus is the mark of our wakened state. We agree with him and take him at his word. We receive what his word offers to us. Through our confession of faith, God's word pervades us and becomes incarnate in us physically and personally. Thus, St. Paul says in Romans 10:8–10,

> "The word is near you, in your mouth and in your heart" [that is, the word of faith that we proclaim]; because if you confess with your mouth that Jesus is Lord and believe in your heart that God raised him from the dead, you will be saved. For with the heart one believes and is justified, and with the mouth one confesses and is saved.

### Daily Death and Resurrection

Jesus calls us as his disciples to deny ourselves and take up our cross daily as we follow him on the way that leads us through death to eternal life (Luke 9:23–24). Our old way of life is over because we now belong to Jesus in body, soul, and spirit. We walk with him in the land of the living (Ps 116:8–9). Our future lies with him. So, too, each new day belongs to him! Each evening we die with him. Each morning we rise with him. Daily we die with him in order to live with him. His death and resurrection reshapes the natural pattern of our lives in the body as we commend our bodies to him and entrust ourselves to him in prayer, both when we go to bed each night and when we get up each morning. C. S. Lewis explains this process of self-surrender eloquently at the end of *Mere Christianity*:

> The principle runs through all life from top to bottom. Give up yourself, and you will find your real self. Lose your life and you will save it. Submit to death, the death of your ambitions and favourite wishes every day and the death of your whole body in the end: submit with every fibre of your being, and you will find eternal life. Keep nothing back. Nothing that you have not given away will be really yours. Nothing in you that has not died will ever be raised from the dead. Look for yourself, and you will find in the long run only hatred, loneliness, despair, rage, ruin, and decay.

But look for Christ and you will find Him, and with Him everything else thrown in.[19]

There are then two sides to our daily devotional self-surrender. On the one hand, we undergo a little death every night by the practice of daily repentance. Each night we experience a little sleep that presages the sleep of death. Each night before we go to sleep, God urges us to confess our sins and seek his pardon. He invites us to throw off the deeds of darkness before we go to bed (Rom 14:12). What's more, as we commend bodies and souls to him before we fall asleep physically, we may ask him to give us his Holy Spirit to put to death all the misdeeds of our bodies, so that they do not vex us at night and are not carried over into the next day (Rom 8:12–13). On the other hand, we also undergo daily renewal by the Holy Spirit each morning when we get up from our beds. Our waking from sleep each morning prefigures the resurrection of our bodies. It is, in fact, a mini-resurrection to life in God's new day. So when we get up in the morning, we need to put on a new set of clothes, the clothing that Christ provides for life in the presence of God the Father. Each morning, we can put on Jesus Christ by confessing him as our living Lord and ourselves as his disciples; each morning, we can clothe ourselves with all his virtues by asking him for them and receiving them from him; each morning, we can clothe ourselves with power from on high as we ask God the Father to give us the Holy Spirit to revive and renew us, to animate and activate us for living and working in his presence.

So we put off the old self each night and put on the new self each new day; we die with Jesus each evening and rise with him each morning. That is how we, in practice, live out our baptism. Our washing in it signifies that the old sinful self, with all its evil deeds and desires, is to be "drowned and die by daily contrition and repentance, and on the other hand that daily a new person is

---

19. Lewis, *Mere Christianity*, 189.

to come forth and rise up to life before God in righteousness and purity forever."[20] That is how we now live day by day in the body by faith in God's Son who gave himself for us and gives himself daily to us as our Lord and Savior.

## Funerals

Funeral customs and practices show how bodies are regarded in any society. They reveal what is commonly believed about death and what happens to people when they die. In this regard, we now see a radical revision of beliefs in the United States and elsewhere in the Western world. Thus, we seldom have real funerals but euphemistic "celebrations of life" that sugarcoat the stark horror of death. These celebrations of life speak about "passing on" rather than dying. The "dearly departed" are not dead, but they are, instead, "deceased." In addition to extravagant eulogies, balloons or doves are often released to signify the liberation of the spirit from the body, the spirit that looks down on us from the sky. In keeping with the growing belief in spiritual release from the body and reincarnation of the spirit in another body, the remains of the deceased are cremated. Worst of all, these and other popular practices all too readily distort Christian funerals and contradict the gospel in them.

The church must not embrace any kind of discarnate spirituality. Instead, congregations should, if at all possible, continue to hold funerals for their members in their sanctuaries rather than in a secular funeral parlor or at a crematorium; funerals with coffins next to the baptismal font, if at all possible, to acknowledge that the wages of sin is death and to celebrate the free gift of eternal life through the Lord Jesus; funerals that do not offer fake hope to the grief-stricken but the sure and certain hope of the resurrection of the body. Even though the Bible does not forbid cremation, the church would do well, in our present context, to encourage the burial of the body on hallowed ground as a powerful,

---

20. The Small Catechism, 412, BoC (360).

countercultural witness to the resurrection of the body, like our ancestors and Christians in the early church. In fact, Christians in Rome held all human bodies in such high regard that they gathered the corpses of derelict people from the alleys and streets where they had died and buried them properly, so that they were not dumped in the municipal garbage heaps with the corpses of dead animals for want of anyone to care for their remains. They buried them in a dignified way because they had been created in God's image. The same belief should inspire us to care for the bodies of those who have died. That, traditionally, was one of the Christian deeds of mercy. At the very least, congregations that own cemeteries should be encouraged to keep them and make good use of them, for those who have died are still part of the congregation. Most of all, we must teach and affirm our hope in the resurrection of the body at every funeral. While we may rightly grieve the loss of those who have died, we must also rejoice with the hymns of praise that celebrate the resurrection of our bodies.

## All Saints' Day

The biblical teaching that bodies of baptized believers are asleep in Christ in preparation for their resurrection from the dead (1 Cor 15:18; cf. Rev 14:13) governs how we remember those who have died. Quite often, grieving believers are tempted to seek inappropriate contact with their loved ones who have died. Some means of contact, like speaking to them or visiting their graves, are relatively harmless. Others, such as seeking a sign from them, keeping a shrine dedicated to them in their homes, or conjuring up their spirits with the help of a medium, are spiritually dangerous. However, a good way to stay in touch with them is with a prayer of thanksgiving for them. Better still, we can stay in touch with them physically and personally in Holy Communion, for Christ's body is the only link between the living and the dead. He is the Lord of them both (Rom 14:9). Both are part of his body. We can also, if we wish, remember them in prayer whenever we receive his holy body in Holy Communion and in a special way annually on

All Saints' Day on November 1 or the Sunday just after. Hebrews 12:24 tells us that in the service of worship we gather together with "the spirits of the righteous made perfect," the souls of those who have reached the destination of their earthly lives in Jesus, the crowd of unseen witnesses that surround us like a cloud in our worship (Heb 12:1).

## Modest Dress

Despite the modern cult of nudity, our contemporaries are obsessed with dress and impressed by how people dress. Even though people have always dressed to keep themselves warm and have always been concerned with how they dress, that concern has, in recent times, turned into an obsession with fashion. So, for example, our daily national newspaper, the *Australian*, which in the past seldom paid any attention to fashion, now has a regular section that is devoted to fashion. It seems to me that, in addition to the desire to attract attention and admiration, our obsession with fashion assumes that our bodies look best when they are best dressed—dressed in a way that covers up our least attractive features and enhances our most attractive features, dressed in a way that shows our shape in the best light and focuses attention on our uncovered faces. Good dress makes us look good and feel good about ourselves.

Our desire to be well-dressed may unconsciously prefigure the resurrection of the body, for when our bodies are raised from the dead, they will not be naked; we will be clothed with incorruptible purity and immortal holiness. Thus, in his great vision of Christ and the church, St. John sees the saints dressed in white linen like the priests at the temple (Rev 3:4–5; 4:4; 6:11; 19:9; cf. 3:18). Christ himself provides them with these bridal vestments (Rev 19:8). Like the vestments of the priests in the Old Testament (Exod 29:21; Lev 8:30), they have been washed and bleached with the blood of Jesus, the blood that makes them pure and holy (Rev 7:14). They disclose their perfect shape and focus the gaze on their faces. Their robes both conceal and reveal their glorified bodies.

So for us, our dress does not just display our social status, identity, and self-regard; it discloses our spiritual status, identity, and honor as citizens of heaven. Since that is so, we do not dress to advertise our general sexual availability but to reserve ourselves for full, sexual self-disclosure in marriage. Our clothes do not just cover our naked sexual organs and physical imperfections from public view; they conceal our inner self with the imperishable beauty that comes from its union with Jesus and his presence in it (1 Pet 3:3–4). That inner self is fully viewed, admired, and enjoyed only by him, just as our sexual nakedness is meant to be viewed, admired, and enjoyed by our spouse. Since we shall be perfectly dressed at the resurrection, we, even now, secretly clothed with Christ's purity and holiness, symbolically bear secret witness to the resurrection of the body by dressing modestly and being well dressed. Our modest dress does not stem from prudish timidity and disgust with our bodies, but from the desire to offer ourselves confidently and fully to Christ and to our spouse. We thereby secretly honor our bodies as hidden members of Christ's body, just as he now secretly honors them and will honor them openly in eternity. Since we have his full approval, we do not need to dress extravagantly or provocatively to call attention to our social status, wealth, or sexuality. We can dress confidently and proudly as sons and daughters of the heavenly King.

As people who are united with the risen Lord Jesus, our life in the body is lived in the light of its resurrection with Jesus and its transfiguration by him. His glory, his radiance, colors all that we now are and all that we once were; it colors all that we do and all that is done to us. It does not just do so because we know that our bodies are destined for the glory of eternal life with God, but because we already now have eternal life. By faith we already now live divine, heavenly lives here on earth. In Jesus we have a foretaste of the future glory that colors and transfigures our present life, the glory that has been prepared for all people from every nation, tribe, people, and language (Rev 7:9). The rich ethnic, tribal, national, and cultural diversity of humanity not only remains but is per-fected in Jesus. Whatever our race or nationality, we all, each in our own way, share in God's multicolored grace (1 Pet 4:10).[21] We all begin to be the people that we were meant to be, created as we are in God's image to reflect the glory of Jesus in some mea-sure. Already now, we have been raised to life with Jesus and are enthroned with him in the heavenly realms (Eph 2:4–7). Since our new life is hidden with Christ in God, we share in his hidden glory (Col 3:3–4). Meanwhile, as we live by faith rather than sight, we have a vision of glory for our bodies that pervades our whole physical existence and fills all of it with eternal significance. What is more, that vision of glory colors our sexuality and shows us its true worth. It puts sex in a new light for us.

---

21. This is the literal sense of the Greek adjective *poikilos* which is usually translated as "manifold," "varied," or "various."

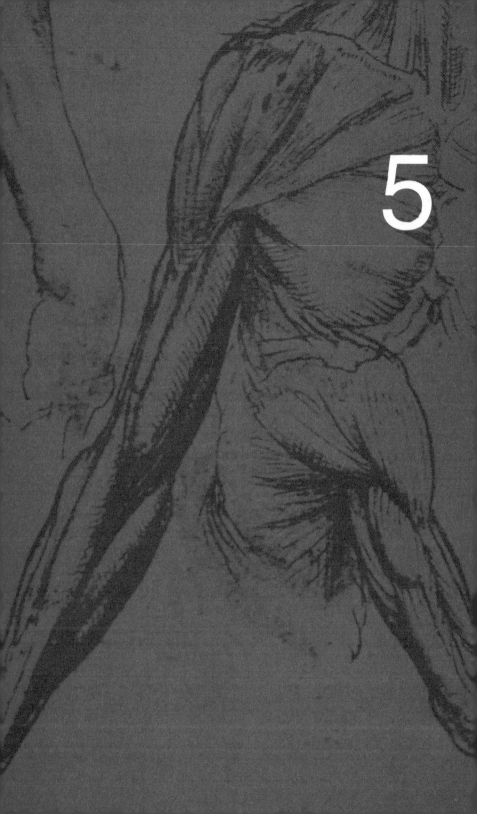

5

# THE SEXUAL BODY

The old Christian teachers said that if man had never fallen, sexual pleasure, instead of being less than it is now, would actually have been greater. I know that some muddle-headed Christians have talked as if Christianity thought that sex, or the body, or pleasure, were bad in themselves. But they are wrong. Christianity is almost the only one of the great religions that thoroughly approves of the body—which believes that matter is good, that God Himself once took on a human body, that some kind of body is going to be given us even in Heaven and is going to be an essential part of our happiness, our beauty, and our energy.

—C. S. *Lewis*

It is, I must confess, hard for me to strike the right note in writing about the sexual nature of our bodies. It is hard enough to do because the matter of sex touches us more deeply, pervasively, and personally than any other aspect of our humanity, except perhaps death. Yet it is even harder for us to consider it in an honest, helpful way because of our own sexual failures as men and women, the limitations of language to convey its complexity, and the current terminology that confuses our understanding and discussion of it.

This book is meant to be a rhapsody on the human body—the body created in God's image, redeemed by Christ, and sanctified for eternal life with God. Yet at this point I must, for a moment, change my song from thankful praise to a sad lament. There is, I reckon, no other aspect of life in the body that has been disrupted so seriously and corrupted so obviously by our fall into sin. There is no other natural, physical gift that has been so evidently misused and commonly abused as this. So when I consider it, my grateful delight in the body must be qualified by repentant sorrow as I pray, "God, be merciful to me, a sinner!"

Now it is true that my sexual sins do not make me a worse sinner in God's eyes than do my other sins. But sexual sins affect me more obviously and comprehensively in my body and soul, my mind and my spirit (1 Cor 6:18). They unsettle my conscience and arouse my guilt. They are, in fact, an index of my sinfully disordered heart. There is then no other dimension of my life in the body that shows how evidently I have sinned in thought, word, and deed. In this regard, my own conscience reminds me how far I have fallen short of God's glory, the glory that he has prepared for me as male person created in his image to be a husband of my wife. As long as I am blind to my own

148

sexual sins against God and my own wife (and other women!), I will not be able to assess the sexual behavior of others as truthfully and compassionately as Christ does. I will, instead, assume the pose of moral, sexual superiority and stand in judgment over others. Yet the plain truth is that I am not their judge. Like them, I am a sinner. But I am a sinner who has been pardoned and purified by Jesus. What's more, I am a minister of the gospel rather than a moral philosopher or moral policeman. My task in what follows is both to teach God's law in order to show his good and gracious will for us in sexual matters, so that we all repent of our sexual sinfulness, and to proclaim his gospel, by which he provides cleansing from the taint of sin and justification for sexual sinners like me.

My sad lament over the ugly ruin of sexual intimacy by all people in their existence east of Eden must also, at the same time, be accompanied and outdone by a paean of praise for God's ongoing gift of male and female sexuality and the joy that he continues to provide for people through it. And not just that! God's even greater gift of sexual chastity to his people and sexual fidelity in holy matrimony far outweighs the ravages of sexual misuse and abuse.

Sadly, we lack the language to extol the beauty of chaste sexuality. Even more than that, our imagination is often too stunted and blunted to appreciate it properly. It is hard to address sexual matters truthfully because the words that we have at our disposal are so inadequate for the task. This is because they tend to focus only on some aspects of our sexuality while failing to do justice to the whole of it, even though we do nowadays speak a lot about it quite explicitly in public. Until modern times, most people were much more reticent about sexuality than we are. In public, they usually spoke about it implicitly and indirectly, if at all. That includes the writers of the sacred Scriptures. So, for example, the authors of the Old Testament speak about "lying together" rather than engaging in sexual intercourse (which is, of course, itself also a euphemism!). Yet it is not as if they were any more prudish than we are. Rather, their public reticence shows that they regarded it as a private, personal matter that could all too easily be degraded by public discourse and open exposure. Despite all our imagined frankness, we, too, still speak about sex matters indirectly. So, for example, we avoid other far cruder expressions by commonly speaking about "making love" or using many other similar idioms.

Over the last fifty years, that public reticence has been gradually replaced by much more explicit discourse about sexual activity. The main problem with this deceptively frank approach is that we have only three other common kinds of language to describe it, none of which is completely truthful. We have the shocking discourse of crude vulgarity that barely disguises its disgust at sex by giving an ugly account of it. Even that ceases to shock after a while; it merely degrades sex and the people who speak of it. In stark contrast with that, we have the technical, anatomical language of medical discourse, which can only describe the mechanics of sexual intercourse. Then we also have the graphic depiction of sexual activity in pornography, which overlooks the sensory, mental, emotional, imaginative, and personal dimensions of sex by its relentless focus on the genitalia. All three approaches tend to demystify sex by reducing it to some part of it. They fail to give a truthful account of the whole. The result is sexual disillusionment and disenchantment.

The most truthful way to understand our sexuality is to speak imaginatively about it, such as is done with the lyrical poetry of the Song of Songs. Lovers do this instinctively, even when they have to resort to romantic clichés. But clichés are still better than most alternatives. Even so, I must admit that such an imaginative approach is a foreign language to most of our contemporaries. But it is worth the effort. It is the best we have!

In the present cultural climate, it is also very difficult for us as Christians to speak truthfully about some controversial aspects of sex, because they have so often been misclassified and misnamed. Despite what Jesus taught about the permanence of marriage, we, quite unthinkingly, refer to the "remarriage" of a divorced person. Even Christians commonly now speak about a "sexual partner" rather than a spouse, let alone a husband or wife. We also have the newly forged social and legal categories of "same-sex marriage" and "marriage equality." Think, too, of the separation of gender from sex, the talk of "sexual orientation," and the description of people as "heterosexual" or "homosexual." It is also common to assert our "sexual identity" and say how we choose to "identify" ourselves "sexually." Together with other terms such as "gender dysphoria" and "sexual reassignment," this new terminology is all part of a deliberate or naïve attempt to reconstruct sexuality in contradiction of the traditional understanding, which corresponds in large measure with nature and the teaching of the Bible, since it has been shaped by it. Like magicians, the advocates of reconstructed sexuality fancy that they can change people sexually by getting them to use the words that match their sexual fantasies. While these ways of speaking may describe certain kinds of sexual behavior, they misconstrue our actual, God-given sexuality.

There is, as always, an element of truth in what they say, because we do use language to discover and name what is real and true in the world that we inhabit. But we cannot use words to remake ourselves according to the image that we, as women and men, have of ourselves or that others have of us. Nor can we deconstruct what God has built into the very nature of our biological bodies and imprinted on them genetically by some linguistic sleight of hand with talk about alternate sexes, different sexual orientations, gender spectrum, or self-chosen identity. God has made us in his image and wishes to remake us in his image, and speak the truth about the devastation of our sexual bodies by the fall and their damaged condition since then. He has given us speech and language as a precious endowment, so that we can understand who we are and what we are. It is the tool that we have to discover the truth of God's creation and our creation in God's image. We identify and classify things by naming them. It is also the tool we have to name and describe the ways that our bodies have been impacted by the fall, and have continued to develop in a post-fall world.

Thus, we hear that even though the Lord God had made the animals and birds, he brought them to Adam to name them (Gen

2:19–20). After God had made Adam's wife, Adam first describes her generically as a "woman" in contrast with himself as a "man" (Gen 2:23), and then names her with her proper name as "Eve," the mother of all living people (Gen 3:20). Yet by naming the animals and his wife, Adam does not make them, nor does he remake them. He identifies what they are and how they differ from each other and him. Most significantly, Adam does not name himself. The Lord God does that for him. God names him "Adam," "Man" (Gen 2:18), and uses that proper noun to name and address him as a person (Gen 3:9, 17). So, if we Christians wish to speak truthfully about our sexuality and portray its beauty, we must speak about it as God does, no matter how hard that may be in a world in which people fancy that they can remake themselves and reconstruct their bodies as they please. We must, most of all in our present social context, speak about sexual chastity no matter how unfashionable it may be.

### THE BEAUTY OF CHASTITY

Chastity is sexual purity. It has to do with sexual reservation for spousal intimacy and fidelity in marriage. It is so important for us because the sexual relationship of a husband and wife, though obviously physical, is also a deeply personal and spiritual matter. For better or worse, it touches and affects us in our souls. It has as much, if not more, to do with the mind than with the body. It affects what we think, how we feel, and what grips our imagination. It has, in fact, more to do with our sense of self as a whole, integrated person than with our male or female bodies.

Sexual purity is vital to the natural ecology of rightly ordered sexuality. As part of our social ecosystem, it enhances the proper working of human sexuality and promotes its fruitful enjoyment. It presupposes that sexual intercourse works best when it is done by the right persons, at the right time, in the right context, and in the right way. Just as we all sense that sexual purity enhances our self-esteem and increases our enjoyment of sexual intercourse, we also all know, quite instinctively and viscerally, that we are polluted physically, emotionally, personally, and spiritually by its abuse. We sense that wrong sexual intercourse makes us unclean because it is disorderly and destructive. Bad sex disgusts us. Like the hit from a drug, it may give us temporary pleasure, but that pleasure does not last. Our addictive indulgence in it feeds a growing appetite that can never be satisfied. It disorders our souls, damages our relationship with our sexual partner, and diminishes our capacity for the ongoing enjoyment of sex in a lasting relationship. In fact, there is no other human activity in which delight can so quickly turn into disgust with ourselves and our bodies. Lasting sexual enjoyment goes hand in hand with chastity.

Sexual chastity is all too often confused with physical virginity. But they are quite different in some ways. A man can be an unchaste virgin, while another man can be a chaste husband. Once lost, virginity cannot be restored. But sexual chastity, when forfeited, can be regained and then even extended from mere physical purity to mental and spiritual purity. It goes far deeper than sexual inexperience and sexual abstinence because it involves the whole self rather than just the body with its sexual organs. Morally, it has to do with the sexual integrity of a man or a woman with their exclusive sexual commitment to each other. Spiritually, it has to do with the purity of the heart that only Christ can provide, the devout heart that has been purified by Jesus (1 Cor 6:11; Eph 5:25–27; Titus 2:11–14; 1 John 1:7, 9), the faithful heart that is governed by self-giving love rather than possessive, sexual lust (Matt 5:27–30). Since it is so closely associated with sexual self-giving, sexual chastity is best learned in the school of Christian marriage.

Whether they know it or not, people who engage in sexual intercourse always give something of themselves to each other. Ideally, a man and a woman who engage in a sexual relationship give themselves totally and unreservedly to each other. Sex is never just sex. Yet such self-giving is not complete at any one point in time, nor on any single occasion. My soul, my sense of self, is not a static fixed entity, but a historical continuum that stretches back and reaches forward in time. Thus, the gift of myself sexually includes my past and foreshadows my future. Since marriage is meant to be a lifelong process of mutual giving and receiving, it calls for chastity before marriage and in it, because both fornication and adultery impair and inhibit sexual self-entrustment. They may, in fact, prevent it from happening or diminish it when it does happen.

Sexual chastity before marriage frees two people to give themselves bodily with their whole past for their future with each other. In a sense, they are in possession of themselves by virtue of their chastity. They have not yet been given to another, but still have themselves, unencumbered, to give wholly to the person they love. There is, theoretically speaking, no part of themselves that is sexually reserved for another and cannot therefore be shared. Chastity, which reserves itself sexually for marriage, clears the way for total and passionate self-offering to another. Its faithfulness creates trust, that precious prerequisite for all personal relationships and for any good marriage. Faithfulness in marriage transforms possessive lust into considerate affection; it subordinates sexual intercourse to a confident, convivial relationship between husband and wife. It personalizes sex, which can otherwise all too easily depersonalize people.

People have always sensed a close link, if not an overlap, between sex and religion. This was especially so in the ancient world with its fertility cults, stories about the marriages of its deities, and notion of sex as a creative, cosmic power. Sex is still the one area of life where apparently secularized people sense something sacred. In it they experience something of the captivating yet frightening power of holiness that has so fascinated and frightened the human race for most of its checkered history. In both religion and sex, people are engaged and gripped more deeply as persons in their souls than in any other areas of experience, except perhaps in the mysteries of parenthood and death. In their experience of sexual passion and rapture, they seem to encounter something mysterious, something powerful that is beyond their control, something that takes them out of themselves and beyond themselves, something that makes them feel more fully and powerfully alive. Thus, the experience of sexual passion and abandonment lay at the heart of much pagan religiosity in the ancient world and its celebration of sexual virility and fertility (1 Thess 4:5).

In contrast with that pagan view, Paul argues in Romans 1:24–25 that people who surrender their bodies to sex as if it were a supernatural, cosmic, divine power do not gain superhuman vitality but actually pollute themselves. They don't just dishonor their own bodies by engaging in sexual impurity; they dishonor God who created them in his image. They exchange the truth of God for the lie of an idol; they worship and serve the creature rather than the Creator. He therefore argues that sexual impurity in all its manifestations involves idolatry and apostasy from the living God (Eph 5:6; Col 3:5). It is an aspect of our rebellion against God and a denial of our creaturely status. It is false worship, for it seeks from another body what no body can give. It makes an idol of the ideal human body and puts it in God's place.

This warning against sexual idolatry can only be understood in the light of God's creation of us in his image as either a male or female person, whether it be for a single life of undivided devotion to him or, most obviously, for cohabitation with each other in marriage. While the sexual chastity of single people reflects Christ's devotion to his human sisters and brothers by their devotion to him, the union of husband and wife prefigures the ultimate, perfect union with Christ and intimacy with each other in the communion of saints. We were made to mirror him in ourselves as persons and, if we are married, in a faithful relationship with our spouse that involves sexual intercourse and culminates in the birth of children. In fact, God not only creates people through the sexual intercourse of a man with a woman, but actually shows us a little of what he is like by the marriage and the family that emerges from it. Since this is so, sexual impurity contradicts our status as people made in God's image and impairs our relationship with him. It dims our vision of God and our view of ourselves as people made in his image. It defiles us and decreases our capacity to give of ourselves in love to him and our spouse. It chokes the natural current of life that is meant to flow into our bodies from the living God and back out into our marriage and family and society.

If sexual impurity damages our relationship with God, then the opposite must also be true. Chastity in marriage and apart from it enhances our relationship with God.[1] In fact, chastity is an attribute of Jesus and God the Father (1 John 3:3). That is what gives chastity its spiritual value. It should therefore come as no surprise that sexual chastity is prized in the New Testament and the early church as something good and beautiful and desirable. Thus St. Paul compares the relationship of the congregation in Corinth to Christ with a pure virgin who is presented to her husband in all her beauty and is devoted entirely to him (2 Cor 11:2–3). Paul also presents himself to the same congregation as a model of chastity (2 Cor 6:7). Likewise, he urges young pastor Timothy to keep himself chaste (1 Tim 5:12) and encourage younger women by treating them with absolute chastity as sisters in Christ (1 Tim 5:2). In fact, Timothy is encouraged to be a model of chastity to all believers in the way he lives with them, speaks to them, and loves them (1 Tim 4:12). Older women are also to encourage younger women to be chaste wives and mothers (Titus 2:5). In a similar vein, St. Peter encourages Christian women who are married to unbelievers to win them over by the beauty of their chaste character and behavior (1 Pet 3:1–6). He also argues that since all Christians have been made chaste and kept chaste by their obedience to the truth of the gospel, they can love each other sincerely and deeply from the heart as brothers and sisters in Christ, without abusing each other sexually (1 Pet 1:22). That's why Paul does not scold the Christians in Philippi for their sexual impurity. Instead, he makes this appeal to their imagination (Phil 4:8): "Finally, brothers,

---

1. While Paul and other early Christian teachers normally use the adjective *katharos* as a general term for what is pure and clean in God's sight, they use the adjective *hagnos* for what is sexually pure and clean in his estimation. It was a common religious term for the sexual chastity of celibate men and women who had devoted themselves sexually to a particular deity.

whatever is true, whatever is honorable, whatever is just, whatever is pure [chaste], whatever is lovely, whatever is commendable, if there is any excellence, if there is anything worthy of praise, think about these things."

Ultimately, the demand for chastity is, as St. Paul affirms in 1 Corinthians 6:12–20, linked with our hope for the resurrection of the body. Since God created the body, and with it our sexuality, our bodies and their sexuality are in themselves good (1 Tim 4:1–5). We are called to be sanctified in body, soul, and spirit for fellowship with God (1 Thess 5:23). This is because our souls are closely and intimately connected with our bodies. What we do with our bodies affects our relationship with God. Any split within ourselves between our bodies and souls damages our spiritual relationship with him. Since our bodies are consecrated as shrines of God's presence and temples of the Holy Spirit, they can be desecrated and defiled by sexual impurity, and thus be made unfit for life with God (1 Cor 6:19). However, our bodies already now share in the eternal life of God and convey something of this physically to others. Thus, we are to glorify God in our bodies, which have been redeemed for union with him (1 Cor 6:20).

Chastity is thus a fine virtue and an excellent gift from God, because in it we have a preview and foretaste of the resurrection of our fully personalized, glorified bodies (see Rev 14:1–5). By the hope of the resurrection, our bodies acquire a dignity and glory that far exceeds the glorification of beautiful human bodies by the depiction of their bare or touched up nakedness. Then they will no longer mask our true selves, as they have since the fall of our first parents, for we will have nothing to hide and nothing to fear from disclosing ourselves. We shall then be fully at home in our bodies. They will be utterly translucent and able to show us fully as we are in Christ. Then, at last, we shall be truly chaste. We shall be as totally and radiantly chaste before God as Christ would have us be and promises to make us. We shall be pure as Christ is pure (1 John 3:3). Our Lord will present us to his Father holy and splendid, without spot or wrinkle or any such thing (Eph 5:27). That, ultimately, is what makes chastity so beautiful and desirable for both single and married people.

## THE GARDEN OF NUPTIAL LOVE

These days, we usually envisage marriage as an intimate, personal relationship between a man and a woman who love each other. It is that! But it is also much more than that, because it involves the bodies of a man and a woman who do not just interact with each other personally but also cohabitate with each other in the same place. Like the home that they establish by their sexual union, it is a place for them to be with each other bodily, a physical state of being for them. So, traditionally, marriage was called an estate, a divinely instituted order that provided a safe place for their sexual union to be protected, nurtured, and to thrive.

Even though I admit that this view of marriage as an estate is much better than the legal view of it as a binding contract between two parties (which it is in part!), that description is a bit too abstract and disembodied for me. I prefer the picture that the Song of Songs provides. Like the garden of Eden, which was the original place for nuptial love as well as loving intimacy with God, marriage is the garden of love, the place of love for the beloved wife and her lover.[2] It is the cultivated, natural environment for their union, a place that is fenced off from the world around it, irrigated by a spring of flowing water, and filled with fruit trees and other lovely, aromatic fauna and flora. Most amazingly, the garden of love is the body of the wife rather than a place apart from her (4:12–15). Yet the lover, her husband, is not its gardener. Even though it is his garden and he is a king, he does not own it (4:16; 5:1; 6:2). Like a locked house, she holds the key that gives him access to it (4:12). He visits it as the guest of his beloved bride, and only at her invitation (4:16b; cf. 5:2–5).

---

2. See also the related picture of the woman's body as her vineyard (1:6; 8:11–12; cf. 1:14; 2:15; 6:11; 7:12).

To change the picture, by offering her body as a garden, she establishes a home for her husband and herself with her body. Through the union of her body with that of her husband, they both have a safe place where they can present themselves to each other, mentally and emotionally, personally and spiritually. Thus, in his commentary on Genesis 2:22, Luther notes that the Lord God "built" Eve from Adam's rib.[3] Her body is thereby envisaged as a building, a house for her to be and a home for Adam to stay in with her. He concludes, "In the same way the wife is still the house for her husband, to which he goes, with whom he dwells, and with whom he joins in the effort and work of supporting the family."

The Song of Songs, surprisingly, focuses mainly on the woman in its vision of nuptial love, which gives the lie to the rather glib, fashionable dismissal of the Bible as a male chauvinist, misogynist book. She is the chief speaker and main character in it. She holds the key to its portrayal of sexual enjoyment. With her body she provides the place for the nuptial union. It cannot exist apart from her body but can only be had with her body. With her body she offers the nuptial union. She, in fact, embodies it. It is worth noting that this focus on the woman is quite in keeping with the story of creation in Genesis 2. That account culminates in God's creation of a wife for Adam and his presentation of her to Adam as his companion.

The Song of Songs also focuses on the place of the five physical senses in its view of nuptial love. It begins with the longing of the bride to be kissed by her lover (1:2) and ends with his desire to hear her voice (8:13). Like a lovely garden, marriage is a place that engages all the five senses of the body in physical, sexual intercourse. They are all employed in making love, and they all combine in order to engage the whole person in lifelong, bodily self-giving. Nuptial love engages the ears of a married couple in an ongoing, intimate conversation that is both physical and mental, emotional

---

3. Luther, *Lectures on Genesis: Chapters 1–5*, LW 1:131–33.

and personal (2:8–15; 8:13).[4] It engages the eyes in seeing and being seen, in visual intimacy and visual enjoyment (4:1–7; 5:10–16). It engages the hands in embracing and being embraced, caressing and being caressed (2:6; 8:3). It engages the nose with the enjoyable aroma of each other's bodies and the sweet fragrance of their desire (1:12–14; 4:10; 7:8). It engages the lips and the tongue in kissing and being kissed (1:3), tasting and being tasted (4:11; 5:1; 7:6–10). All are equally important. They are all part and parcel of their sexual union. Thus, while nuptial love is intensely physical, it is, or at least should be, also equally emotional and personal. By satisfying the senses, nuptial love enlists them in its cause and integrates them with each other. It refines their use and prevents their abuse. So nuptial love is given and received by the whole body with all its senses. It is full-bodied communication between two persons of the opposite sex who are meant to complement each other in every way.

### THE HOUSE OF MARRIAGE

In his teaching on marriage, Jesus asserts that in every marriage, God joins every man and woman together with each other (Matt 19:6; Mark 10:9). With this assertion, Jesus touches on the most profound dimension of marriage. It is God who serves as the marriage celebrant in every wedding, no matter where, and when, or how it is contracted. Just as he brought Eve to Adam, so he presents each wife to her husband as his gift to him. He unites them with each other. He is at work in every lawful marriage and in the life of every married couple. Even if, in some cultures, parents may arrange the marriage, or even if, as in our culture, a couple may choose to marry each other, God nevertheless officiates at their wedding.

---

4. The poem reinforces the primacy of speaking by presenting us with a series of speeches in which we overhear the woman as she speaks to her lover and about him in seventy-one verses, the man as he speaks to her in forty verses, and the comments of other onlookers in a few other verses.

The far-reaching implications of God's role in their marriage is spelled out cryptically by Genesis 2:24: "Therefore a man shall [will] leave his father and mother and hold fast [cleave] to his wife, and they shall [will] become one flesh."[5] This sentence may be construed both as a statement of fact and a directive. It explains how a couple enters into the marriage that God provides for them. The onus here is placed on the man as the husband. Entry into the nuptial union properly comes in three stages that correspond with its social character, its binding status, and its sexual purpose. Their ordered sequence ensures that it works as God intends.

Contrary to popular custom in the ancient world and many societies to the present day, which expect the woman to leave her parents and relinquish her attachment to them, God requires the man to "leave" his father and mother in order to establish a new household with his wife. This is vital to the success of their marriage, for unless a man separates himself from his parents, he will not be free to give himself to his wife and receive her as an equal partner in their marriage. If his parents do not relinquish him, they will, consciously or unconsciously, interfere with his marriage and undermine it. Like the parents of the bride, his parents must allow him to marry her, give their blessing to his union with her, and recognize that his primary allegiance now belongs to her.

Contrary to popular custom, which requires the woman to devote herself to her husband and to cleave to him, God requires the man to commit himself to her in the covenant of marriage with binding promises of fidelity in the rite of marriage. His commitment to her is primary. It provides a sure and certain basis for her ongoing commitment and entrustment to him. This is what makes their relationship a marriage. It cannot work as it should, nor is it likely to last, without his public commitment to her.

Contrary to common practice, which assumes that sexual intercourse is the best entrance into a good sexual partnership (which

---

5. The phrase "and he said" in Matthew 19:5 could refer either to what Jesus said or what God said.

may then be confirmed by the rite of marriage), God requires a man and a woman "become one flesh" only after the man has left his parents and committed himself publicly to his wife in the covenant of marriage. They become one flesh through sexual intercourse, which may, in due course, result in the conception of a child who is also one flesh with them. Even though we rightly regard the first act of sexual intercourse as the consummation of the marriage, that is not entirely true, because the wife and her husband "become" one flesh by their ongoing sexual cohabitation. As they live together, work together, and fit together with each other, they become one flesh. That's a lifelong process rather than just a single event.

These three aspects of marriage have been usefully compared with the three sides of a triangle.[6] I would like to add another biblical picture by comparing marriage to a home for a married couple (Ps 127:1; Prov 14:1; 24:3). Its foundation is God's word, which institutes and maintains a marriage. The husband's separation from both his parents are the walls of the house. The husband's commitment to his wife and her consequent commitment to him are the roof. Sexual intercourse establishes the bedroom as the safe, private heart of their house. Their house is not built on sexual intercourse; it is built for it, for their sexual union to flourish.

### SEXUAL HOLINESS

Many Christians have a bad conscience about sex, often more so than about anything else that they do. They are not sure whether God approves of it or not. They are even less sure whether he approves of their sexual behavior, let alone their desire for sex and their attitude to sex. That uncertainty is stoked by the devil, who often concentrates his condemnation in this regard. He switches from tempting them to sin and excusing their sexual sins to damning them for their sexual activity and their desire for sexual

---

6. See Walter Trobisch, *I Married You* (New York: Harper and Row, 1975), 11–24, 33–48, 71–83.

intercourse. His aim is to portray God as a sexual killjoy and give them a bad conscience about their sexuality.

The biblical teaching about sex is meant to rectify this. It does not set out a comprehensive code of sexual ethics. Even where it does teach about sexual morality, it does so pastorally. Its purpose is to deliver a good conscience to God's people—people who break the sixth commandment and sin in thought, word, and deed, people whose conscience is burdened by lust and sexual transgression. Most of all, it does so by its positive teaching on holy matrimony and holy singleness.

Like sexual intercourse, marriage belongs to the order of creation. It was created by God and blessed by him. He established marriage as a life-giving, life-sustaining order in his ordered world. So, before the fall, both sexual intercourse and marriage were good and pure in his eyes. Even after the fall, marriage still retains much of its original power. Despite its abuse, it has not lost its inherent beauty, so much so that some in same-sex relationships desire it for themselves and vainly try to mimic it. What's more, right sexual intercourse between women and men in marriage does not make them physically or spiritually unclean. It remains God's good gift for all people. As such, like everything else that God has created, it is good (1 Tim 4:4). Only its abuse pollutes the bodies and souls of those who engage in it.

Even though marriage belongs to the order of creation, Christian marriage belongs to the order of redemption as well. It then becomes a holy state and can rightly be called holy matrimony. Paul explains how this happens in 1 Timothy 4:1–5. There he warns Timothy against spiritual gurus who forbid marriage and the eating of certain kinds of food, such as meat, because those foods were held to prevent would-be spiritual highfliers from reaching higher levels of disembodied spirituality. Such teaching, says Paul, is demonic because it spurns what God has created. In that context he provides this foundational teaching on the sanctification of marriage and sexual enjoyment in marriage. He says, "For everything created by God is good, and nothing is to be rejected if it is received with thanksgiving, for it is made holy by the word of God and prayer" (4:4–5).

Since marriage belongs to the natural order, the divinely established order of God's creation, it is good. But it is not in itself holy. It becomes holy when it is sanctified by the word of God and prayer. That happens in two ways. On the one hand, by its use of God's word in proclamation, prayer, and blessing, the Christian rite of marriage turns ordinary, common marriage into holy matrimony. It thereby becomes a holy estate in which the couple are not just blessed by God but also sanctified by his Holy Spirit. This dual status of marriage is evident in the three usual biblical readings in the service for it: Genesis 2:18–24 and Matthew 19:4–6 on God's institution of marriage, and Ephesians 5:21–33 on the nature and purpose of Christian marriage. On the other hand, the marital union continues to be sanctified by the word of God and prayer through the couple's regular participation in corporate worship as well as through their home devotions. By their daily devotions they are kept holy as they say grace before and after meals, as they hear and meditate on God's holy word, and as they thank God for each other and pray for themselves and their marriage. God's holy word protects the marriage from all kinds of sexual impurity that threaten to pollute their marriage and desecrate its holiness (Heb 13:4). Their faith in the triune God fills their marriage with thanksgiving, so that it is tinged with the hidden beauty of holiness.

Christ offers two remedies for sexual impurity that apply equally for married and unmarried persons, remedies that provide them with a good conscience. On the one hand, he cleanses his disciples from sexual impurity through his remission of their sins, both the sexual sins that they have committed and the sexual sins that have been committed against them. Through baptism, his holy absolution, and his cleansing blood in Holy Communion, he restores and maintains their purity and chastity. On the other hand, besides cleansing them by the washing of water with God's word in holy baptism, he also sanctifies them though it (Eph 5:25–27; cf. 1 Cor 6:11). By faith they share in Christ's own holiness (1 Co

1:30). Since through faith in him they are sanctified by him (1 Cor 1:2; Acts 26:18; Heb 2:11), they are holy in him (Phil 1:1; 4:21). God's word sanctifies them (John 17:18). So, too, does the body and blood of Jesus (Heb 10:13, 29; 13:12)! God the Father sanctifies them completely in body, soul, and spirit (1 Thess 5:23). In his sight they are as holy as his holy Son (Eph 1:4). With their bodies they are both part of God's holy temple, the place where he meets with his people (1 Cor 3:16–17; 2 Cor 6:16; Eph 2:19–22; 1 Pet 2:4–5), and members of his holy priesthood, which serves him in his temple (1 Pet 2:5, 9; Rev 1:5–6). And since they are holy, God calls them to live holy lives (1 Pet 1:14–15). That call extends to their whole life in the body, including their sexuality.

Paul explores the call to sexual purity and sanctification in 1 Thessalonians 4:1–8, where he instructs both single and married Christians on how to please God with their sexual behavior. He tells them how they can have sex with a good conscience:

> Finally, then, brothers, we ask and urge you in the Lord Jesus, that as you received from us how you ought to walk and please God, just as you are doing, that you do so more and more. For you know what instructions we gave you through the Lord Jesus. For this is the will of God, your sanctification: that you abstain from sexual immorality[7]; that each of you know how to control his own body in holiness and honor, not in the passion of lust like the Gentiles who do not know God; that no one transgress and wrong his brother in this matter, because the Lord is an avenger of all these things, as we have told you beforehand and solemnly warned you. For God has not called us for impurity, but in holiness. Therefore whoever disregards this, disregards not man but God, who gives his Holy Spirit to you.

God's basic purpose for all men and women as people with sexual bodies is their sanctification. He both calls them to be holy and

---

7. Literally, "fornication."

makes them holy. He sanctifies their bodies. That includes their sexual organs.

Believers' holiness is meant to shape their sexual behavior, so that they please God (1 Thess 4:1). Since their bodies are holy, they must abstain from fornication, any kind of sexual intercourse apart from marriage. Fornication pollutes them and desecrates their holiness. Since their bodies are holy, they must exercise sexual self-restraint and keep control of their sexual organs.[8] Unlike pagan unbelievers, they know that they must control their bodies and honor them because they belong to God. He has honored them by sacrificing his Son to redeem and sanctify them for life with him. They exercise physical and emotional self-control so that they can give their bodies to God and, if they are married, to their spouse as well. Since they are brothers and sisters of Christ in God's holy family, they must not cross the proper sexual boundaries in the congregation and exploit other members of their family sexually. Since the congregation is holy, it is meant to be a sexual sanctuary, a safe place that is established and protected by the Lord Jesus. That is why Paul adds a stern warning. If they abuse any members sexually, they can be sure that the Lord Jesus will judge their wrongdoing and correct them, because they have defiled their fellow saints and desecrated their holiness. The holy context magnifies the gravity of the offense.

Paul's teaching in this passage has, I reckon, seldom been more relevant to the church than at present. In recent times, the church has been greatly damaged by the sexual sins of its pastors and its people. To be sure, what has happened in the church mirrors what is happening in the world around it. But that is no excuse! Since we are all called to be holy, we cannot tolerate sexual abuse and must not excuse it in the church. Instead, we must confront it and deal with it appropriately, so that our congregations are sexual safe places for all their members. Every congregation is to be a sexual

---

8. The phrase that is translated by "his own body" is "his own vessel" in Greek. Here Paul seems to make a pun of its two senses as the male sexual organ and the body of his wife as its recipient.

sanctuary. If we disregard the call to sexual sanctification, we will disregard God's Holy Spirit, who sanctifies each congregation and all its members.

The sexual sanctification of all Christians, whether single or married, results from their participation in the service of worship. In response to God's service of them, they are called to "present" their bodies as a living sacrifice to God the Father, their priestly offering that is holy and well-pleasing to him (Rom 12:1). Here Paul recalls his fuller treatment of that subject earlier in Romans 6:12–23. Because the Christians in Rome have been brought from death to life together with Jesus, their bodies and all the members of their bodies belong to God the Father. That includes their sexual organs! When they were slaves to sin before they were baptized, they, in their reckless pursuit of sexual pleasure and their destructive quest for freedom, "presented" the members of their bodies to injustice and unrighteousness (6:13), to impurity and ever-increasing lawlessness (6:19). But now that they have been redeemed from slavery to sin and death, they are God's servants, his royal courtiers, agents of his righteousness. As recipients of his grace, they are now to "present" all the members of their bodies to him for them to be freed from sin and sanctified for eternal life with him. They therefore rely on him for their purity and their holiness. An important part of that offering is the dedication and presentation of their sexual organs to God. Their genitals, too, are included in their service of God. In practice, we "present" our bodies with all their members to God for purification and sanctification as we receive the body and blood of Jesus penitently and faithfully. As Jesus "presents" himself bodily to us, we there and then present ourselves to him and his heavenly Father. We put out bodies at his disposal and entrust each part of them to him.

## GOOD SEXUAL DESIRE

Like sexual intercourse, sexual desire is a good gift from God. Since he invented it, he fosters it and approves of it. In the Apology of the Augsburg Confession, Melanchthon notes that the desire of one sex for the opposite sex is an ordinance of God.[9] It is something that has been ordained and is still sustained by him. It is produced by God's creative command that male and female should be fruitful and multiply on earth. God wants them to desire each other sexually. Such natural desire is right and good. It pleases God. It must, however, be distinguished from the sexual lust that came into play after the fall. Lust is a disordered, possessive desire, the self-centered desire for personal sexual gratification at the expense of another person. In the long run, lust actually diminishes and damages sexual desire, which, by its very nature, can be fleeting and is often wayward.

In 1 Thessalonians 4:5, Paul speaks rather helpfully about "the passion of desire" in connection with his teaching on sexual sanctification. He does not use passion in its modern sense as a term for strong emotion or for ardent commitment to some cause. Rather, he employs it here and in Romans 1:26 and Colossians 3:5 in its ancient sense as a rampant emotion that overwhelms and overpowers us. We experience it as a disorderly force that overtakes us so strongly that we lose our emotional self-control, such as with an outburst of anger or an attack of anxiety. Thus, lust is a sexual passion that transforms a considerate lover into a hapless, helpless victim of sexual desire. It is both addictive and destructive—addictive because it demands increasing indulgence without the delivery of satisfaction, and destructive because it burns up the lustful person physically, mentally, and emotionally. Like all evil desires, it corrupts the whole person with its deceptive allurements that fail to deliver what they so luridly promise (Eph 4:22; 2 Pet 1:4).

Jesus warns his disciples about the danger of lust in Matthew 5:27–30.[10] He maintains that lust is a matter of the heart. The source of lust is not the sexual attractiveness of a woman or a man. It

---

9. Apology of the Augsburg Confession 23.7.12–13, BoC (249–50).

10. For an analysis of this passage see Jeffrey A. Gibbs, *Matthew 1:1–11:1*, Concordia Commentary (Saint Louis: Concordia, 2006), 286–89.

does not come from the look of a person, but from the heart of an onlooker who surveys another person as a sexual object. It involves imaginary sexual intercourse with a person of the opposite sex apart from marriage, rather than the physical act of adultery, which may or may not result from it. Jesus therefore gives this stern judgment that charges each of us with adultery: "But I say to you that everyone who looks at a woman with lustful intent has already committed adultery with her in his heart" (Matt 5:28). That also applies to every woman. Jesus uses God's prohibition of adultery in the sixth commandment to identify lust as the secret source of adultery as well as its secret enactment. Even though the object of lust is the body of another person, it is the product of a disordered heart with its pornographic imagination. Therefore, the heart needs to be reformed before there can be any change in sexual misconduct.

Since adultery in the heart is the root of actual adultery, it needs to be uprooted there. Jesus dramatizes the severity of the problem by describing that change as a kind of amputation. The inner eye that replays an imaginary sexual scenario on the screen of the mind and the inner hand that makes imaginary sexual contact with an imagined partner must be cut off to prevent the whole person from going to hell. The eradication of lust requires radical spiritual surgery.

Jesus does not explain how this can be done. It is, in fact, an impossible task. To be sure, we can, and must, discipline our minds and our bodies by not looking lustfully at another person. But that does not change the heart. In fact, sexual repression usually arouses the pornographic imagination and inflames lustful desire. It all too often makes the bad much worse. Self-discipline cannot perform the required surgery on the heart and mind. Only Christ can do that. He alone can create a new heart and renew a right spirit in us (Ps 51:10). He is the surgeon who gives us a spiritual heart transplant in baptism (Ezek 11:19; 36:25–27). There he removes the old self with its misbehavior and its corruptive desires and provides us with a new, God-like self with a new, holy, spiritual mentality (Eph 4:22–23). He is the only one who can kill off all the sexual disorder that comes from our sexual idolatry: all fornication, impurity, lust, evil desire, and sexual greed (Col 3:5). He transforms us sexual idolaters from the inside out.

Since our old self has been put to death together with Jesus and we have been raised with a new self together with him, we must now "count ourselves dead to sin and alive to God in Christ Jesus" (Rom 6:3–11). We do so by daily confession of sin and daily prayer for the Holy Spirit. By daily contrition and repentance, the old self with its wrong sexual misdeeds and evil sexual desires must be drowned off, so that the Holy Spirit can raise up a new self to live before God in righteousness and purity, a new self with good sexual desires and right sexual behavior.

Thus, our sexual transformation, which begins in baptism, continues for as long as we live in the body here on earth. Through our positive and negative sexual experiences, God reconfigures our imagination, refines our desires, and reshapes our behavior. He uses our sexual successes to encourage us and make us grateful for what he actually provides. He uses our sexual misdeeds to lead us to repentance and the reception of forgiveness. Most of all, he uses our sexual weaknesses and failures to turn to him in prayer and ask for his Holy Spirit to empower us to live chaste lives and transform us as his holy people.

So then, our sexual transformation depends on our reception of his Spirit and all the fruit of the Spirit in regular worship and in our daily devotions. In fact, public worship provides the best kind of sexual therapy for us as God's children, since by our participation in it we gain a good conscience that prevents guilt from impairing the proper enjoyment of sexual intercourse in marriage or destroying our contentment with our unmarried state. The baptismal therapy of our daily devotions, in which we confess our sins and receive the assurance of forgiveness from God's word, builds on what we receive in worship. The couple that prays together will, by God's grace, stay together and grow together.

## Transforming the Sexual Imagination

The transformation of sexual desire is correlated with the purifica-tion of the imagination, because positive sexual desire depends in large measure on our rightly ordered imagination. God has made us in such a way that our eyes are attracted to the person that we desire. This has been so from the beginning, when God presented Eve to Adam for his admiration of her. Visual stimulus, visual disclosure, and visual intimacy play a vital role in normal sexual intercourse. In fact, it could be said that, for most men and many women, the eyes are their most important sexual organs. That is most apparent in the symbolic function of nakedness since the fall. Visual attraction and visual self-disclosure are closely asso-ciated with bodily self-giving in sexual intercourse. Quite simply, we undress to engage in sex. We modestly keep our nakedness for our spouse and jealously reserve the nakedness of our spouse for ourselves. That is normal! That is natural! That is part of God's design! In its legislation for marriage, the Old Testament acknowl-edges the importance of this by describing a man's sexual contact with a woman as uncovering her nakedness (Lev 18:6–19; 20:11, 17–21). Her nakedness is not meant for public sight, but only for her spouse. Since a married couple is one flesh, her nakedness belongs to her husband, and her husband's to her.[11]

Like all other aspects of sexuality, the currency of visual inti-macy has been depreciated and debased by sin. Sinful husbands and wives no longer have eyes only for their spouse. They do not delight in the naked sight of each other. Instead, they regard each other critically. They tend to be ashamed of their own bodies and displeased with the actual, physical appearance of their spouse. They assess the sexual attractiveness of another body and strip it naked in their imagination. By idolizing that imaginary body, they spurn their own spouse in favor of another imagined body. That

---

11. See John W. Kleinig, *Leviticus*, Concordia Commentary (Saint Louis: Concordia, 2003), 386–87.

then decreases their desire for their actual spouse, who cannot ever measure up to their lurid, wild fantasies.

That phenomenon is exploited by pornography, which is the visual depiction of fornication for sexual arousal. It is, of course, nothing new and has been around since the early history of humanity. But it has, over the last three decades, increased its wide reach and secret power through the internet. Now all kinds of sexual scenarios are available for private, personal viewing to anyone who seeks physical and emotional comfort from it. Unlike good literature and art, which depicts nudity in an honest, wholesome, and constructive fashion, it displays naked genitalia explicitly engaging in the full range of disordered sexual acts to stimulate the body sexually, apart from the actual body of another person. While it seems to focus on the body, it, in fact, presents its viewer with disembodied sex and virtual sexual intercourse. It disconnects sex from the actual body of another person and turns it into an imagined, mental activity that is best expressed by solitary masturbation.

As has been shown in many studies, the regular use of pornography does immense damage. Most obviously, it arouses perverted desires that cannot be satisfied by normal sexual intercourse. It reprograms the brains of young people and desensitizes all who keep using it, so that they are no longer sexually aroused by the actual presence and touch, the smell and the taste, the speech and sight, of a real body, but instead require artificial stimulation in their imagination to awaken and sustain sexual desire. Like a drug that delivers a short high to its user that is followed by an emotional slump, it delivers a charge that does not last but requires ever-increasing indulgence to maintain its diminishing intensity and ward off the ever-increasing severity of its consequent low. The chemical transformation in a porn-addicted brain impairs normal sexual arousal and the natural, physical sexual response to another person. So, oddly, indulgence in pornography does not actually awaken normal sexual desire—it switches it off. Instead of increasing healthy sexual enjoyment, it decreases it. It does not enrich the sexual imagination but actually impoverishes it by its narrow focus on the physical mechanics of sex. In short, it peddles fake sex. The pornographic display of sexual activity is, paradoxically, not explicit enough, rather than too explicit, because it shows so little of what actually happens when a married couple makes love with each other.

There is so much more that could be said about the physical, mental, and personal destructiveness of habitual indulgence in pornography. But that goes beyond the scope of this study, which considers how God regards our bodies and what we do with them. In his eyes, pornography is just another instance of idolatry, the worship of the human body rather than him as its Creator (Rom 1:18–25). God deals with this perversion of the natural order by handing fallen humanity over to the lusts of their hearts. He lets people get their own way and makes them stew in their own juice. He lets them defile and dishonor their bodies to bring them to their senses and discover the truth about their bodies, which have been created in God's image to share in his holiness. While pornography pollutes unbelievers and believers, it also desecrates the holiness of believers and so opens them to the accusation and condemnation of the devil. He oppresses them by giving them a bad conscience that is filled with guilt and shame and self-disgust. What they need more than anything else is God's absolution for their idolatry and failure to serve him with thanksgiving.

Spiritually speaking, indulgence in pornography and pornographic fantasies is much more a matter of the first commandment than of the sixth. Those who indulge in it do not value God's approval, nor do they fear his disapproval; they do not love God but love unnatural sexual stimulation more than him; they do not trust in him to provide comfort and enjoyment in marriage or apart from it, but rely on imaginative self-stimulation for sexual comfort and enjoyment. Our fascination with pornography therefore masks a deeper issue, our suicidal rebellion against God and our service of his creatures rather than our life-receiving service of him. Liberation from its pernicious grip comes from the exercise of faith in God, faith that confesses its sexual sins in a confidential context, seeks remission from them, and prays for God's help in overcoming sexual temptations. That's what the godly person does in Psalm 119:37 with this prayer: "Turn my eyes from looking at worthless things; and give me life in your ways."

Yet it is not enough merely to shun pornography and avoid indulgence in pornographic fantasies. What has been damaged must be healed by good pastoral care. Pastors must offer private confession and absolution to cleanse the guilty conscience from the stain of pornography. The shameful soul must be covered with Christ's purity and be assured of God's approval. Then the disordered imagination can be healed by the contemplation of loveliness rather than ugliness.

The Old Testament provides us with a good antidote to the corruption of the sexual desire with the Song of Songs.[12] Since it is the inspired word of God, it has the spiritual power to purify and sanctify our sexual imagination and our sexual desire. It does not get us to repress our sexuality, but helps us to order it, so that it operates in a way that pleases God and our spouse as well. It shows us how God views sexual desire and sexual love in marriage as a radiant reflection of Christ's union with the church as his lovely bride. By the inspiration of the Holy Spirit, it enlightens our eyes to see the beauty of human sexuality in the light of the beauty of holiness, and vice versa.

### Sexual Admiration

The Song of Songs presents us with a set of poems that aid us in right sexual contemplation and enjoyment of the naked body. In them, both the husband and the wife address their spouse with words of admiration and praise. We have two poems in which the husband delights in the naked body of his wife and praises the beauty of its main parts. In 4:1–5, he moves from her eyes to her

---

12. Two commentaries that do this well are by Christopher W. Mitchell (*The Song of Songs*, Concordia Commentary, [Saint Louis: Concordia, 2003]) and Robert W. Jenson (*Song of Songs*, Interpretation, [Louisville: John Knox, 2005]).

hair, to her teeth and her lips to her temple and her neck, before he finally comes to her breasts. In 7:1–5, he moves upwards from her feet, the only part of her that is dressed, to her thighs and navel, to her belly and her breasts, to her neck and her eyes, before he finally comes to her head and her hair. We also have one poem inserted between them in which the wife responds to her husband's appreciation of her by praising his not-so-obviously naked body. In 5:10–16, she begins her perusal of him with his golden head and dark hair, and then moves downwards to his eyes and cheeks, his lips and arms, his torso and legs, before she returns to his mouth as the sweetest part of him in order to discover what he will say or whether he will kiss her. The most amazing thing about these poems is their stunning use of the same imagery used by pagan poets to praise the idols of their gods in the ancient world—but used here to describe the human body made in God's image. They subvert visual idolatry with verbal praise for the actual body of the speaker's spouse.

These poems help a husband and wife use their imagination to appreciate each other sexually and to show their appreciation with outspoken admiration. They focus on what is attractive and beautiful about each part of the body, rather than merely on the appearance of their sexual organs. They encourage them to awaken and enhance affectionate sexual desire by expressing their delight in their naked bodies and appreciation of each part of them. Most remarkably, they are God's word, speech that is inspired by the Holy Spirit and inspires its speakers and hearers with the Holy Spirit. When married people use this poetry to meditate on each other physically and sexually, God himself orders and refines, purifies and sanctifies, their imagination and their desire for each other. They then see each other as God sees them and hear his voice as he speaks to them through their spouse. They desire each other in a way that pleases God and love each other as Christ loves them. As they fix their imagination on each other's actual bodies, the sexual fakery of pornography is unmasked by God's word and replaced by actual sexual enjoyment. In faith and love, they hear

God speaking to them and see him offering their spouse to them as a gift from him.

This is how Luther describes that mutual appreciation of each other remade in God's image:

> You should look on your wife as if she were the only woman on earth—not a single other woman existed; and you should look on your husband as if he were the only man on earth—not a single other man existed, so that no king, yes, not even the sun should shine brighter and light up your eyes as much as your wife or your husband. Because right here you have God's word, which promises you this woman or this man. This word of God gives you this woman or this man, saying, "This man shall be yours; this woman shall be yours. This pleases me greatly! All angels and creatures rejoice because of it." There is no greater adornment than God's word, with which you look on your wife as a gift from God.[13]

Such appreciation of the spouse cannot but arouse a sense of gratitude, gratitude to one's spouse and gratitude to God for one's spouse as his good gift in marriage.

Paul touches on this briefly in Ephesians 5:3–5. There he addresses the Christians in Ephesus as "saints," holy people who share Christ's holiness. Since they are holy, they must avoid all sexual disorder and lewd banter. All that is to give way to thanksgiving. In their sexual conduct, they are not to be greedy grabbers but grateful thanks-givers. All married people have been much more richly blessed by God in their marriage than they ever realize (Prov 18:22; 19:14). They therefore have no cause for disdainful disparagement and disappointed complaining. Instead, they have good reason to thank each other and God for what they daily receive and enjoy in their marriage. He purifies and sanctifies them, so that they can serve him and each other with thanksgiving.

---

13. "Wedding Sermon" (January 8, 1531), WA 34,1:52.13–21; translated by Todd Hains.

There is, I think, no lasting and deepening sexual enjoyment for Christians without such thanksgiving.

## SEX WITH A GOOD CONSCIENCE

While nothing diminishes sexual enjoyment quite as much as a bad conscience, nothing else also enhances it more than a good conscience, a clean conscience freed from guilt and shame, accusation and condemnation, disgust and self-reproach. God therefore gives us a good conscience so that we can enjoy what he intended for us by making us men and women.

In his word he assures us that he invented sex and sexual intercourse. Since he created us with sexual bodies, our sexuality is in itself good. Its proper use is good. The only bad thing about it is its abuse. It can therefore be received as a good gift from him that is best enjoyed by our appreciation of it and thanksgiving for it.

By his word he institutes marriage as the proper context for a sexual relationship between a man and a woman. He also establishes the terms for entry into it as well as for life in it. He thereby shows us what pleases him in the use of our sexuality and what makes for a good conscience in marriage. We need not be in doubt about his approval and blessing of us if we fit in with what he provides for us in his ordinances.

By his word as law that exposes sin and as gospel that forgives repentant sinners, he helps them to admit their sexual transgressions and seek his grace and grants them pardon and full release from the crippling burden of guilt. By it he also discloses the shame and hurt from sexual abuse by others and provides cleansing and healing for sexually abused people through their vindication by Jesus. His pardon and cleansing are the only sure foundation for life with a good conscience. It frees us from the compulsive urge to engage in sexual self-justification and sexual self-condemnation.

By his word, God not only unites a couple in marriage as its true celebrant but also sanctifies it through their bodily union with Jesus and his bodily presence with them as the third party to it. By his word and its use in meditation and prayer, he gives them his Holy Spirit to transform them into faithful, self-giving lovers and refine their thoughts and emotions, their imagination and desire, so that they reflect Christ to each other in the nuptial union. Through their sanctification, they benefit from their good conscience, because they see their bodies as God sees them and feel as he does about their sexual fidelity.

God does all that and much more so that his people can have a good conscience in all their bodily life on earth. Each husband and wife is therefore urged to enjoy life *with* their spouse in the whole of their fleeting life under the sun, for that is God's allotted portion for them in their work and in their leisure (Eccl 9:9).

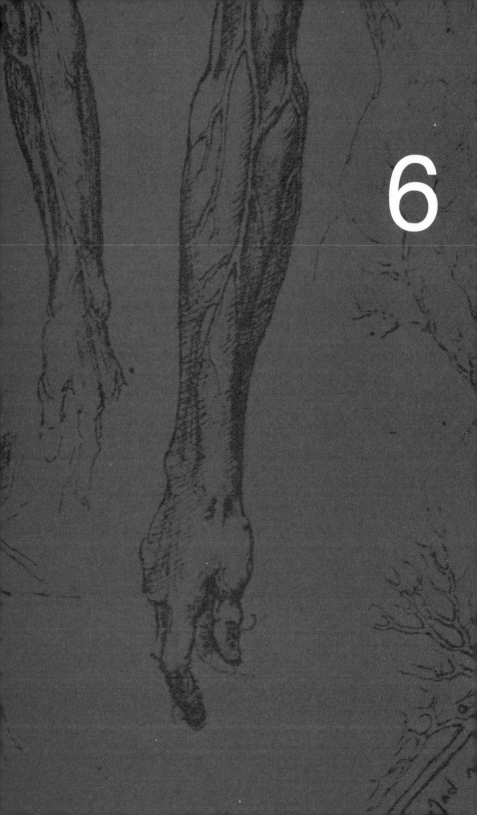

6

# THE SPOUSAL BODY

Both celibacy and marriage have their own
different forms of service and ministry to the Lord.

—*Clement of Alexandria*

If therefore purity refers to something that is
permissible and approved by God, then marriages
are pure because they are approved by the Word
of God. ... Thus, as virginity is impure in the
ungodly, so marriage is pure in the godly on
account of the Word of God and faith. ... For we
are justified neither on account of virginity nor on
account of marriage but freely on account of Christ,
when we believe that on account of him we have
a gracious God.

—*Philipp Melanchthon*

Traditionally, a betrothal differed from marriage as a pledge of exclusive fidelity in a relationship between a woman and a man before their actual marriage. It was a provisional state in which a couple prepared for married life, and a provisional time in which they got to know each other as they learned how to communicate with each other.

The image of betrothal was used by God in Hosea 2:19–20 to depict his relationship with his people in the new covenant and also by Paul in 2 Corinthians 11:2 to describe the relationship of the congregation in Corinth with Christ as her husband-to-be. That image is, in many ways, a good picture of the union between Christ and his disciples, because it applies equally to those who are married and to those who are single. Both share in the same general betrothal. Both equally await the consummation of their relationship. Both are preparing for their full one-flesh union with Jesus.

This study is much indebted to the exploration of the theology of the body and its bearing on human sexuality by Pope John Paul II.[1] He has done more than any other theologian in recent times to expound this topic scripturally and philosophically. His central claim is that the bodies of all men and women are essentially spousal. They were not just designed for sexual intercourse and human reproduction but also, and even more basically, for bodily self-giving love, whether it be in singleness or marriage. And more than that! Since both men and women were made in God's image, they were made for a spousal union of self-giving love with Christ as their common bridegroom.

---

1. Karol Wojtyła (John Paul II), *Male and Woman He Created Them: A Theology of the Body*, translated and edited by Michael Waldstein (Boston: Pauline), 2006.

So God created and redeemed and sanctified their bodies to share in his love bodily and give of themselves bodily to him and others, partially now and completely in eternity. And all this is theirs only in Christ and as a gift from him.

Marriage is therefore provisional. So, too, is singleness! Both foreshadow and reflect the full one-flesh union of Christ with the church and each believer as his beloved bride through their participation in his death and resurrection. Their betrothal will be consummated in eternity. Then all those who share in his resurrection will celebrate their bodily union with Christ in his wedding supper (Rev 19:7, 9; 21:2).

## THE MYSTERY OF MARRIAGE

In the musical *My Fair Lady*, Eliza Doolittle chides her inept suitor: "Don't speak of love! Show me!" Since marriage is a physical sexual union of a man and a woman, nuptial love needs to be shown physically. It cannot only be a platonic union of two souls with a soulmate. It is not enough for a married couple merely to feel in love with each other. Their love must be spoken and enacted. They need to give themselves personally to each other, so that they can give themselves physically to each other. By showing their love with a physical act of self-entrustment, they show something of Christ's love and hint at how it is given, received, and reciprocated.

Paul explores this spiritual dimension of marriage most eloquently in Ephesians 5:22–33. There he speaks about marriage as a mystery (5:31). It is hidden from normal perception and rational reflection on what we perceive. It remains hidden even when it is discovered. Although a mystery resembles a secret as something hidden and unknown, it differs from a secret because it remains hidden and can only ever be partially known, even when it is disclosed. In fact, the more you experience a mystery and know about it from experience, the more wonderful and mysterious it becomes. That is supremely so for the mystery of marriage. It is in itself a natural mystery that hides within it an even deeper supernatural mystery, the mystery of Christ's union with the church.

Every human marriage prefigures, foreshadows, and reflects the union of God's incarnate Son as the heavenly Bridegroom with his earthly bride. But that mystery was hidden and undisclosed until his incarnation and remains hidden from those who are unbelievers, no matter how good their marriage may be. That is so even though God unites every husband and wife in every marriage that is in accordance with natural law, the law by which he creates and maintains proper order in the world and conveys his blessing to the whole human family. Yet while the marriage of pagan or unbelieving men and women to each other is valid and pleasing to God, its mystery is only manifest to those who have faith in Jesus and are sanctified by their faith in him. Through his word and Holy Spirit, God discloses that mystery to believers who have been united with Jesus in baptism. So married Christians participate in both the natural mystery of marriage and the supernatural mystery of faith. In fact, their union with Christ and faith in him as their Lord transforms their union with each other, so that increasingly the relationship of the wife with her husband matches the union of the church with Christ, and the relationship of the husband with his wife corresponds ever more closely with the union of Christ with the church.

As Paul indicates by his paraphrase of Genesis 2:24 in Ephesians 5:30, their participation in these two aspects of this mystery and their experience of it hinge on both the one-flesh union of husband and wife in marriage and the one-flesh union of Christ and the church in holy baptism. Both have to do with a divinely instituted order for the transmission and reception of God's blessings, the order of marriage with the husband as the head of his wife and the order of salvation with Christ as the head of the church (5:23). Yet marriage is much more than a mere metaphor for our union with Christ. That gets things back to front. Christ's union with the church and its members shows us the true nature and purpose of marriage, which even after the fall into sin still reflects the nuptial union of Christ with his bride. He himself reshapes the marriage of baptized believers, so that it embodies and discloses the mystery of his self-sacrificial love.

The primary mystery is the union of the incarnate Christ as the head with the church as his body and all those who belong to the church as his members. The church does not and cannot exist apart from him, just as the human body and its members cannot exist apart from the head. Nor does Christ exist apart from the church. That union depends entirely on him. It is established and maintained by him. He loved the church, before she ever loved him, and still loves her, even when she no longer loves him. He transforms her by cleansing her from the stain of sin and sharing his own holiness with her. Since he is her head, he now nourishes and cherishes her as his own body. He does not exercise his headship by dominating her and demanding services from her, but by serving her and giving himself to her. The church, in turn, is happy to be subordinate to him as her head in a divinely instituted order in which she depends on him, trusts in him, and receives everything from him, whether it be his demonstrative love, spiritual nourishment, or affectionate attention. By his love for her, Christ images God the Father to her. He shows her his Father's heart. Who would not be happy to submit to such a loving head? Who could not but respond to such a loving head with ardent love and warm devotion?

The secondary visible manifestation of the mystery comes from the one-flesh union of Christ with the church. It is the mystery of Christian marriage in which husband and wife are both one flesh with each other and one flesh with Christ. The reception of God's blessings in marriage depends on respect for the order that he has established for it to work and flourish, his order for the bestowal and reception of nuptial love, his order for mutual and reciprocal self-giving. In the order of marriage, the husband is the head of the wife. He is not her boss but her benefactor. He devotes himself to her and her welfare. He takes responsibility for her well-being and takes the lead in giving himself to her. Like Christ, he offers himself and his love to her. The husband does not demand her love as his right, nor claim sexual services from her. Rather, he woos her with his steady devotion and unwavering faithfulness to her. He shows his love for her by his whole relationship with her rather than just in sexual intercourse. His body is for her and her only. In the words of an old marriage vow, he "worships" her with his body. He loves her, even when she feels that she no longer loves him or cannot love him as she knows she should. He nourishes her physically by providing for her; he protects her and cares for her personally by considering her needs (1 Pet 3:7). He cherishes her by paying attention to her and valuing her more highly than anyone else in his life. He never regards her apart from himself and himself apart from her.

She, in turn, values him as her head and fits in with him by appreciating what he does for her and gives to her. She is happy to be subordinate to him by taking her place in God's order for her under him and together with him, like a queen beside her royal husband (Eph 5:22, 24; Col 3:18). Above all else, she respects him as her husband (Eph 5:33), without accusation and condemnation, and honors him because he represents Christ to her (5:22). This is so because both of them are in Christ.

What surprises me most about this instruction is the apparent imbalance in the relationship. The onus in the marital union rests on the husband as the head of his wife (5:23). Yet only one thing is required of him as a husband, something that is impossible apart from Christ and his Holy Spirit. He must love his wife as Christ loves the church (5:25–28). By loving her demonstrably and self-sacrificially, he courts her acceptance of him and encourages her willing subordination to him as her head. Likewise, only one thing is required of the wife as his partner. She must honor and respect him in thought, word, and deed (5:33). By her respect for him, she encourages him to give of himself to her. Where and when they both do this, the image of God has begun to be restored, for by their mutual love they reflect the love of God bodily and show what he is like bodily.

## SINGLE DEVOTION

Since God created human beings in his image as male and female, their marriage reflects the physical union of Christ with the church. Yet marriage is not the only way that Christian men and women resemble him and show something of his likeness. They also do that in a single, unmarried state. That, too, has God's approval. After all, Jesus himself never married. Neither did the great prophet Jeremiah (16:2), nor the great apostle Paul (1 Cor 7:6–8).

The single life is not at all abnormal and uncommon; it is quite normal and common. All married people were single before they were married, and half of them will once again be single after the death of their spouse. According to the latest figures, more than half the population of Australia is single. Yet, even though the single life serves its own God-given purpose and has its own beauty, its importance receives far too little attention in the church.[2]

While Genesis 1 describes the creation of Adam and Eve together at the same time, Genesis 2 depicts the creation of Adam, the first human being, before the creation of Eve. By Adam's original solitude God shows us that this is the primary state of every human being. All people are created first of all as distinct, complete persons each with separate bodies. Their bodies separate them from the animals and other humans; they disclose that they are separate persons, each and every one with their own souls. By their interaction with God and the world around them, they become aware of themselves as persons, each with a unique relationship with God, and as agents who are able to act in their own right. That helps us understand how God views single people. Like Adam before the creation of Eve, those who are not married enjoy the primary mode of human life in the body that even those who marry share before they marry and still share when they are married. That original solitude is an essential part of our humanity. Each single person reminds us of that.

---

2. For a recent reflection on this, see "Being Single," in *Human Sexuality: Three Key Issues (Background Paper)*, CTICR Doctrinal Statements and Theological Opinions 3.H., Lutheran Church of Australia, 2014, 11–16.

We live in a society that belittles the unique contribution of single men and women in many different ways. The worst slight is that those who are sexually inactive are viewed as somehow inferior or even odd. They are not real women or real men. Yet that is quite untrue. We do not become real women or real men through sexual maturity, sexual intercourse, or parenthood. Our manhood or womanhood is given to us genetically at conception. Our masculinity or femininity does not come from our engagement in sexual intercourse. That may, in fact, damage it. It belongs to us even if we are sexually inexperienced and sexually inactive. It is our birthright as human beings. At most, sexual activity confirms our sexuality. It does not at all establish it.

Since that is so, the sexual status of single men or single women is just as significant as it is for those who are married. It is always in play and always adds something good in every situation. Just think of the role of unmarried uncles and aunts. Think, too, of the significance of relationships between brothers and sisters and cousins of the opposite sex. That is also true for the friendships of single people with those who are married, whether it be of the opposite sex or the same sex. They are all a source of enrichment and fulfilment quite apart from any kind of overt or covert physical sexual interaction. That applies even more for those who are single Christians. In all of their contacts with people of either sex, they mirror something of Christ to the people who surround them. They are meant to embody and model true friendship and self-giving love that transcends erotic attraction and interaction.

Sadly, we live in societies where friendship has become difficult for most people, if not almost impossible for young people, whether it be with people of the same sex or people of the opposite sex. This is because our obsession with sex and our sexual identity darkens and distorts all our relationships. The love of a man for another man or a woman for another woman and the love of married women and men for someone other than their spouse is regarded with suspicion as latently or blatantly erotic. When all relationships are sexualized, friendships are greatly diminished and often undone. In that context, the church is to be a safe place sexually that contributes much to the recovery and promotion of friendship for friendless single people.

Single men and women have a very significant part to play in every Christian community. They remind us that the church is God's holy family rather than an association of families and married couples. All members of God's family are brothers and sisters with each other, because they have God as their Father and Jesus as their brother. So unlike the human family and marriage, which are provisional because they belong to this age, our relationship with each other as brothers and sisters in Christ is eternal (cf. Mark 3:33–35; 10:29–30). Thus, in the New Testament, fellow Christians are most commonly called brothers. All Christians enjoy fraternal friendship and love with the other members of their congregation and the church at large (Rom 12:10; 1 Thess 4:9; Heb 13:1; 1 Pet 1:22; 3:8; 2 Pet 2:9). Close fellowship with another Christian is the most profound kind of friendship that we can enjoy in this life because it is eternal. So single Christians show us that the spiritual friendship of believers transcends sexuality, marriage, and the family.

In Matthew 19:10–12, Christ surprises his disciples and us with his countercultural teaching on the single life. He transforms the term "eunuch," which was commonly used as a contemptuous description for single people, by adopting it as a badge of honor for single people. In response to his claim that God did not sanction divorce, the disciples had remarked that it would therefore be better not to marry at all. Jesus agreed with them, but with the provision that it was only better for some people. The single life was itself a vocation, a gift from God (Matt 19:11; see also 1 Cor 7:7). He then adds that there are three kinds of the single life that each have their contribution to make.

Some people, says Jesus, are born "eunuchs," men and women who were unequipped or ill-equipped for sexual intercourse. This could be for lack of sexual organs, the possession of both kinds of sexual organs, or the total absence of sexual desire. Even though they are treated with contempt in most societies, and even though they were excluded from the priesthood (Lev 21:20) and participation in the temple service in ancient Israel (Deut 23:1), Jesus accepts them and affirms their worth. We must, too! They are no less human and valuable than sexually functional men and women. They, in fact, remind us all that since the fall we have all been damaged sexually by sin so that our bodies no longer function as they should.

Some people are made "eunuchs" intentionally or accidently by other people. They have been sexually disabled in some way, whether it be by castration or some other kind of genital mutilation, ill health, or the experience of incapacitating sexual abuse. Jesus also accepts them and affirms their worth.

Last, some people have made themselves "eunuchs" for the sake of God's kingdom. They have freely and willingly chosen a single state of life as part of their calling to serve God. That kind of celibacy is a special spiritual gift, a gift of grace that is given only to some men and women. It cannot be required of anybody or imposed on anyone; it is given to them by God and received by them in faithful obedience to their calling. It is a holy, spiritual state of life in God's kingdom, the kingdom that has been ushered in by Jesus. It brings its own demands and its own rewards. In fact, the Lutheran confessions claim that this kind of celibacy "is a gift that surpasses marriage," a gift that frees a person from domestic distractions and demands for undivided, wholehearted devotion to Christ.[3] It surpasses marriage because it is a gift of grace from God, a spiritual gift rather than a natural endowment (1 Cor 7:7). By their single-minded service of God, those who have been called to this kind of single life reflect Christ's own wholehearted service of his heavenly Father in his unmarried life on earth.

What, then, is the purpose of God's call to celibacy for the sake of his kingdom? That is spelled out most fully by St. Paul in 1 Corinthians 7:7–8 and 25–35. The purpose of celibate single life

---

3. Apology of the Augsburg Confession 23.39–40, BoC (253).

is threefold. First, it frees single people to serve the Lord more simply, directly, and wholeheartedly than married people, whose loyalty is necessarily divided between pleasing their spouse and pleasing their Lord. So, for example, Paul could not have served as the apostle to the gentiles if he had been married and had to care for his wife and their children. Secondly, it acknowledges that the chief allegiance of all Christians is to their Lord, who has reclaimed them totally for himself to live and work with him. It is, lastly, a reminder that marriage, even at its best, is a provisional reality limited to this age. The union of husband and wife prefigures the ultimate, perfect physical union with Christ and intimacy with each other in the communion of saints. So, the celibacy of single Christians is a byproduct of their physical devotion to the Lord and an aid to it. It reminds us of the ties of eternal, fraternal friendship and love in the church as his body. Its devotion to Jesus bears witness to the devotion of Jesus to his heavenly Father in his earthly life as a man. Like matrimony, faithful singleness is a God-pleasing, holy way of life (1 Cor 7:34).

## REAL UNITY IN REAL DIVERSITY

In Matthew 19:4–5 and Mark 10:6–8, Jesus recalls Genesis 1:27 and 2:24 in order to teach the Pharisees about divorce. Together with his assertion that humans cannot separate those whom the Lord God has joined in marriage, he also teaches us about two other aspects of marriage: its origin as God's creation and its nature as a one-flesh union.

Marriage is not a human invention. It did not evolve in the course of human history to protect mothers and nurture children. It did not arise in settled societies as a human institution that was sanctioned legally and religiously to safeguard the property of men and pass it on to their descendants. No, the Lord God, the Creator of heaven and earth, created it. What's more, he did not establish marriage after the fall into sin to minimize its consequences. He instituted it at the beginning when he created humanity. The marital union of husband and wife is as much part of God's foundational order for the world as the creation of day and night. It is part of God's provision for the survival, nurture, and propagation of human life. He therefore determines what it is and what it is meant to provide. So, no matter how hard they try or how much they disrupt God's order, no human government and no human enterprise can change its nature and thwart its purpose, neither by legislation, indoctrination, or physical enforcement. Marriage is, quite simply, something given. And it remains given as long as human beings survive on earth.

Right from the beginning of human life on earth, God created humanity with its sexual polarity. He created human beings as either male or female for correlation with each other. They are both equally and entirely human. As men and women, they are both made in God's image and have both been equally corrupted by sin. As part of the human family, they both have the same vocation whether they are married or not. Together with all other men and women they have been delegated and empowered to rule over the fish, birds, and animals and to care for the earth with its vegetation as the main source of food for themselves and the animals. Yet they also have different roles to play with each other as physical partners in the procreation and nurture of their descendants. Even if they are unmarried, they have something special to contribute as single women or men. They are called to work together with other women and men in taking care of children, people around them, and their natural environment.

Even though God created each human being as either male or female for the purpose of procreation, the propagation of children does not exhaust his purpose for them in their sexuality. The second chapter of Genesis adds a second dimension to their sexuality. They were created for sexual community and companionship in marriage. That was God's added blessing for them. He decided that just as he did not live in solitude, it was not good for them to live in solitude. So he created Eve from Adam to be Adam's sexual companion (Gen 2:18, 20). Their companionship differed from their association with the animals and friendship with other people in two ways: they were created to be coworkers and correspondent partners.

On the one hand, Eve was to be Adam's "helper." By his use of this term, God designated her as his active partner, his helpmate, a coworker with him in the common enterprise of their marriage. On the most elementary level, they needed to cooperate with each other in sexual intercourse and procreation. Yet it went beyond that and included everything that they did as a couple. They were both meant to work together as interdependent partners for the benefit of each other and their children, if they had any, and subduing the earth by farming it well to increase its productivity. Their sexual differences equipped them to work together in their marriage, each in a different way for their common good.

On the other hand, God also created Eve as Adam's counterpart, his proper spouse. She was to be "fit for him" as his opposite, his match, his other half, someone different from him sexually and yet like him personally, like two halves of the same circle. Thus, they were each meant to make up for what the other lacked both in procreation and in their convivial nuptial union. They were meant to challenge and enrich each other with their differences. They were, quite simply and yet profoundly, meant to complement each other as sexual partners and nuptial coworkers. Most significantly, their complementary sexuality as male and female persons meant that they could become one flesh, a single physical community, without ceasing to be different persons. True unity in diversity! Oddly, they discovered themselves as unique persons with their own unique identity and character in their nuptial union. Thus, their sexual partnership promoted their development as persons who each in their own way reflected something of God's image to each other and their social context.

God's purpose in creating Adam and Eve as a man and a woman with male and female bodies also extends beyond their sexual union. It includes his creation of Eve with the physical and personal capacity to be a mother who begets children with God's help (Gen 4:1). Thus, already before she bears her first child, Adam recognizes that she has been made to be "the mother of all living" people (Gen 3:20). He therefore names her "Eve," which means life-giver or life-transmitter. He thereby also discovers his own character as a potential father. So, just as her femininity involves motherhood, so his masculinity involves fatherhood. By his paternal masculinity and her maternal femininity, they further reflect the image of God as Father as well as the image of his incarnate Son, whose body is the church, the mother of the faithful (Gal 4:26).

## SEPARATING WHAT GOD HAS UNITED

When the Pharisees ask Jesus whether it is lawful to divorce one's spouse for any cause, Jesus recalls God's original creation of humans as male and female and their one-flesh union. From that he concludes, "So they are no longer two but one flesh. What therefore God has joined together, let not man separate" (Mark 10:8b–9).

There are two ways in which humans try to separate what God has united, one ancient and the other modern. The ancient attempt is by divorce, the modern by the separation of gender from sex.

God unites a couple with each other bodily in marriage. He does that in every marriage, no matter how it is enacted. Since God unites them, Jesus decrees that no one should separate them from each other, except for God himself. A divine act of creation can only be modified or undone by its divine Creator. This means that in God's eyes, a "divorced" couple is still physically one flesh, even if they refuse to acknowledge that fact and no longer live together as husband and wife.

So the biblical teaching on divorce is really quite simple for any Christian, even if its practice is seldom straightforward and often painful to observe. To be sure, Jesus acknowledges that, through Moses, God permitted divorce for the Israelites because their hearts were hardened to God and each other (Deut 24:1; Mark 10:4–5; cf. Matt 5:31). But that was not part of his original design for marriage before the fall of Adam and Eve away from God. Nor is it his will for his holy people in the new covenant. God wants every Christian couple to stay together as long as both of them are still alive. What's more, he deals with their hardened and offending hearts by providing pardon and the power of the Holy Spirit to remain faithful to each other.

In his teaching on divorce, Jesus does not speak as a law-giver, a new Moses. Instead, he speaks to his disciples as their pastor who teaches them the sixth commandment and applies it practically to them (Matt 5:27–32). He makes it clear that God does not approve of either divorce or marriage to another person after a divorce, but instead regards it as a violation of the sixth commandment. Since the original marriage is still in force in God's eyes, it is an act of adultery. That is the focus of his teaching. Thus, any man who divorces his wife makes her commit adultery, unless she has already been faithless to him (Matt 5:32a); any man who divorces his wife and marries another woman commits adultery against his former wife (Matt 19:9; Mark 10:11; Luke 16:18a); any man who marries a divorced woman commits adultery against her former husband (Matt 5:32b; Luke 16:18a). Likewise, any woman who divorces her husband and marries another man commits adultery against her former husband (Mark 10:12). Most surprisingly, Jesus does not regard the two parties in a divorce separately but always together with each other. He considers them as still married, even if they are divorced. Therefore, when Jesus considers divorced people, he concentrates on the damage done to their marriage and their spouse.

In this teaching Jesus does not speak as a teacher of Christian ethics who is concerned with marital misconduct, nor as a marriage counselor who is concerned to save troubled marriages, but as a pastor to the consciences of his disciples. He teaches the sixth commandment in order to lead them to repentance and show them what pleases God. His main concern is to deal with their guilt by using the sixth commandment to diagnose their sin and to give them a good conscience by teaching the gospel. That is most necessary for their spiritual well-being, for, I think, there are few sins used so effectively by Satan to burden consciences and destroy the assurance of salvation as sexual infidelity that results in the breakup of a marriage. People who have been wounded by the severe fracture of divorce need to be led sensitively and gently to repentance for their part in it, and to faith in the blood of Jesus, who cleanses them from their sins against their former spouse and from the sins of their former spouse against them.

Jesus does acknowledge that divorce occurs and will occur among his disciples. Yet he frustrates us by failing to provide clear moral and practical guidelines to negotiate a failed marriage, just as he frustrated the Pharisees by failing to tell them in what circumstances it is lawful for a man to divorce a woman. The closest that he comes to that is in Matthew 19:9. There he teaches that a husband who has married a single woman, after divorcing his wife because she has had sexual intercourse with another man, does not commit adultery against his former wife. Yet, even then, he does not actually sanction divorce, but says that he may marry another woman with a good conscience. That pastoral exception, however, does not change God's decree that no one shall separate those whom God has united in marriage.[4]

### Gender

Another way of separating what God has united is the present project in the Western world to disconnect personal gender from biological sexuality. Gender used to be the grammatical term for the classification of nouns, pronouns, and adjectives as masculine, feminine, or neuter. We have some remnants of that in English with its personal pronouns, he/him, she/her, and it, and their corresponding possessive adjectives, his, her, and its. It then became a colloquial term for the sex of a person and the characteristics and roles that were regarded as typically masculine or feminine in any given society.

But now we have a new definition of gender that rejects its connection with the sex of a person and discounts the natural,

---

4. For a further discussion on Christ's teaching on divorce, see Jeffrey A. Gibbs, *Matthew 11:2–20:34*, Concordia Commentary (Saint Louis: Concordia, 2010), 942–62.

God-given sexual polarity of male and female. Increasingly, gender has come to describe the kind of mental sexual identity that people choose for themselves apart from the biological sexuality of their bodies. According to that way of thinking, my gender is determined by how I feel and regard myself as a sexual person and my body, and how I want others to regard me sexually. This notion of gender has rapidly become a foundational dogma for the dominant philosophy of sexuality in our society. Thus, I am not stuck with the gender that was assigned to me genetically with my chromosomes and disclosed at birth by my sexual organs. Apart from that, I can choose to identify myself with the opposite sex; identify myself with both genders to various degrees, in different ways, and on different occasions; or to identify myself with neither sex. As if that were not confusing enough, many theorists now also argue for gender fluidity across a whole spectrum of possibilities in which there are no distinct gender classifications. With that fluid definition, gender becomes a vague, unhelpful term that no longer has a clear sense and sharp profile. Worst of all, identification by gender no longer provides a sure basis for a person's identity. The result is uncertainty and confusion.

Many who belong to the cultural elite of our society now separate gender completely from sex. For them, gender has become a social, mental construct subject to human manipulation and transformation. It has to do with how one feels about oneself and one's body. If I feel out of kilter with my actual body and regard myself as a member of the opposite sex, then I suffer from gender dysphoria. The best solution to that condition is to remake the body hormonally and surgically in order to match that gender. Yet even after sexual reassignment by surgery, the body has not really been changed genetically and biologically. It remains the body of a man or a woman, despite the cosmetic alteration of its sexual organs and the ongoing hormonal treatment required to maintain the desired secondary sexual characteristics.

The separation of gender from sex violates God's order for humanity with its polarity of men and women. Both the account of human creation in Genesis 1:27 and its reaffirmation by Jesus in Matthew 19:4 and Mark 10:6 teach that God created humanity in his image as male and female. In Hebrew, the terms "male" and "female" describe both their biological sexuality (Lev 12:2, 5, 7; 15:33), which they share with all the animals (Gen 6:19; 7:3, 9, 16), and their corresponding gender, their sexual identity (Lev 27:3, 4, 5, 7; Num 5:3). Likewise, their Greek equivalents cover both physical sex and personal gender. Both are assigned to them by God in his creation of their bodies. So both their sexual status and their gender are aspects of their creation in God's image. Their creation as male and female is not secondary to their humanity; it is essential to their nature and vocation as human beings. As men and women with male and female bodies, they have been made to represent God, each in their own way, and mirror his character, each according to their unique characteristics.

At present, our children and grandchildren are bearing the brunt of gender confusion and reconstruction. Now more than ever, we need to help and protect them so that they are not severely damaged by what they confront at school and in popular culture. We need to express our appreciation for them and their appearance as boys and girls and teach them to appreciate their own bodies, most of all in adolescence when they are so often uncomfortable with their developing sexuality, confused by the contradictory demands of our society, and dissatisfied with their bodily appearance. They need to have affectionate, appreciative male and female role models to counter the sexual deceptiveness of popular culture and integrate their identity as a man or a woman with their actual genetic sexual status.

Despite what is happening in the world around us, we Christians cannot separate the sexual mind from the sexual body, nor can we separate our gender identity from the actual sexual construction of our bodies. God has joined gender together with sex; they belong together. If we separate them, we violate our humanity and damage our bodies sexually; we obscure our identity as women and men made in God's image. Yet, even so, in God's eyes we still remain as he created us. Just as he regards a divorced person as still married to their former spouse, so he regards a so-called transgendered person according to their original sexual status and treats them accordingly.

## UNITING WHAT GOD HAS SEPARATED

When God created the world, he ordered it by separating similar entities from each other, such as the light from the darkness, the day from the night, the dry land from the sea, the birds from the fish, human beings from the land animals, and women from men. By separating these created entities, he established the balanced polarities that energized the dynamic, life-sustaining order of the world. God commissioned Adam and Eve, and us, to care for the earthly part of that ecosystem and ensure that it was not disturbed and disrupted. That order includes the sexual polarity of men and women, something that is required for human reproduction and yet is able to be so easily damaged. Just as we humans violate God's natural sexual ecology for us as men and women by separating what he has united in marriage and human sexuality, so we also violate his sexual ecology by taking what he has separated sexually and uniting it in fornication and in sexual intercourse with a person of the same sex.

Fornication is sexual intercourse with a person outside marriage. The Greek word for it is derived from the term for a male or female prostitute. But it is not limited in the New Testament to the sale of sexual favors in a commercial transaction; it also includes the demand for sexual intercourse from someone other than one's spouse. It is a term for all kinds of sexual intercourse apart from marriage. It also refers to the pornographic imagination that feeds on it and is fed by it.

Although the New Testament clearly prohibits fornication in many places,[5] the reasons for its prohibition are seldom given.

---

5. See Acts 15:20, 29; 21:25; 1 Cor 5:1, 9; 6:9; 2 Cor 12:21; Gal 5:19; Eph 5:5; Col 3:5; 1 Thess 4:3; 1 Tim 1:10; Heb 12:16; 13:4; Rev 22:15.

That is rather puzzling, because it was so countercultural in the ancient world, just as it now is in much of the Western world. The New Testament teaches that if fornication goes unrepented of and unpardoned, it disqualifies the fornicator from receiving their heavenly inheritance (1 Cor 6:9–11; Rev 22:15). Since it produces spiritual impurity (2 Cor 12:21; Gal 5:19; Eph 5:5; Col 3:5), it results in God's judgment (1 Thess 4:3; Heb 13:4; cf. 1 Cor 10:8). St. Paul explains why this is so in 1 Corinthians 6:12–20.[6] He tackles this topic there in order to dissuade the male members of the church in Corinth from consorting with prostitutes in order to fulfill their sexual "needs." Surprisingly, the reasons that he gives are much more theological than moral.

Paul argues that sexual intercourse does not just satisfy certain basic bodily needs, such as eating or drinking (6:13). It has been designed to produce a personal, bodily union between a man and a woman in marriage. It is a personal union because the human body is inseparable from a person, rather than something existing apart from a person. You cannot then take a woman's body without interacting with her as a whole person; you cannot detach her body from her soul. Even though people usually identify themselves with their bodies, they all too often falsely fancy that the physical sexuality of another person exists apart from that person. Yet it is in our sexuality that we most obviously experience the unity of ourselves as persons with our bodies.[7] Thus, Robert Jenson, commenting on Song of Songs, rightly remarks:

---

6. For a closer examination of this passage, see Gregory L. Lockwood, 1 Corinthians, Concordia Commentary (Saint Louis: Concordia, 2003), 210–22.

7. It seems to me that the devil tempts us to engage in fornication in order to get us to dissociate our souls spiritually from our bodies and pursue various kinds of discarnate spirituality, such as in paganism, spiritualism, Gnosticism, Hinduism, and Buddhism.

The gnostic temptation, to see persons as of one order and bodies as another, is constant in human history and by no accident afflicts especially our sexual lives. For sexuality is the point where God has made our persons and our bodies one.[8]

Paul also argues that the sexual body of a believer now no longer belongs to him. It belongs to the triune God. Since his body has been united with the body of Christ in baptism, it is owned by him (6:15, 20). The body of each Christian is a member of Christ's body, because he purchased it by his death for its redemption. God the Father, who raised the body of Jesus from the dead, will raise up the bodies of all those who belong to Christ (6:14). Their bodies are therefore destined for eternal life with him. By their union with Christ they have become one spirit with him; they share his Spirit (6:17). So the body of each believer is now a temple of the Holy Spirit, a holy shrine for God's Spirit (6:19–20). Just as the choir of Levites glorified God, present with them in glory at the temple in Jerusalem in songs of thanksgiving and praise, so believers are now called to glorify God in the temple of their bodies and thus show his glory to the people around him. Thus, God's high regard and holy purpose for the body of each believer is the basis for his prohibition of fornication.

Since the body of each Christian belongs to Christ, fornication is a misalliance between two incompatible parties, a misalliance between a body that is united bodily with Christ and the body of a sexual partner that does not belong to the fornicator. It joins what God has separated. As a result of that bodily union, the holy body of the believer is polluted and desecrated. The fornicator is guilty of sacrilege; he sins against Christ who has redeemed him, against the Holy Spirit within him, and against his own body that does not belong to that woman (6:18). Worst of all, in this instance it joins his holy body with the unclean body of a pagan prostitute (6:15).

---

8. Robert W. Jenson, *Song of Songs*, Interpretation (Louisville: John Knox, 2005), 62.

Thus, fornication wrongly unites what God has rightly separated. It unites the body that belongs to Christ with the body of a woman who is not married to him. It makes Christ a party to that act of pollution and desecration.

## Same-Sex Intercourse

Like fornication, sexual intercourse with a person of the same sex unites what God has separated.[9] He created human beings as male and female for nuptial union with each other in marriage, an extra-verted union with the opposite sex rather than with a person of the same sex. That divinely given order is violated by the copulation of a man with a man or a woman with a woman. It is also subverted by the promotion and practice of marriage between people of the same sex. Same-sex marriage is not marriage, because it unites what God has separated. Even if the marriage of two people of the same sex is sanctioned by political legislation and popular culture, God does not regard it as a marriage. It is a fake marriage that borrows the trappings of a real marriage to justify its existence. Since God has not instituted it, the church cannot bless and sanctify it as if it were a true marriage.

It seems to me that the present controversy over same-sex inter-course and same-sex marriage is fraught with much confusion in the public arena and in the church. People are confused about how to understand these issues and assess them. This confusion stems in large measure from how we speak about them and describe them. The language used determines our understanding because it frames our discussion of these matters. Thus, we quite commonly separate same-sex attraction from opposite-sex attraction as two different

---

9. While in the previous chapter I discussed sexual desire in general and its sanctification and only implicitly handled sexual orientation and original sin, in this book I do not address the question of same-sex sexual desire. On this question, particularly regarding Christians who experience enduring same-sex sexual desires, see Matthew Lee Anderson, "Sex, Temptation, and the Gay Christian: What Chastity Demands" (June 20, 2019), mereorthodoxy.com; Johanna Finnegan, "Labels and Evangelism" (February 25, 2019), johannafinegan.com; Finnegan, "The Sinfulness of Homosexual Desire Is Not an Argument against Spiritual Friendship, Revoice, or 'Celibate Gays' " (March 15, 2019).

states of being and so classify people as either homosexual or heterosexual. But that is, in fact, a misleading way of thinking. Both of these terms are modern inventions that now describe the sexual identity of people rather than their sexual activity.

The notion of homosexuality as a mental, psychological state was devised in the nineteenth century to describe the "abnormal," pathological state of people who were sexually attracted to their own sex rather than the opposite sex.[10] Homosexuality was therefore regarded as a mental sickness, a pathological mental state that resulted in the desire for "abnormal" sexual intercourse. In contrast with homosexuality, heterosexuality was the natural condition of a healthy man or woman. In that philosophy, the focus of attention shifted from the traditional, moral assessment of sexual acts to the evaluation of someone's sexual mentality and the sexual orientation of a person. More recently, it has been used to classify people according to their supposed sexual identity. They are now classed as homosexual or heterosexual people. Even though the notion of homosexuality as a mental sickness has been largely rejected, the distinction between homosexuality and heterosexuality as mental, emotional, personal states still remains. But now both are commonly regarded as two normal, natural, equally valid kinds of sexuality. Simple justice, it is claimed, requires that we recognize the equivalence of same-sex marriage with opposite-sex marriage.

Two serious problems arise from identifying men and women as either homosexual or heterosexual, let alone basing marriage legally on their self-chosen sexual identity. First, in this approach, people derive their personal identity from their sexual orientation and its expression, rather than from their humanity as men and women. So, these adjectives are now used to describe who I am rather than what I do. The way that I identify myself sexually, or

---

10.  "Homosexual" was first coined as a general term in German by Karl-Maria Kertbeny in 1869. It was then used as a technical term by German psychiatrists and psychologists for the sexual orientation of people toward their own sex. It was first used in English by Craddock's translation of Kraft-Ebing's *Psychopathia Sexualis* in 1892 and then adopted by Havelock Ellis in 1901 in his *Studies in the Psychology of Sex*.

that others identify me sexually, determines who I am. My sexual identity, my gender status, is held to be part and parcel of my intrinsic personal identity. It becomes an essential foundation for my sense of self. I derive my being from it. Thus, while I can change my sexual behavior, I cannot change my sexuality. That's how I really and truly am. It makes me the person that I am, the person that God made me to be. I am stuck with it and cannot ever escape its claims on me. Should I deny my true sexual identity, I would violate my very self. It would be suicidal for me.

It is, I maintain, misleading and unhelpful to identify a person as either homosexual or heterosexual. We are sexual people who can engage in heterosexual or homosexual acts or even in both kinds. But that does not determine who we are. Neither homosexuality nor heterosexuality are states of being. At best, they describe how we think and feel, how we act, and why we act as we do. At worst, they are false categories that do not correspond with the complex realities of male and female sexuality, let alone with God's purpose for us as sexual agents.

Even if we can't change the public discourse on this topic, we as Christians have no reason to accept it uncritically by speaking rather carelessly about people as homosexuals. Or even as heterosexual persons! Most of all, even though we must reject all same-sex intercourse as sinful in God's sight, just as we reject all other sexual sins, we should not condemn people for their supposed homosexual identity, let alone their sexual orientation or their physical attraction to people of the same sex. That would only drive them to despair at their seemingly hopeless condition, or to reject God's word. Rather, our focus should be on the salvation of their souls by repentance for their sexual sins and the cleansing of their conscience through the blood of Jesus. We are all sinners who need to be pardoned for our sin.

Second, the identification of myself as either heterosexual or homosexual largely absolves me of responsibility before God for my sexual behavior. Thus, if I am a homosexual person, then it is right for me to act in a way that is consistent with my sexual identity, provided that I do so respectfully, considerately, and lovingly. Conversely, it would be wrong for me not to do so. I have a right to do so. After all, that is how God made me. If I am a normal, heterosexual person, then it is right for me to act according to my sexual nature by engaging in fornication, accessing pornography, having anal intercourse with my spouse, committing adultery, and divorcing my spouse if he or she does not satisfy me sexually. What's more, as a Christian who accepts the teaching of the church, I can self-righteously regard myself as morally superior to all so-called homosexuals by virtue of my heterosexuality. Thus, the careless use of these terms only adds to our moral confusion and spiritual disorder.

Like the Bible, the tradition of moral teaching in orthodox Christianity does not classify human beings as heterosexual or homosexual persons. Like God himself, it regards them as men and women, male and female. What's more, in its teaching on sexuality, the Bible focuses on what people do and how they behave sexually. Thus, in Leviticus 18:22 and 20:13, God prohibits a man from lying with another male person as with a woman. That refers to what we would now call anal sexual intercourse of one man with another. In Romans 1:26–27, Paul distinguishes between the natural and unnatural function and use of male and female bodies in his description of same-sex intercourse as an unnatural use of their sexual organs. In 1 Corinthians 6:9 and 1 Timothy 1:10, he recalls the language used by God in Leviticus when he describes men who have sexual intercourse with each other as "males who lie with males," men who go to bed with other men. That term is also used more narrowly in 1 Timothy 1:10 to describe the active partner in anal intercourse in contrast with his receptive sexual partner. The Greek word for the passive partner refers to an effeminate man.[11] Thus, the Scriptures do not speak abstractly and gen-

---

11. The traditional English translation of these terms by "sodomite" and "catamite" are too obscure to be of any use because they presuppose familiarity with the Old Testament and classical Greek mythology.

erally about a homosexual state or a homosexual identity but quite concretely and realistically about same-sex activity.

So, in the interest of truthfulness, it would be best if we Christians did not speak about people as either homosexual or heterosexual and did not regard homosexuality and heterosexuality as states of being. Like God, we should regard all sexual offenders as sinners; they are all men and women made in his image, corrupted by sin, judged by God for what they have done, and in need of his merciful pardon.

### The Assessment of Same-Sex Intercourse

How, then, should we regard sexual intercourse between two people of the same sex? Since it is impossible to cover the many aspects of this controversial topic in this study, I shall restrict the discussion to what is said about it in the Bible.[12] The texts that teach about it are Leviticus 18:22 and 20:13 in the Old Testament and Romans 1:25–27; 1 Corinthians 6:9–11; and 1 Timothy 1:8–11 in the New Testament.[13]

The prohibition of same-sex intercourse is given in two different contexts in Leviticus, which show why it is forbidden.[14] The prohibition in 18:22 considers it in the context of the order of creation. That prohibition recognizes that same-sex intercourse was commonly practiced and condoned by pagans both in Egypt and in Canaan (18:1–2, 24–29). But like all other sexual offenses, it violated God's life-giving decrees for all humankind, not just for the Israelites (18:5).[15] They applied to every human being. Their violation polluted the offenders and the land itself (18:24–30).

---

12. For further discussion of this topic, see *A Plan for Ministry to Homosexuals and their Families* (The Task Force on Ministry to Homosexuals and Their Families, The Lutheran Church—Missouri Synod, 1999), and the excursus "Homosexuality" by Gregory L. Lockwood in *1 Corinthians*, Concordia Commentary (Saint Louis: Concordia, 2003), 204–9.

13. See also the likely allusion to it in Jude 7–8.

14. See John W. Kleinig, *Leviticus*, Concordia Commentary (Saint Louis: Concordia), 385–89, 431–39.

15. Here the Hebrew term *ha'adam* refers to humanity as a whole and each human being as a descendant of Adam.

They thereby became unclean in God's sight. The prohibition in 20:13 considers same-sex intercourse between two men and other sexual offenses within the holy order of Israel as a liturgical community. That prohibition belonged to God's sanctifying statutes, the statutes by which God made his people holy and kept them holy (20:7–8). Since the Israelites were holy, they were required to avoid the sexual impurity of their pagan neighbors, so that they did not defile God's sanctuary and desecrate his holiness (20:24–26; cf. 20:4).

The prohibition of same-sex intercourse is reaffirmed by Paul in two places. In 1 Timothy 1:10, he connects it with the sixth commandment and couples it with the prohibition of fornication. These acts were closely associated in the ancient world because they usually involved the use of young female or male slaves. Paul claims that the sexual intercourse of a man with another man is contrary to the sound teaching of law and gospel. In 1 Corinthians 6:9–10 it is listed with fornication, idolatry, and adultery as unrighteous offenses that disqualify offenders from inheriting God's kingdom.

In Romans 1:25–27 Paul gives us this rationale for the prohibition of same-sex intercourse:[16]

> Therefore God gave them up in the lusts of their hearts to impurity, to the dishonoring of their bodies among themselves, because they exchanged the truth of God for a lie and worshiped and served the creature rather than the Creator, who is blessed forever. Amen. For this reason God gave them up to dishonorable passions. Indeed, their females[17] exchanged the natural use (of the male) for what was contrary to nature.[18] Likewise also, the males, abandoning the

---

16. Here I give my own translation of these verses.

17. In this and the next verse, Paul speaks about females and males rather than women quite deliberately to allude to Gen 1:27 and God's creation of sexual order for human beings. All current translations overlook that allusion by speaking about women and men.

18. See the discussion on this key term in Michael P. Middendorf, *Romans 1–8*, Concordia Commentary (Saint Louis: Concordia, 2013), 145–50.

natural use of the female, were inflamed in their craving for one another, so that males performed the improper act[19] on a male and received back on themselves the due penalty for their error.

Here Paul's teaching about same-sex intercourse is part of his introductory discussion on God's righteous judgment of both gentiles and Jews that culminates in his conclusion that God regards all people equally unrighteous in his sight (Rom 3:19–20). In that context, Paul teaches us six things about our topic.

First, he argues that same-sex sexual acts violate the natural order, the order that God established by his creation of human beings as male and female (Rom 1:26–27). The arrangement of their sexual organs shows that they were made for sexual intercourse between a man and a woman. To put it crudely, a penis was made for a vagina of a woman rather than an anus or mouth of a man. Sexual intercourse with a person of the same sex is therefore an "error," a deviation from what is right, a misdeed that has practical, negative consequences for those who go about sex in that way (1:27).

Second, rather unusually for his time, Paul also speaks about the passionate sexual intercourse of a woman with a woman (Rom 1:26). Yet unlike the modern tendency to regard sex between women as equivalent to what is done by men, he recognizes that men differ in what they do with each other and in the negative consequences of what is done. Thus, in contrast with the sexual intercourse of a woman with a woman, he describes anal intercourse as an improper, shameful act that is performed by one male on another male, a compulsive act that brings with it its own penalties (1:27).

Third, like all other sexual sins, same-sex intercourse is an act of idolatry, for thereby women and men revere and serve their own created body rather than its Creator (Rom 1:22–25). It

---

19. This euphemism describes a sexual act that deviates from the proper mode of behavior. The use of the definite article most likely indicates that it alludes to either anal or oral intercourse.

violates the body that has been made in God's image and likeness. The glory of the body, made in God's image and crowned with his glory, is exchanged for the corruptible beauty of a mortal man (1:22). The body of the sexual partner becomes an idol, which is supposed to supply what only God can give. Ironically, the adoration of that body does not actually honor it; rather, it dishonors the body and degrades it (1:24).

Fourth, like all other sins, it meets with God's disapproval and incurs his righteous judgment. That does not just happen in the final judgment at the end of the world but begins already now. God lets men and women get their own way with their own sex and do as they please. He hands them over to their offenses (Rom 1:26). They get what they want. But in that, they suffer the negative consequences of their sexual acts by enslavement to their disordered cravings. They receive the due penalty for the error (1:27). God does this to show them the truth of his word and so bring them to repentance.

Fifth, like all other sexual sins, it does not just pollute the body; it pollutes the heart (Rom 1:24). The result of such improper behavior is an unclean conscience that knows what has been done is not right in God's sight—a bad conscience that needs to excuse what has been done and seeks to gain public approval for it, a guilty conscience that spurns God's law, expects his judgment, and fears his condemnation.

Sixth, God does not classify men and women as either heterosexual or homosexual people. He judges all men and women alike in their sexual misbehavior without regarding one kind of it as more sinful than another. Thus, in his eyes, fornication and adultery are just as unrighteous as same-sex intercourse. Each of us is without excuse before God (Rom 2:1; 3:19–20). We cannot justify ourselves by condemning the sexual misbehavior of others. We all need to repent of our sexual unrighteousness and receive cleansing from our impurity.

In Romans 1, Paul teaches that God has forbidden same-sex intercourse because it is a kind of idolatry. But in 1 Corinthians

6:9–11, he speaks about what God has done to help those who have engaged in it.[20] After listing the offenses that exclude people from God's kingdom and the inheritance that God provides for its citizens, Paul declares that even though some Christians in Corinth had committed these sins, including same-sex intercourse, God had rescued them from their consequent entrapment. They and all believers have been washed clean by the waters of baptism, sanctified by the Holy Spirit, and justified by the remission of sins in the name of Jesus. They therefore are now pure and holy and righteous in God's sight.

That, too, is the case for all those male members of the congregation who had previously engaged in sexual intercourse with other men. And women with other women! They have all been set free from their former sexual way of life. Even though they might still be attracted to other men or women, like former fornicators and adulterers who might still be bothered by sexual temptation, they now have divine help and power to overcome these temptations and live in chastity. The most important thing for them is that since they belong to Christ, they are now pure and holy and righteous in the sight of God the Father. As sons and daughters of God, they derive their identity from him rather than from their sexuality. Best of all, they can stand before him with a good conscience because they know that he is pleased with them. All blame and shame are gone! No disgust and despair any longer! They have no reason to fear his disapproval, and every reason to expect nothing but good from him.

### A PROVISIONAL STATE

Even though marriage is one of God's greatest gifts to human beings, it exists only in this world as an essential part of human life in the body. Like childhood, it is a provisional state. While every actual marriage is made by God as its celebrant, in heaven

---

20. For a fuller discussion of this passage, see Gregory L. Lockwood, 1 Corinthians, Concordia Commentary (Saint Louis: Concordia, 2003), 196–203.

there are no marriages as we now know them. That truth is rather puzzling, since the Scriptures teach us that Christ will restore the whole of the fallen world and raise the bodies of all believers to eternal life with him in his new creation. If it is provisional, what will happen to our male and female bodies and to those of us who are one flesh with our spouse in marriage?

In Luke 20:27–40 Jesus teaches us a little about the state of our sexual bodies and their marital union with other bodies after the resurrection. There he makes two points relevant to this discussion. First, because we will then have immortal bodies that cannot die, there will be no need for sexual reproduction to replace ourselves when we die. Thus, there will be no marrying and giving in marriage in the new creation. Instead, we will be like angels as sons of God the Father. We will be as radiant and splendid, lucid and translucent, lovely and lively, beautiful and wonderful as the angels. Yet, unlike them—but like Jesus, the resurrected Son of God—we will still have bodies. Despite our transformation into his likeness, we will still be the same persons as now, and recognizable as such. We will still be women and men, but perfectly so. We will know our former spouse as our husband or wife, just as we will recognize all those who are near and dear to us now. And we will all enjoy the same perfect, physical fellowship with all our brothers and sisters in Christ as with our spouse, but without sexual intercourse.

Second, the Lord Jesus is the God of the living, who all share in his divine life. That includes us and all of God's people, because we all share in his resurrection. Like him, we are all sons of God the Father. We are all one flesh with Jesus and one flesh with each other through him. We are all part of a supernatural physical and spiritual community that includes Abraham, Isaac, and Jacob, as well as every other member of God's family. When we are raised from the dead together with our bodies, we, then perfectly united with his body, will all share the same communion with God the Father as Jesus, a spiritual intimacy of body and soul that supersedes the intimate life of husbands and wives even in the very best of marriages.

So, marriage is a provisional way of life that helps us envisage eternal life in union with Christ our heavenly bridegroom (Eph 5:25–27, 32; see also Rev 19:7; 21:1; 22:17). It will finally give way to the enjoyment of perfect union with him and the whole communion of saints in body, soul, and spirit. In that life with Jesus, we will not be disembodied but even more perfectly embodied than we are now. Thus in this life, holy matrimony, the marriage of two believers, gives us a preview and foretaste of our perfect bodily union with Christ and each other. Those who are now one flesh and one spirit with each other and Jesus, as well as those who are not married but are also united with him, will be forever one with him and all the saints in the life to come. Like any earthly marriage, that nuptial union and communion will involve their convivial, bodily life with each other. But there will be no sexual intercourse in heaven—and no desire for it at all! There, the greedy, self-possessed sexual body will become a receptive, self-giving body in and through its nuptial union with Jesus, a body that is perfectly equipped to receive the love of God the Father and love as it is loved by him. That bodily union is prefigured, however imperfectly, by the sexual union of two bodies in every marriage. That is why Paul says that even in this life, those who have wives should live as if they had none (1 Cor 7:29).

So, when God considers the sexual union of a husband and wife in marriage and the devotion of an unmarried person to Jesus, he sees in them a preview of Christ's union with his beloved earthly bride. That gives both marriage and a single life its eternal worth! Inspired by the vision of our heavenly union in Revelation 19:6–9 and 21:1–4, and prompted by the Holy Spirit, as encouraged in Revelation 22:17 and 22:20, whether single or married, we who are corporately the bride of Christ say, "Come. Amen. Come, Lord Jesus!"

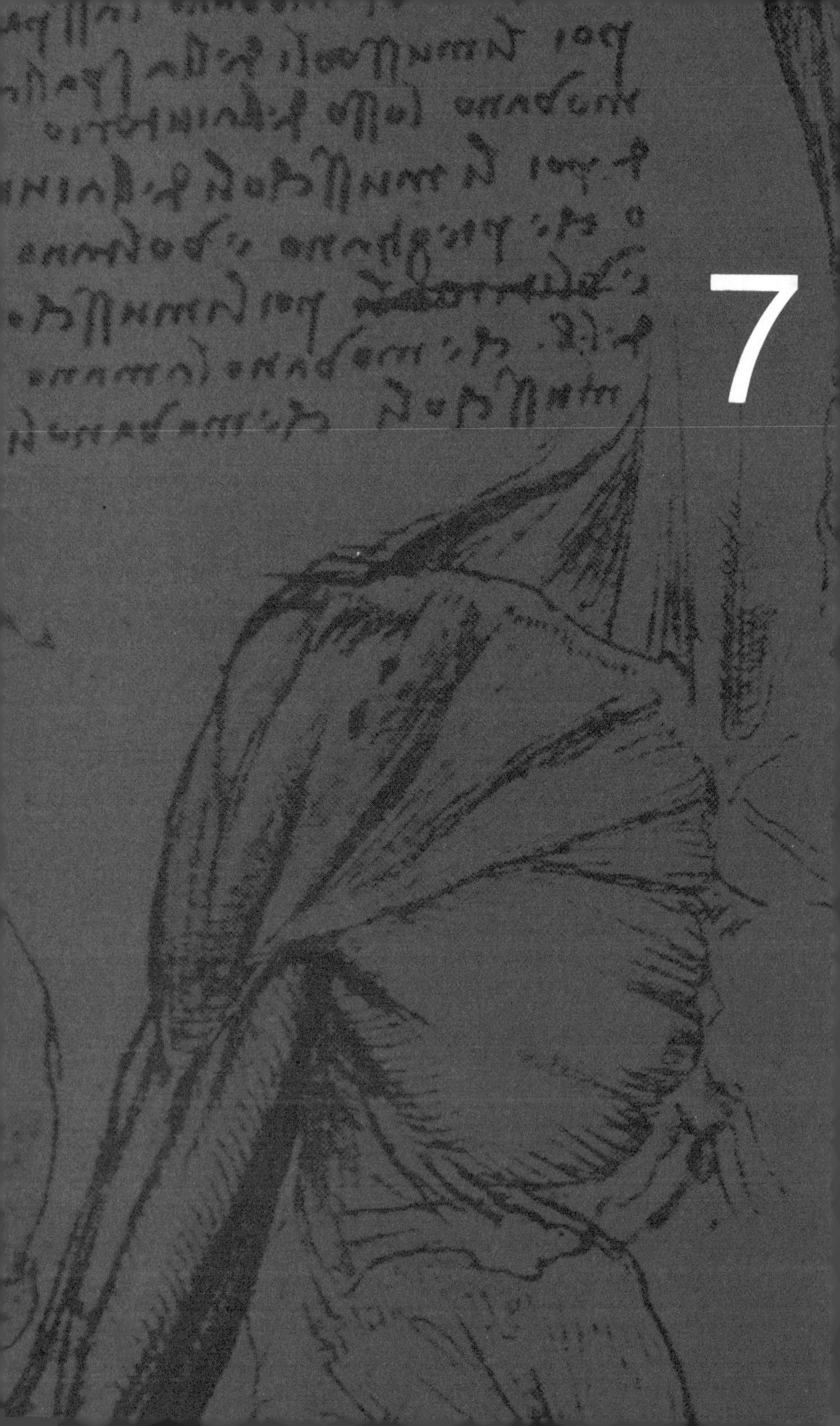

# 7

# THE LIVING BODY

Thus, the most precious treasure and the strongest consolation we Christians have is this: that the Word, the true and natural Son of God, became man, with flesh and blood like that of any human; that he became incarnate for our sakes in order that we might enter into glory, that our flesh and blood, skin and hair, hands and feet, stomach and back might reside in heaven as God does, and in order that we might defy the devil and whatever else assails us. We are convinced that all our members belong in heaven as heirs of heaven's realm.

—*Martin Luther*

**A**ll human life on earth shares the same common condition: it is lived in the body. We were conceived with embryonic bodies in the body of our mother. We were born with bodies, grow up in them, and have them for as long as we live. We identify ourselves with our bodies. We use our bodies to associate with others and interact with our environment. We enjoy life and health with our bodies and suffer sickness and pain with them. Our bodies locate us geographically and socially here on earth. Like us, they cannot exist by themselves because they depend on the world and the people around them for their nourishment and growth, survival and safety. We mature and age and die with our bodies. So human life on earth is, always and only, life in the body.

Our spiritual life on earth is also life in the body. It is the life that we live with the triune God, Father, Son, and Holy Spirit. More correctly, it is the life of Jesus in us, our life of faith in him, his eternal life that he shares with us, as we live for a short while in our bodies here on earth.

Like our physical life, our spiritual life comes from the living God. He made us in his image so that we would not just resemble the animals and other human beings with their bodies; he made us to resemble him in body, soul, and spirit. He wanted us to receive his love and share it bodily with each other. So, even when we humans turn away from him in suicidal disregard, he does not turn away from us. He continues to protect us and provides for us in our bodily journey from the womb to the tomb. Even if we do not believe in him as our God, we still live and move and have our bodily being in him. He is not far from any of us, even if we are far from him. Through what we experience with our fragile bodies, he shows us how dependent we are on others for our livelihood and on him for our existence.

Yet God is not satisfied with keeping us physically alive for the enjoyment of a transitory life with each other and his creatures. He wants us to become fully alive with a spiritual life as well. God the Father therefore sent his one and only Son to live a full human life in human flesh and die a human death, in order to rescue us from eternal death and share his own divine life with us. He raised his Son from the dead in order to raise us up with our bodies for eternal life with him. His incarnate Son now interacts with us physically by speaking to us, regenerating us by water and the Holy Spirit, and giving us his life-giving body and blood for our spiritual nourishment. Through these physical means he also now sanctifies our bodies so that they are living temples for him, holy shrines for his life-giving Holy Spirit. And the goal of all that is eternal life that begins already now by faith here on earth and is fulfilled in God's new creation. So we Christians always have life in the body, from its inauguration to its consummation. It is the life of faith in Jesus who lives in us. As Paul explains in Galatians 2:20, "It is no longer I who live, but Christ who lives in me. And the life I now live in the flesh I live by faith in the Son of God, who loved me and gave himself for me."

Well, why does God expend so much effort and work with such patience in creating, preserving, and redeeming our human bodies? After all, they are of little value in themselves and in the grand scheme of things. They have such a short natural life and are so subject to decay; they are so fragile and vulnerable, limited and dependent, compared with the holy angels. No matter how long our bodies live and what they accomplish, they will die, and their deeds will be undone. Why, then, does he hold our mortal bodies in such high regard?

In my opinion, the greatest statue that has ever been crafted by any human sculptor is Michelangelo's statue of David. It is a perfect depiction of a nude male body. Yet its origin was anything but perfect. It was made from a huge block of white marble that had been brought with much difficulty and great expense from Carrara to Florence to be made into a statue for the beautiful cathedral in the city. The sculptor, who had begun work on it, died before he got very far with it. He had shaped it rather roughly, leaving a misplaced, inverted, V-shaped gap between where he had intended to carve the legs. Two other sculptors were commissioned to complete the statue after his death. But they gave up on it because of the misplaced incision and the imperfections in the stone that threatened its stability. It lay unused for 25 years before Michelangelo took over. The all-too-apparent faults in the slab presented creative possibilities to him. He saw its potential and used its imperfections to sculpt a masterpiece.[1]

God is like that with us and our human bodies. He takes them and turns them into masterpieces, works of his divine art. Despite their apparent lack of worth, he makes them worthy of eternal life with him and all the angels. He created our male and female bodies in his image to resemble him in our bodily existence. He made them so that he could remake them into the image and likeness of his beloved Son. Even though they had been scarred and marred by their suicidal rebellion against him, he redeemed and sanctified them through the incarnation of his Son, who loved us and gave himself for us. Through baptism, our earthly bodies are now one flesh with Jesus in this life, like a bride with her groom, just as our bodies will be united with his glorified body forever in the life to come (Eph 5:29–32). Since we are one with him in body and soul, he now presents us with our holy, blameless bodies to God the Father as we live by faith in him (Eph 5:25–27).

## THREE PERSPECTIVES ON THE BODY

God the Father now sees us from three different points of view. He sees us as we once were apart from his Son, as we now are in his Son, and as we will be together with his Son. But not in that

---

1. See "David, by Michelangelo" at www.Michelangelo.org.david.jsp.

order. His final vision of us comes from his purpose for us, which colors how he now sees us.

First of all, he sees as we will be when we are face to face with him together with his Son in the life to come. He regards us already now, provisionally, as perfect people with our resurrected and glorified bodies. He sees us in glory with Jesus and the angels, pure and holy, without spot or wrinkle or any such blemish. And as he considers us, he is pleased with what he sees, and that makes him very proud of us.

Second, he regards our present bodies in that light because he now sees us as hidden in his Son, dressed up, as it were, with him, one flesh with him in his glory. He considers us as people who have been covered with the righteousness and purity, the holiness and beauty, of Jesus. So when he looks at us and our bodies, he sees Jesus in us and us in Jesus. Our life is now hidden with Christ in God (Col 3:3). Our bodily union and communion with Jesus may be hidden from our eyes, but not from God's sight. He is not ashamed to be called our God (Heb 11:16), just as Jesus is not ashamed to call us his brothers and sisters (Heb 2:11). God approves of us and is just as pleased with us as he is with Jesus. He therefore says to us and each believer, "You are my beloved son; you are my beloved daughter; I am well pleased with you."

Third, even though our heavenly Father admires us as the beautiful bride of his Son, he does not overlook our sin and gloss over its gravity. He sees our sin much more clearly than we ever do. He considers all our misbehavior as well as our mistrustful heart that motivates it. He regards our sin in the same way that Michelangelo regarded that damaged slab of marble. He does not reject us because we are sinful and unclean; rather, he uses our sin to bring us back to him and remake us in the image of his Son. He puts our sinful self to death together with Jesus, in order to raise us up as new people together with Jesus. He therefore sees us as sinners whom he pardons and transforms more and more fully, so that we are worthy of eternal life with him.

## THREE HOMES

So how then shall we regard our bodies that have been so wonderfully made and even more wonderfully remade? There are many possible ways to consider our bodies in the light of God's regard for them. However, I would like to complete my rhapsody on the body by telling you how I consider my own.

For me, the key is recognizing that my body is always located somewhere in its journey on earth—not anywhere, or everywhere, but somewhere. It can only be in one place with certain people and certain things at any point of time. If it is now here in this place, it cannot be there in that place. But it does not remain, like a tree in the ground, in only one place. Day by day it moves from place to place. Yet each of these places is not equally important. The most important place at any stage of my life is my home. It is my point of orientation, the place where I am. I visit many other places, but I do not live there. My home is the place where I live.

In all, I have had three homes. Yet each of these has been located in a number of different geographical places and in an even larger number of houses. My three homes are the personal places where my body is at home with those who are one flesh with me. They are the places that God has assigned for me to be during my life in the body. They are my home with my parents and siblings, my home with my wife and our children, and my home with Jesus and his heavenly Father and all my fellow saints. They show where my body has come from, where it is now, and where it will be forever.

My first home was and is with my parents and seven siblings. It is my first home because God has created me with my body through my father and my mother. My body comes from them and is still connected with them in countless ways, even though they are both now dead. From a human point of view, I owe my body to them; it is as it is largely because of them and their ancestors. Even though I have lived with them in three different houses in three separate places, I have had only one family home. My home was always wherever my mother was living with my father. Whenever I was there with her, my body was at home in that place. That is where it still belongs. That is where I belong, even though it no longer exists as an actual place. The geographical relocation of my first home in different places and its physical demise have given me a foretaste of my final home. So I thank God the Father for my first temporary home that foreshadows my third eternal home.

My second home is with my wife, Claire, and our four children. It is the second location that God has provided for my body, by giving her to me in marriage. I am now one flesh with her and at home with her. My body belongs to her, just as her body belongs to me. My home is wherever we have lived together as a married couple. Even though we have occupied ten separate houses in four different cities, I have had one home with her for more than fifty years. She is the fixed, unaltered physical point of orientation for me with my ever-changing body. The temporary marital union of my body with hers in a changing world is a foretaste of our permanent one-flesh union with our Lord Jesus. So I thank God the Father for giving me a second home for my body with her and a preview of my third home through my union with her.

My third home is with Jesus and his Father. That home is the house of the heavenly Father, which belongs to Jesus as his Son (Luke 2:49); it is his home that he shares with us and all the saints (John 14:1); it is that place where Jesus is at home with us and where we are at home with him (John 14:23). His home is the church that, like him, is located both in heaven and on earth. His home became my spiritual home when I was baptized and has remained my spiritual home ever since. In the church, I live my life in the body together with Jesus. Like the houses that have served as places of residence for me at various stages in my life, I have been a member of nine different congregations. Yet all the while I have belonged to only one church; I have had only one heavenly home here on earth. Since my baptism, the heavenly home for my earthly body has been the one holy catholic and apostolic church, which is located in the city of God, heavenly Jerusalem (Heb 12:22–24). That has been my true home even when I was living in different places here on earth.

My body has been wonderfully made and even more wonderfully remade for life with Jesus in that heavenly home. That is where it belongs. That is where it longs to be at rest. That is the goal of its journey here on earth. That is where it will at last be at home forever. So I cannot but thank my heavenly Father for providing that eternal home for my body through his Son, both now in this age and forever in the age to come. I am indeed fearfully and wonderfully made! So, too, are you and all people on earth.

# EPIGRAPH SOURCES

Chapter 1  C. S. Lewis, "Membership," in *The Weight of Glory and Other Addresses* (Grand Rapids: Eerdmans, 1972), 41.

Chapter 2  A. F. C. Vilmar, *Dogmatik* (Gütersloh: Bertelsmann, 1874), 1:332–33. Author's translation.

Chapter 3  Ignatius, *Letter to the Smyrnaeans*, 1.2–3; 3:1–2. Author's translation.

Chapter 4  Martin Luther, *Selected Psalms 2. Psalm 110*, LW 13:243.

Chapter 5  C. S. Lewis, *Mere Christianity* (Glasgow: Collins, 1977), 88.

Chapter 6  Clement, in *Alexandrian Christianity: Selected Translations of Clement and Origin*, Library of Christian Classics 2 (Philadelphia: Westminster, 1954).

Philipp Melanchton, "Apology of the Ausgburg
Confession, article 23 on 'The Marriage of
Priests' 33, 34, 36," Kolb-Wengert edition of *The
Book of Concord*, 252f.

Chapter 7  Martin Luther, "Seventh Sermon on John 1"
(1537), LW 22:110.

# AUTHOR INDEX

# SUBJECT INDEX

# SCRIPTURE INDEX

## Old Testament

## New Testament